A POET'S
TRUTH

A POET'S TRUTH

Conversations with Latino/Latina Poets • Bruce Allen Dick

The University of Arizona Press
Tucson

The University of Arizona Press
© 2003 The Arizona Board of Regents
First Printing
All rights reserved

∞ This book is printed on acid-free, archival-quality paper.
Manufactured in the United States of America

08   07   06   05   04   03   6   5   4   3   2   1

Library of Congress Cataloging-in-Publication Data
Dick, Bruce, 1953–
   A poet's truth : conversations with Latino/Latina poets / Bruce Allen Dick
      p. cm.
   ISBN 0-8165-2275-8 (cloth : alk. paper) — ISBN 0-8165-2276-6 (pbk. : alk. paper)
   1. American poetry—Hispanic American authors—History and criticism—Theory, etc. 2.
American poetry—20th century—History and criticism—
Theory, etc. 3. Poets, American—20th century—Interviews. 4. Hispanic American women
authors—Interviews. 5. Hispanic American authors—
Interviews. 6. Hispanic Americans in literature. 7. Poetry—Authorship. I. Title

PS153.H56 D53 2003
811'.509868—dc21

British Library Cataloguing-in-Publication Data
A catalogue record for this book is available from the British Library.

Publication of this book is made possible in part by the proceeds of
a permanent endowment created with the assistance of a Challenge Grant from the National
Endowment for the Humanities, a federal agency.

To my father, David Coolidge Dick, 1925–94,
to my mother, Betty Emily Dick,
and to Gabriella, Melanie, and Julien, for being there

Contents

Acknowledgments

This collection of interviews would not have been possible without many people's help and support. I am indebted foremost to Virgil Suárez, who has shown genuine interest in this project and provided valuable assistance from the start. I'd also like to thank Luis Rodríguez, who encouraged me in the early stages of the project, and the other thirteen participants in this collection for their patience, guidance, and support. Silvio Sirias should be recognized for helping plant the seed, and the title of the book was inspired by a line from the interview with Judith Ortiz Cofer. I am especially grateful to my colleagues in the Department of English at Appalachian State University (ASU), especially Susan Weinberg, who helped edit portions of the manuscript. I also thank Mark Vogel, Leon Lewis, Cece Conway, Edelma Huntley, Elaine O'Quinn, Katherine Kirkpatrick, Dan Hurley, Amy Greer, Janet Smith, Dave Haney, Ray Wonder, Nacho Garcia, Tom Rauch, David Ferreira, Tony Grahame, Lila Porterfield, Kemp Jones, Valerie Midgett, Ed Midgett, Karl Van Ausdel, Alfred Pritchett, and my brothers James, Scott, and Bobby Dick for their helpful suggestions, advice, and support. David Larry deserves special recognition for his technical assistance. A number of graduate students assisted with various phases of research, including Joe Boykin, Greg Deleruyelle, Sandy Hartwiger, Kris Heiks, Beth Leysiefer, Chris Saunders, Natalie Serianni, David Howell, and John Tedder. The ASU Graduate School and the College of Arts and Sciences provided financial support over the past two years, and the University Research Council supplied a generous grant to cover various project expenses. As usual, the excellent staff at ASU's Belk Library assisted me in every stage of this project. Most important, I thank Gabriella Motta-Passajou, my wife, for giving me the time and space I needed to complete this book. Her suggestions along the way have proved invaluable. Finally, thanks to Mel and Jules for keeping me young.

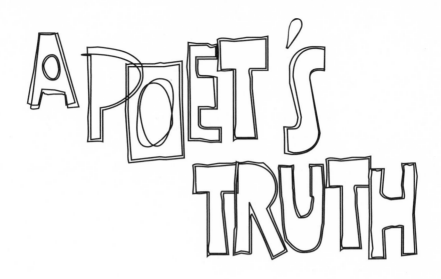

Introduction

This collection of interviews provides a forum for fifteen contemporary Latino poets to discuss their work, to comment on a number of related topics that help identify their place in American literature, and to take a stand on the wide range of social and political issues affecting Latinos throughout the United States.

The idea for this collection dates back to the early 1990s, when I first started focusing on Latino poets and novelists in the classroom. My students were captivated by these writers and asked me to find ways to bring them to campus for public readings. Within a few years, several of these authors—among them Virgil Suárez, Gustavo Pérez Firmat, and Benjamin Alire Sáenz—had participated in the Visiting Writers Series at Appalachian State University, where I teach. With another colleague, Silvio Sirias, I interviewed some of these writers and began pursuing ways to publish the conversations as a book. Because the interviews spanned the entire decade, though, the nine conversations we collected unfortunately became dated. I never stopped thinking about the collection, however, for I was convinced that both individually and collectively these writers had important and timely things to say. Finally, during our first major snowstorm of the new millennium, Chicano poet Luis Rodríguez visited our community for a series of readings. I jumped at the opportunity to interview him. Luis's inspiration prompted me to renew the project, which developed into this collection of new interviews, all conducted since January 2000.

The most difficult challenge in compiling this book was deciding which poets to include. Anthologies published in the past decade—among them *After Aztlán: Latino Poets in the Nineties* (1992), *Paper Dance: 55 Latino Poets* (1995), and *¡Floricanto Sí!: A Collection of Latina Poetry* (1998)—attest to the large number of Latino poets writing in the United States today. Several poets in these texts easily can stand beside the fifteen poets represented here. In determining my selections, I finally decided to focus solely on Chicano, Puerto Rican, and Cuban writers. The prolific authors from these three groups represent the vast majority of published Latino poets.

Another criterion was whether the individual author had made a mark in poetry *and* had enjoyed success in other literary forms. For me, as the interviewer, this focus provided further information from which to draw questions and to gain a more thorough definition of the individual writer's views. Thus, of the fifteen poets included here, six are also novelists; seven are authors of short fiction; seven are essayists; at least three have written children's books; one is a journalist; another is an accomplished scholar and critic; and six have written memoirs. Nonetheless, because of space constraints, I framed most of my interview questions around poetry. In addition, I wanted to call attention to the quality of poetry these writers have produced and to record their comments on how they view themselves within the broader territory of American poetry. At the same time, I queried them about their other writing. The answers add to the tone of each interview and present a more complete picture of each writer's work.

Finally, I sought a balance between established and emerging poets. For example, Victor Hernández Cruz has been publishing poetry since the 1960s. A handful of poets in this collection developed their craft in the 1970s and began publishing poetry within a few years. Others have published most of their work during the 1980s and 1990s, a few only recently in the past five years. Although some poets are better known than others, all are active writers who continue to produce important and vital works.

In order to expedite these conversations, I had to rely on a number of different arrangements. Owing to schedules and individual preferences, some of the interview responses were given in person, whereas others were written or given by telephone. My original conversations with Virgil Suárez and Gustavo Pérez Firmat were too dated for this project, so I conducted new interviews with both writers via e-mail. I also used e-mail for the interview with Victor Hernández Cruz, who lives part of each year in Morocco, the other part in Puerto Rico. I conducted nine interviews in person: Sandra María Esteves and Miguel Algarín in New York City; Aleida Rodríguez, Ricardo Pau-Llosa, and Carolina Hospital with Carlos Medina in Miami; and Judith Ortiz Cofer in Athens, Georgia. The conversations with Luis Rodríguez, Demetria Martínez, and Benjamin Alire Sáenz took place at

Appalachian State University in Boone, North Carolina. The remaining three interviews—with Martín Espada, Leroy Quintana, and Pat Mora—took place over the telephone. The time frame for the fifteen interviews spans approximately seventeen months, from January 27, 2000, to June 18, 2001.

These interviews are of interest for several reasons. First and perhaps most important, they represent an ongoing legacy of Latino/a writers and poets. By the 1880s, building on indigenous cultural traditions fused with a literary heritage dating back to the sixteenth century, when Spanish explorers, traders, settlers, and clergy first recorded their memoirs, Latino/a writers were publishing in almost all of the popular genres of the day. They wrote in either Spanish or English, sometimes mixing the two languages. By the 1920s, writing to a new influx of Mexican and Caribbean immigrants, these authors addressed both how to preserve their native heritage and how best to assimilate into their newly adopted land, a discussion that has continued to this day. Later, a great wave of writers either discovered their voices in the Chicano and Puerto Rican civil rights movements of the 1960s or in exile in the United States during the early years of the Castro regime, profoundly influencing the generations of writers collected here. Although these poets have achieved wide recognition for their works and many hold positions at prestigious U.S. universities, all are aware of their literary roots.

A key thread linking these writers is their connection to the families and communities from which they sprung. As most of these interviews reveal, the authors celebrate their varied heritages and work to preserve them through writing, teaching, and public speaking. Protecting civil rights for all Americans is a further concern. Chicana writer Pat Mora believes that "the work of the poet is for the people." Lawyer-turned-poet Martín Espada speaks "on behalf of those without an opportunity to be heard." A former priest, Benjamin Alire Sáenz argues that we "don't deal well with poverty in this country, period. . . . Democracy is important, and anything that opens up a space for democracy and that lives up to this whole notion that all people are created equal—I take that very seriously." When a writer's family and community are threatened, the individual writer is threatened, and although these writers dwell at various points on the political spectrum, all of them are conscious of their surroundings and address the problems they see there.

Each writer in this collection also talks at length about the craft of his or her poetry—the influences and the process behind it. They also speak candidly about the difficulty in publishing poetry, particularly in an industry and for a reading public that often marginalizes poets. Martín Espada applauds the recent "publishing boom" that a number of Latino fiction writers are experiencing but points out that "the same benefits have not panned out for Latino poets." In her interview, Cuban poet Carolina Hospital argues that Latino writers "still have to convince publishers that there will be a readership for [their] material. [The publishers'] attitude is that 'we have plenty of non-Hispanic authors writing out there, so why should we take a chance with a Hispanic one?'" She also mentions that she has "had problems getting work published because it doesn't focus exclusively on [her] being Cuban." In the same conversation, Carlos Medina, who coauthored with Hospital the recently published novel *A Little Love,* argues: "I think [publishers] still have a limited view of the world. And I think it's their burden to broaden their view, not ours. I think that the so-called ethnic writers are ahead of the time, ahead of the curve, and I think that the publishers are still thinking in terms of niche and compartmentalization." Although the writers collected here generally agree with Virgil Suárez that poets "navigat[e] alone," they also accept this solitary journey as part of the territory. If they suffer a writing block in one form, they weave in and out of genres until they discover one that works for them at that time. Whether they are writing poetry, fiction, children's books, articles, essays, or memoirs, they find a way to give voice to their continuing concerns.

Despite these commonalities, these fifteen writers demonstrate the diversity one finds among Latino poets. Commercial publishers often categorize Latino writers as a homogeneous group of people who share common values and goals. Most of the poets in this collection do share similar interests, but they dispel this myth of uniformity by emphasizing differences between as well as within communities of Chicano, Puerto Rican, and Cuban writers. The issues of labeling and identity provide the most striking areas of disagreement found among these three groups. Martín Espada speaks for several writers in this collection who believe their "ethnic voice" transcends their birthplace or allegiance to a particular group or country. "I've always felt Latino in addition to being Puerto Rican," Espada responds in his interview. "As far as I'm concerned, any human identity is multilayered. . . . I am Latino and Puerto Rican, just the same way that I am a father and a husband. Those identities coexist. . . . I've always believed, politically and aesthetically, that Puerto Ricans have to reach out to other Latino groups, creating bridges and bonds, because we are still small in number." Sandra María Esteves echoes this point about the complexity of a multilayered identity when she describes herself as "Puertorriqueña-Dominicana-Borinqueña-Quisqueyana-Taino-Africana." Victor Hernández Cruz also believes this collective identity can be traced back as far as Africa. He explains: "The European culture that came to the Spanish-speaking Americas was the Spanish culture of the Mediterranean coasts, and this culture had been under Islamic Moroccan influence for many centuries. So things we consider Spanish are really things that are North African, which by extension are either of Berber or Arabic origin or even sub-Saharan since [the black African] has been a factor in this region." He believes all Latinos are "swimming in olive oil."

On the other hand, Cuban writer Gustavo Pérez Firmat argues that the idea of Latino identity "is a statistical fiction." Although teaching second- and third-generation Latino students at Columbia University has softened his stand, he explains in his interview that for him "nationality is way more important than ethnicity" and that "the term *Latino* erases [his] nationality." For Cuban Ricardo Pau-Llosa, the "preservation of language" often distinguishes one group from another. He states: "I was stunned, though perhaps should not have been, in the 1980s, when I cocurated a traveling exhibition of Latino art, to encounter Chicanos in Los Angeles and Texas who appeared very nationalistic, very 'Mexican,' but didn't speak a word of Spanish. I was the white, Anglo-looking curator with an international career and outlook, indistinguishable from the evil capitalist and so forth, and they were the ethnic Latinos who dressed the part, but I spoke Spanish fluently, and they could speak only the language of their supposed oppressors." Pau-Llosa argues elsewhere that "considering myself a *Latino* in the current American context of that term is absurd."

All of the other writers in this collection take a position on this topic, although they are not as polarized in their views. For Virgil Suárez, we are "all bicultural . . . in that we grow older each day, and we have to live thinking about the person we were yesterday and the person we will become tomorrow." Most of the poets agree with Luis Rodríguez that "it depends on the context." Rodríguez accepts a number of different labels: Latino, Chicano, American writer, native writer, English-speaking poet. "Obviously, I'm a writer. . . . It's a complicated issue," he explains, "but I think it's important to address it, not deny it."

The poets in this collection also highlight differences among members within each particular ethnic group. For example, Chicana/o poets such as Demetria Martínez, Pat Mora, and Benjamin Alire Sáenz often explore common themes that include the U.S.–Mexico border, desert terrain, Catholicism, and the mixed cultural heritage associated with southern Texas and the American Southwest. But Leroy Quintana, a Vietnam veteran, focuses much of his poetry on his war experience. In his interview, he also discusses the difference between northern New Mexico, where he was raised, and the southern border of the United States, which has influenced so many Chicano and Chicana writers. "It's important to know that this experience of crossing the Río Grande into a new life is quite foreign to people from northern New Mexico, who have no connection to Mexico. Students will ask me what state [in Mexico] I or my parents are from, and I have no answer for them. New Mexico was settled long before the *Mayflower,* and people have lived there for many, many generations." Similarly, Chicano poet Luis Rodríguez grew up in urban centers far removed from these other geographic and cultural environments and typically examines different subject matter in his writing.

Although the Puerto Rican writers in this collection express some form of loyalty to Puerto Rico, those born or raised in New York City often identify with a "Nuyorican aesthetic," which is more aligned with the politics and multiculturalism of New York. Their daily concerns and national views often differ from those of Puerto Rican writers such as Judith Ortiz Cofer, who lives in Georgia. "I think the Nuyorican poets are willfully and willingly a very specialized group of people who have a vision," Ortiz Cofer explains in her interview, "and it has to do with living in the universe of New York City. . . . I didn't experience that, and for me to try to be a part of that would be ridiculous. . . . I happen to live in the South." She speaks for many writers in this collection who examine their ethnicity: "And so being Puerto Rican is just who I am, but I could live in Connecticut, and I'd still be Judith Ortiz Cofer, the so-called Puerto Rican American writer. You can call me anything you want but don't keep me from doing anything I want." In his interview, Miguel Algarín, who has lived most of his life in New York, says: "I'm not interested in having people say they're Nuyoricans. But it's still funny for me to come to the Nuyorican [Poets Cafe] and hear a white male say, 'Hey, I'm a Nuyorican poet; I'm on the team.'. . . The term *Nuyorican* lost its intimidating aspect and kind of became inclusive instead of exclusive. But Nuyorican is also the northern Latino man and woman recognizing that they *are* the mainstream, that they *are* the majority or at least among the majority."

All of the Cubans in this collection were born in Cuba and thus take some kind of stand against Castro and the Cuban Revolution. Miami-based writer Ricardo Pau-Llosa considers it his "ethical and moral duty to denounce" Castro's Cuba, which he describes as a "horrible dictatorship." He states that "as a poet, I feel that part of what I do is keep the record straight, go back to what the facts are, and from there build a poetic assimilation of those facts." Virgil Suárez is not as severe in his criticism of Castro, but he does mention that there are "more Cubans living in exile or who have been killed because of the revolution than are actually living currently on the island." Aleida Rodríguez, who spent part of her youth in Illinois and now lives in Los Angeles, alludes to Cuba only sparingly in her writing. "I've also always thought my writing should reflect my imagination, not my identity, per se," she points out, "and expressing an imagination without borders has been my lifelong goal—fields without fences. Openness." Even though she refuses to accept "the ghetto of ideas assigned" to her by critics and other writers, she does remember some of her childhood experiences in Cuba, including one that convinced her parents to leave Cuba: "Some representatives of the government came into our classroom one day and said to us, 'Pray to God for a dish of ice cream.' We put our hands together, but nothing appeared. Then they said, 'Pray to Fidel Castro for some ice cream,' and while we had our heads bowed and eyes closed, they went around and put little dishes of ice cream on our desks. My parents pulled me right out of school when I came home with that story and applied for visas."

In light of recent census reports documenting the dramatic increase among Latino populations in the United States, this collection of interviews is timely. Scholars will find a wealth of biographical, intellectual, and literary material collected here for the first time. For teachers, this text will complement anthologies of Latino writers as well as individual collections and other types of books written by Latino poets. Students will be able to read firsthand accounts of how poets and writers view their own work. They also will find helpful suggestions on such subjects as self-publishing, work schedules, and editing. This book of interviews is not limited to a specialized academic market, however. Because these authors address a number of concerns beyond their writing, it should be accessible to any individual interested in learning more about Latino cultures in the United States and about the excellent writers produced within those communities.

Miguel Algarín

*B*orn in Santurce, Puerto Rico, Miguel Algarín moved to the United States when he was nine years old. Working his way through graduate school in the 1960s, he taught literature at Rutgers University before founding the Nuyorican Poets Cafe, a popular gathering spot for artists, writers, and musicians in New York City's Lower East Side. Long heralded as the spokesperson for Nuyorican writers, he published, with Miguel Piñero, the first significant anthology of poetry by New York Puerto Ricans. Algarín has produced theater, directed films, and written for television. He also has published six volumes of poetry and translated Pablo Neruda's *Song of Protest* from Spanish to English.

This interview was conducted at the Nuyorican Poets Cafe on March 2, 2001. Algarín talks at length about his own poetry, which dates back to the late 1970s. He also recalls the origins of the Cafe, discusses the meaning behind the term *Nuyorican,* and talks about Latinos outside the Nuyorican tradition.

SUGGESTED READING

Nuyorican Poetry: An Anthology of Puerto Rican Words and Feelings
coedited with Miguel Piñero
(New York: Morrow, 1975)

Mongo Affair: Poems
(New York: Nuyorican Poets Cafe, 1978)

On Call
(Houston: Arte Público Press, 1980)

Body Bee Calling (from the 21st Century)
(Houston: Arte Público, 1982)

Time's Now
(Houston: Arte Público, 1985)

Love Is Hard Work: Memorias de Louisaida
(New York: Scribner, 1997)

Dirty Beauty
(forthcoming)

⌄ *We know about your connection with the Nuyorican Poets Cafe, but there's not much information available on your life before the Cafe. Could you bring us up to date to the early 1970s, when the Nuyorican Cafe first opened its doors?*

Some people think I started out by writing Shakespearean scholarship, but Shakespeare had come to me before scholarship. I received Shakespeare through the stage by producing him, by putting on an extravaganza of his, such as *Julius Caesar* set in Africa, Mali, the thirteenth century. That's what Rome Neal, other folks, and I did here, at the Nuyorican. But this really started strong in the 1980s. In the 1960s, I was in the university studying, and toward the 1970s I was working on translations of Neruda. My main priority at this point was honing my mind. I was working toward my doctorate at Rutgers and studying at Princeton under Professor Joseph Frank, who was working on Hegel's aesthetics. This was the graduate life I was living in New Brunswick, New Jersey. At each school, there was a department devoted exclusively to comparative literature back then, and I wanted my doctorate in it. Later I started teaching at the university level, in New Brunswick. I secured myself a position there and aimed at getting back into New York. But it had been a great era of being away from New York and looking at the intellectual history of western Europe, and it prepared me to deal with that intellectualism, which is somewhat where we are here in the United States, even today.

⌄ *And in the early 1970s, you opened the Nuyorican Poets Cafe, which is still going strong. Can you talk briefly about the Cafe's origins? What motivated you to open the Cafe?*

In the early 1970s, I moved back to New York from New Brunswick. Once I was in New York, I was living in the Lower East Side once again. I started to let friends into my apartment who were writers. Before long, there were many people dropping by. To have ten or twelve people in a small apartment is a lot. To have double that number or triple is a whole lot. I realized that I was going to have to move out of my living room and into a larger space. I queried about the Sunshine Tavern, across the street, which had closed down. I was told that it would cost $125 a month. I got the community folks to come and shore up the walls, and then we moved in a couple of months later. Just like that! But what I really managed to save was *me*. I had been going to bed at two or three or four in the morning and getting up at eight the next morning to teach a class in New Jersey. It was impossible to continue doing that. Remember, writers write and live at night, but I had to live at night and during the day, too. I was tired. When I moved the literary hangout across the street, I named the space the Nuyorican Poets Cafe. It opened on Sixth Street, but then I moved it to Third Street. It became my public living room. And that's how I found sleep.

 ∨ *So it's been on Third Street going on twenty something years?*

Since 1981, 1982, 1983, somewhere around there. We closed for renovations and then reopened in 1988. I was doing theater elsewhere, but billing the productions under the Nuyorican Poets Cafe Theater.

 ∨ *Have you ever thought about renovating or expanding again?*

There is a high-rise, luxury apartment building getting ready to go up in the vacant lot beside us. Two-room apartments for $2,500 a month. Why? Because the building will be standing next to the Nuyorican, which incidentally still charges $5 at the door for most events.

 ∨ *How is the Cafe accepted in the community? Do you still get much local support?*

Yes, except for the time I fought with the gardeners in the back. But gardens are a celebrated cause. Of course, today the people who used to live near the Nuyorican, our original supporters, can no longer afford to live on the Lower East Side, close to the Cafe. They have all moved to the outskirts of the Bronx and Queens. But that's why I want to keep the door at $5—so those original supporters can still afford to come inside the Nuyorican. If you still want these people who have been pushed out to the edges, you keep the door price affordable to them.

 ∨ *In the introduction to **Nuyorican Poetry**, you write that the "poet has to invent a new language, a new tradition of communication." Are you talking about all poets, or is this statement a direct reference to Nuyorican poets? Is this what defines the Nuyorican voice—a new language? A tradition of communication all its own?*

I'm talking about all poets. That's where we all have to be in order to be free with each other. To know that language is a tool and that we have to clean it up. Clear, clean, pure. But that's the writer talking. As the producer of this place, the Nuyorican Poets Cafe, I look at people using language in all kinds of ways—in theater, in testimonials, in poetry. This place is a language risk, however, because when you get up on stage, you're at a great risk. You come to be uncomfortable. You have to get up in front of people, and they are your judges.

> ⌄ *Is this **Nuyorican** label as relevant today as it was twenty-five years ago, when you helped discover the term? Or have most of these poets branched out to establish their own unique aesthetic or voice?*

Of course poets branch out. Look at Reg E Gaines. He read here about ten years ago—had maybe four or five or six poems in his pocket—but he was so brilliant with what he had, he went like a train going full steam and landed up on Broadway with *Bring in the Noise, Bring in the Funk*—working with George Wolfe. He'd say he learned his trade at the Nuyorican Poets Cafe, though. Paul Beatty, Luis Cuzman—the Cafe has the reputation of drawing the community indoors and giving it a voice.

> ⌄ *So is the Nuyorican Poets Cafe separate from this idea of a Nuyorican voice?*

Hey, haven't you heard? Anyone can be a Nuyorican Poets Cafe writer. Do you think I am going to sit down and say, "Only Puerto Rican poets can read here?"

> ⌄ *I'm just trying to define or identify the term. I've talked to other poets from Puerto Rico who refuse to be pigeonholed into the Nuyorican label.*

That's clear, isn't it? I accept that. There's a North American literature frost— Emerson, Thoreau—those writers were all writing in a new voice but using the old form, English. It's different cultures. The southern novel is not like the northern novel of Maine. So I'm sure we're all going to say we're something else. I'm not interested in having people say they're Nuyoricans. But it's still funny for me to come to the Nuyorican and hear a white male say, "Hey, I'm a Nuyorican poet; I'm on the team." And I say, "Wow." The term *Nuyorican* lost its intimidating aspect and kind of became inclusive instead of exclusive. But Nuyorican is also the northern Latino man and woman recognizing that they *are* the mainstream, that they *are* the majority or at least among the majority. They certainly speak Spanish, which is the most predominantly spoken language in the Western Hemisphere.

> ∨ *The Nuyorican spirit that you've conveyed in your poetry—it's*
> *obvious, too, that it reaches outside, into other Latino cultures. Rudolfo*
> *Anaya has written an introduction to one of your books, for example.*

The original Nuyorican poets would travel thousands of miles over land to be with the Chicano poets when they would hold powwows in the late 1970s in the Southwest and in Texas. The Chicanos know us. We mean something to them, as they mean something to us.

> ∨ *As a Nuyorican, do you feel a closer link or connection to a certain*
> *Latino group over another? To the Chicano over the Cuban? Put*
> *another way, is there a Latino group outside Puerto Ricans who might*
> *be more prone to appear at your café?*

Cuban theater people have done work here. Cuban music dominates the waves here. When we deal with rhymes and beats, this music holds the place together. Cubans, Dominicans, Chicanos, Salvadoreanos. We've had a Chilean pass through. So, clearly, the Nuyorican, the Latino man and woman from the North do not have to worry about defending or talking down the mainstream because they *are* the mainstream.

> ∨ *Let's switch to your own poetry. You've been publishing poems for*
> *more than twenty-five years. How do you see your poetry evolving and*
> *changing over time? The early poetry seems more focused on*
> *New York, whereas your later work is more universal or at least set*
> *outside of New York. And then your last collection, your last book,*
> ***Love Is Hard Work***, *is . . .*

My last *book*, because I never write collections of poems. As you can see, my books are divided into sections, into themes. Did you understand why I called part of the book "Nuyorican Kaddish"? I'm using a Jewish term and manner of observing the dead because we of the Nuyorican school of the 1950s and the 1960s went to school with Jews. Allen Ginsberg influenced us a great deal. *Kaddish* influenced me. Mikey Piñero especially loved that poem. That's why I used the word *kaddish.*

ⱽ *So your poetry has changed thematically?*

Theme is one aspect of my poetry that has changed. But that's only one way of looking at it. Of course, it's changed, though. Awesome change. *Body Bee Calling (from the 21st Century)* was a poetic odyssey into a science fiction version of the poetic mind. It is the responsibility of the poet to stay afoot with science. Poetry and science have always embraced each other. Unfortunately, there was a break off somewhere, which leaves art disconnected from a body of information that changes. It's left with no reference points and new ideas. I fell upon *Body* because I was looking for a reunion between language for poets and language for engineers and rocket scientists. Science is very important for the thematic growth of language. If it weren't for scientific, electronic thinking, we would be missing half the new language additions that have appeared in the Oxford dictionaries over the past twenty years. It's not enough to cry over racism or poverty or any of these things. They are just by-products.

You have to raise the issues, asking, "At what point is there still a self, an original Miguel Algarín, son of Miguel and María Algarín? After three-quarters transplant, am I still that lady's son or my father's son, or am I the son of everyone else? Aesthetically, am I still born of my mother, when three quarters of my body is transplanted here?"

The Nuyorican aesthetic takes in those biological and ethical questions that are still in the air, as much as anything else. I'm jotting down for other Latino poets to come some places where certain things have happened, where certain things are international—Paris, Morocco, Tangier. In the 1960s, I was not living in the Lower East Side. In the 1960s, I was living in central Jersey, where I was playing student and teaching. That's when all the intellectual stuff was happening. The development of the Nuyorican mind is the development of the Puerto Rican mind as it awakens in its trajectories through the intellectual history that dominates the nation. We're part of a bigger scheme. It's interesting to me that the things we said brought us so much attention. Like Miguel Piñero with *Short Eyes*. It stopped the nation—to look at men behind bars.

But the evolution . . . Verbs, nouns, adjectives, prepositions—nothing keeps the same weight, value, or balance. They shift as your needs shift, as your conditions shift. I'm fifty-nine years old. When I was forty, I was writing from a different perspective. I can tell you that specifically the difference was in crafting verbs, nouns, object relationships. But maybe you don't like these obtuse answers. I look to the structure of the language, just like the ballet dancer uses his arms and toes and body to emote. Those are his punctuation and grammatical structure. A choreographer vehemently insists on this move after this move after this move. So the evolution of my poetry has to do a lot with how I choreograph its grammatical energy.

> ⌄ *You came to the United States when you were nine and assimilated quickly. Did you ever go back to Puerto Rico to live?*

No, I never went back to live. I go back to Puerto Rico knowing so many more things than I knew, however, but I go back infrequently. I find that I don't want to engage in any intellectual dialogue about whether the word *Nuyorican* really creates a new entity. Puerto Ricans are definitely not Nuyoricans. I don't care about that kind of issue, though. I can't get involved in that. It's what you *can* do. That's what's got to be judged. To get into a dialogue about independent Puerto Rico or dependent Puerto Rico: Who gives a fuck? Who needs another nation? Of all things, this fucking world needs another nation that's going to be starving worse than Haiti? What are we talking about? The Nuyorican Puerto Rican is defining the natural, cultural aesthetics of the nation by being humble and allowing himself or herself to be invaded. And absorbed. Yet we don't give up a thing because we are citizens. We don't need a green card. We never had to swear off anybody and to swear ourselves to this nation. The Chicanos are very aware of that—that we come with this thing called citizenship.

> ⌄ *Are you conscious of a balance in your books? Sometimes your poems are long, sometimes spiritual.*

Do you know what I'm doing? I'm studying grammar. Grammar. The space between me, Miguel, and you. And that's an enormous space to cover. It's huge. I don't mean because you're white and I'm Puerto Rican. I mean that it's a space that needs to be covered. The emotion in me has to hit you.

> ⌄ *In the poem called "Talking," you write: "A poem must complete the full cycle of release." What exactly do you mean?*

That's about the body's chemistry and electricity. The emotional states seem more like circuits that are actually short-circuited, that come out as a crisis of the body— as electrical circuits. When you short-circuit, the light goes out. When you short-circuit in the knee, that goes out, too. So the body's chemistry and the electricity are what the cycle is. I have a poem about this.

> ⌄ *The "Conversation with Silence" poems . . .*

Grammar. "I see, / you see, / and when I see what you see, / the space between you and I disappears, / but I still despair, / because I don't know if you've done what I did / in order to see what you see." That's "Conversation Number 5 with Christ." It was just a grammatical exercise in going from first person to second person to third person, the Holy Trinity.

> ⌄ *Did these poems come to you at a time when you were working with*
> *some of the southwestern Chicano poets?*

Yes, they did, and we still are working together. I visited with Rudolfo Anaya and Jimmy Santiago Baca. There was a lot of contact. There still is with other people, with different scenes. They're my family. Baca's wife knows my sister. I've spent time at Anaya's house. They knew my mother. I think you can call that a contact point, the Southwest and the Northeast. I live here. The Chicanos live there. It's a vast country. We can communicate with each other though.

But not with the Cubans, at least on the same level. The white government of this nation has cut off contact with Cuba. All contact or lack of contact with Cuba has been made politically. To me, that's not so interesting—heavy political messages that you would be connected to if you became a Cuban defender or pro-Castro. But I didn't need that. The Cubans who stayed behind were making their point. Ninety miles away from the coast of the United States and they are communists. They got some balls, man. Castro made 85 percent of Cuba literate. The black Cubans, the brown Cubans—many of them became doctors and lawyers and went to universities. He freed the Cuban nation from the American stronghold that was present at the time. The sinister fear of communism was raging in this country in the 1940s. Then we had the McCarthy trials. Castro is outrageous, a ballsy guy.

> ⌄ *I'd like to return to Anaya and something he wrote in the introduc-*
> *tion to **Time's Now**, one of your books of poetry. He says that for you*
> *"love is the truth." This power of love is reflected in much of your*
> *poetry, including some of your recent portraits in which you remember*

your father and friends. In your poetry, is love, as Anaya writes, that
"endless space" where "all the islands come together"?

It's a beautiful image that he writes about me. Love for me, as I say, is hard work.
If you do your work, though, you can come together and stay together.

ᵥ *Your poetry also expands beyond the streets of New York, as I men-*
tioned earlier. Are you conscious of balancing your books by reaching
out into the "global quarrels" you identify in a poem such as "A Defi-
ance"? Are you also motivated by events that happen to be current at
the time you write?

I've been there. I've been to El Salvador, to Central America. But I'm talking as a
Nuyorican, and so I have the television talking to me twenty-four hours a day,
whatever is happening in Central America. The Salvadoreanos were having a civil
war. You have to understand that it doesn't matter if I'm living in New Jersey or
New York to want to say something back to the people who are killing each other,
raging with hatred. We can't help but know those things because we're in the communication capital of the world.

ᵥ *In some of your Central American poems included in* **Time's Now***,*
you openly attack the Reagan administration. In one poem, "While
Morazán is on the evening news: first part," you write: "Who to love is
the White House dilemma / while El Salvador explodes." What are your
feelings toward the new Republican administration?

I'm still getting over the pardons that Bill Clinton gave away. By that logic, any one
of the black kids on the street corners of Brooklyn who gets arrested for selling
crack should also have gotten a pardon. We don't know where the Bush administration is yet. All he's promised is a tax cut of $1.6 trillion.

ᵥ **Love Is Hard Work** *was published in 1997. As I've mentioned, the*
collection contains some very intimate portraits about your father,
about losing him. There are other poems about your family and friends.
Was this a difficult collection to put together? It's such a heartfelt book.

Yes, very difficult. I've been around long enough to see a lot of people come and
go. I used to have two parents. Now I have none. When my mother died, it was

very shocking. To this day, I can dial her number, and there will be a woman speaking to me. And she'll say, "Oh," and start talking to me as if I'm her son. I was still being taken care of, somehow, when she was alive. You never know how to be a man until your mother dies.

> ⌄ *You've also been a translator—the Neruda* **Song of Protest**. *Have you translated other works?*

No, no, that's the main one. I've done other poems, but translating wasn't for me because both of these languages exist in my mind as total entities, as total representations of me. Spanish and English. The point here is that bilingualism is ill-defined. Theoretically, in the schools at least, bilingualism means that you learn in your own language until you get English down strong enough to learn in it. It's a way of dropping something instead of keeping it—keeping that second language equal and growing. This nation is making this point about English, but there are hundreds of millions of people south of the border who speak Spanish. Are you kidding me? Soon as the powers of state change, don't be surprised if Spanish is voted the national language here. I can live in New York for days and weeks without hearing a word of English; I can go all day speaking Spanish. As a matter of fact, I often do.

> ⌄ *Are you conscious of going in and out of languages when you write? Some of your poetry—several of your poems, actually—uses both Spanish and English interchangeably.*

Yes, they do. Right now, though, the languages refuse to integrate in my mind. Spanish is claiming its own space; English is claiming its own space. They're demanding separation of state. Actually, in the book I'm writing now, Spanish and English are in two struggles. Each language wants each to know, to me as writer, that they express themselves in original and self-engendered power in you.

> ⌄ *It seems like you've been doing this for a long time, haven't you? Some of your poetry even back in the 1970s blends both languages.*

You're right, but now in this book it's demanding that I separate them.

ˇ *Is this a conscious decision, then, when you write?*

It's a current state of mind. As I finish off this new book, *Dirty Beauty,* both languages are being *prima ballerina absolute,* and they're fucking with my brain.

ˇ *One last question. What do you teach now at the university? Courses in Latino literature?*

No, I teach white people their culture! That's how I make my living. I'm still at Rutgers teaching Shakespeare, but I also teach ethnic literature in the United States. I bring all these poets together that have come through the Nuyorican Cafe, and I teach them. I teach those poets because they have something unique and vibrant to say.

Martín Espada

The son of a Puerto Rican father and a Jewish mother, Martín Espada was born in Brooklyn, New York, in 1957. Besides practicing law, he has worked as a news correspondent in Nicaragua, an advocate for the mentally ill, a clerk in a hotel for transients, a groundskeeper in a baseball park, and a bouncer in a bar. His work-related experiences, in particular those as a legal services lawyer and as an advocate for the poor, often inspire his poetry. Espada is presently a tenured professor in the Department of English at the University of Massachusetts, Amherst.

This interview took place by telephone on April 16, 2001. Espada addresses a number of concerns, among them problems facing Latino immigrants today. "The true borders of Latino experience are and always have been the borders of racism," he argues, and "the fact that now we have more visibility in the media [does] not change the basic condition of most Latinos in this country, [does] not change the racism that keeps those Latinos in their place." Espada also talks about his roles as an activist lawyer, a teacher, and a poet.

SUGGESTED READING

The Immigrant Iceboy's Bolero
(Madison, Wisc.: Ghost Pony Press, 1982)

Trumpets from the Islands of Their Eviction
(Tempe, Ariz.: Bilingual Press/ Editorial Bilingüe, 1987)

Rebellion Is the Circle of a Lover's Hands
(Willimantic, Conn.: Curbstone Press, 1990)

City of Coughing and Dead Radiators: Poems
(New York: W. W. Norton, 1993)

Poetry Like Bread: Poets of the Political Imagination from Curbstone Press
(Willimantic, Conn.: Curbstone Press, 1994)

Imagine the Angels of Bread: Poems
(New York: W. W. Norton, 1996)

El Coro: A Chorus of Latino and Latina Poetry
(Amherst: University of Massachusetts Press, 1997)

Zapata's Disciple: Essays
(Cambridge, Mass.: South End Press, 1998)

A Mayan Astronomer in Hell's Kitchen: Poems
(New York: W. W. Norton, 2000)

⌄ *In the introduction to your recent anthology,* **El Coro: A Chorus of Latino and Latina Poetry***, you write that this "is a bewildering moment in history to be Latino and a poet." What exactly do you mean by "bewildering"?*

Well, basically what's behind this statement is that there are more opportunities for Latino writers than ever, but there's still a long way to go. There are many ways in which I can answer that question. As far as the Latino publishing boom is concerned, I think it's now a well-known fact that Latino fiction is everywhere, and deservedly so, but the same benefits have not panned out for Latino poets. Of course, I'm not speaking of that hybrid kind of writer who writes both fiction and poetry, but of those who tend to focus predominantly on their poetry, who define themselves first and foremost as poets. This boom has not benefited them, and we have to ask, "Why?"

The most obvious reason that leaps to my attention is economics. Based on what I know, being one of the few Latino poets who is published by the New York publishing industry, I think money is paramount. There is a perception in the publishing world, New York and elsewhere, that poetry doesn't sell—in particular Latino poetry. Publishers believe there's no market for it. Slowly it's dawning on the people in the publishing industry that that might not be the truth, but for many years that has been gospel. And it's circular logic because if you don't attempt to sell Latino poetry, of course it is not going to sell, and then you can argue that it is not going to sell. So you begin with that dilemma.

An even more significant problem is that the publishing industry has been very resistant to hiring Latinos and placing Latinos in positions of power. As long as Latinos themselves are not making publishing decisions from within the mainstream publishing industry, then there will always be certain kinds of contradictions, gulfs, and misunderstandings. The time has certainly come because everyone knows the big news about the 2000 U.S. census—that the Latino population is at least thirty-five million in this country, which makes this one of the largest Spanish-speaking countries in the world. In fact, thirty-five million is almost certainly a serious undercount, given the situation with undocumented Latinos in this country. Some organizations estimate that the real total is more like forty million. How can the New York publishing industry refuse to hire Latinos under these circumstances? How can the publishing industry in general refuse to hire Latinos in the face of figures like that?

So I still have an issue with the publishing industry itself. There are many people within the industry who are interested in Latino literature, who are willing to publish Latino literature. But I don't want to see this as something we are handed by the publishing industry. I want to see sharing of power and sharing of resources, which means hiring Latinos for visible positions within the publishing industry, positions that really do make a difference in terms of decision making. So I also take that into account when I say this is a bewildering moment to be Latino and a poet.

What this problem also raises is the whole issue of tokenism. What do you do if you're a token? And this certainly is an issue that transcends literature. My father was a political activist in Puerto Rican New York in the 1950s and 1960s. He was tokenized routinely: the only one on the committee, the only one invited to the meeting. And I remember him talking to me about the phenomenon of tokenism because he realized I would have to deal with it. He did not envision in what setting I would deal with it; he didn't know I was going to do what I do today, but he would tell me about what it meant to be a token and how to deal with it. There are several ways to respond when you feel that you're being tokenized. One is not to participate at all. Another way is to make a scene. Still another way is to try and be as effective as possible within that role. My father indicated to me a long time ago that that is what he tried to do. As he put it, "If you're gonna be tokenized, you better be one hell of a token." I've been tokenized so many times you could use me to ride the subway in New York.

You get used to it after a while; you get used to the strange sensation that, for Latinos, "one" is both the floor and the ceiling. You get used to being the only one on the panel, the only one invited to such and such a conference, to such and such a book fair. And you realize after a while that there is an agenda being imposed from without, and it might have something to do with appearances, something to do with the organizer's desire to be serving a particular constituency. It happens often enough that you do notice it when it occurs; it is strange when you are tokenized, and you have choices to make all of a sudden: Do I participate in this? Do I name it for what it is? Do I try to be as effective as possible? How do I handle it?

Another place where I've seen it happen is in the private-foundation world. I sat on a committee of a private foundation giving out more than a million dollars to individual writers, and I was appalled by what I saw. I was appalled by the fact that I had been chosen as a token. When you play the numbers game like that and you're tokenized, one of the things you're up against—in a committee, let's say— is that you are going to be outvoted: four to one, four to one, four to one, four to one. You can be as persuasive as the most brilliant orator, but it does not matter. Clearly two blocs have been created for political reasons, and you are in the smaller bloc. Once again you look up and realize "one" is the floor and the ceiling when it comes to Latino participation. And yet I managed in my way to be effective because at one point I actually put what was obvious on the table—namely, that this particular program had been running for five years, had given grants to fifty writers, all of whom had to engage in a community project, and not one of those writers was Latino. Not one of those dollars—five million up to that point—not one of those dollars had been given to the Latino community because obviously if the writer is not affiliated with the Latino community, well, the dollars don't make their way to those places.

So I actually said this out loud at a committee meeting. The people in charge were mortified. Sure enough, this led to a Latina writer being chosen by this particular program. She ended up getting a huge grant, more than one hundred thousand dollars, and being affiliated with a community organization. I did not want to sit across from famous poet X and muss his hair, but I ended up doing it because it was my responsibility to bring certain kinds of issues to the table. That is one of the by-products of being tokenized—it is an oppositional kind of thing. That means that people walk out of there saying, "What is wrong with that guy? He's got a real chip on his shoulder." Suffice it to say, you're not going to be invited to any more of their reindeer games. But that wasn't my doing, and it wasn't my intention to go in there and cause a conflict. The conflict is inherent in the situation; the conflict is inherent in being tokenized.

⌄ *Let's switch to your own writing. In your essay "Zapata's Disciple and Perfect Brie," you mention that you started writing poetry as a way of explaining "myself to myself." Do you still use poetry this way—as a means toward self-actualization? Or have you gravitated completely*

to "speaking on behalf of those without an opportunity to be heard,"
as you mention in the same essay?

Well, I think I do both. When I write an autobiographical poem, I'm revisiting that part of my life, and I'm trying to ask and answer questions that perhaps I couldn't ask or answer when these events occurred twenty or thirty years ago. So certainly it's about that—explaining myself to myself—and I think it always will be. On the other hand, almost from the beginning, even when I began writing poetry as a teenager, I was interested in "poetry of advocacy." I was interested in speaking on behalf of those without an opportunity to be heard. That to me was a natural outgrowth of being surrounded by people who were consigned to silence. I'm referring, of course, to the Puerto Rican community; I'm referring to the community in Brooklyn where I grew up; I'm referring to my own family. Certainly, being able to observe this perpetuation of silence meant that I felt a responsibility from the beginning to break that silence.

From the beginning, I was always interested in the idea of justice, hand in hand with the poetry. To this day, I think that that is probably the single most important idea in my work, not justice per se, but actually the struggle for justice, being able to talk about justice in philosophical terms, in aesthetic terms, in practical terms. There is no human society that I know of that has solved this problem—the problem of how to make justice. And so I think we as writers and as citizens should dedicate ourselves to thinking about it and speaking about it. I see nothing out of the ordinary when I write a poem where justice is the theme.

v *Is this what motivated you to go to law school as well?*

Certainly. Going to law school was a decision I made because I wanted to realize a commitment to the community, to try and bring some justice to that community. It seemed a practical solution. I had some paralegal experience, and if you work as a paralegal, you feel as if you're lacking; you feel as if there are some holes in your experience and your training that can be filled by going to law school, and then, ultimately, you will become a better advocate.

No one around me had any idea what was possible. None of us, certainly no one from my family, had ever heard of an M.F.A. program. I had never heard of an M.F.A. program. I did raise poetry as something I wanted to continue doing, but the people close to me basically rejected that idea. They didn't think—as much as they admired what I did with my writing—that it would go anywhere tangible, that there was any way of turning it into employment, that there was any way of turning it into some commitment to the community. This was not part of our frame of reference. So it was frustrating for me, but when I went to law school, I went with the assumption that poetry was going to become a secondary part of my life.

Then something happened to me that changed all that. It happened in my second year of law school. Just before I went to law school, I had my first book published, which was a little chapbook, and nobody really noticed, and in fact that provided more evidence to me that I was going to have to move on and make law my profession. Yet in my second year I encountered a striking contrast. During the summer of that year—I'm talking about 1983—I was working for the Migrant Legal Action Program in Washington, D.C., doing outreach in Spanish among farmworkers in Maryland and Delaware, explaining their legal rights to them— troubleshooting, essentially. This was an internship, and, as an intern, I was not there for the money; I was there for the experience. It was a good thing I wasn't there for the money because I was paid thirty-five dollars a week for thirty-five hours a week. A dollar an hour, for legal work, in 1983, not 1938. So I was broke, and I came home broke. The only thing that saved me that year—and now I'm talking about the academic year, that takes us into 1984—was that I won a fellowship from the Massachusetts Artists Foundation in poetry. It paid me five thousand dollars. And all of a sudden, a light bulb the size of a watermelon went off in my head: I can have two careers; I can do both of these things. I used to tell people that if the law didn't work out, I always had poetry to fall back on. And I did.

> ∨ In "The Empire of Queen Ixolib," another one of your essays, you write that through your poetry you can "build [your] father a museum of words, where a glass case displays the seat on the bus where he said 'no.'" It seems to me that you do this in a lot of your poetry, especially your more overtly political poems—"build . . . museum[s] of words" around the silent majority in order to preserve their moment, sometimes their heroic stand, in time. Is this an accurate assessment of your work?

I would say that it is, generally. The idea behind the phrase you quoted, the image, refers to a time I visited the Smithsonian Institution. I believe it was the History Museum, in fact, where I did a reading with several other Latino writers. I saw there the original seats from the Woolworth's counter where they [the civil rights activists] began the great sit-in in Greensboro. I imagined what it would have been like if my father and many other thousands of anonymous others who sacrificed and struggled and sometimes died for civil rights in the South during the 1950s and 1960s could be honored in the same way. What if we could find that bus, what if we could find that seat, what if we could put it in glass, and what if we could display it in some museum like the Smithsonian? Because for every seat taken from a Woolworth's counter and displayed in a museum, there are thousands and thousands of other seats and artifacts coming from the civil rights movement that none of us will ever see. So the reason for writing that essay—for that matter, the reason behind writing the poem called "Sleeping on the Bus"—was to honor not only my father but all of those nameless and faceless, anonymous people who sacrificed and suffered and went to jail and sometimes died to change the world.

Today when people talk to me about what is visionary, what is impossible in terms of social change, I always point them—direct them—back half a century ago to the southern United States, saying, "My father was put in jail in Biloxi, Mississippi, in 1949 for not going to the back of the bus." One of his realizations sitting in jail was that he wanted to spend the rest of his life fighting this sort of thing. Indeed, because of his efforts, because of the efforts of thousands of others, there were major changes throughout the southern United States, which ended a legal system of segregation that at one time people thought impregnable. When we talk about what cannot be changed in this society, it boils down to a matter of imagination. When someone tells me that we cannot have fundamental social change, that, to me, is a failure of the imagination. Sometimes I have to come full circle back to history in order to point to the future.

ᵛ *In the introduction to* **Trumpets from the Islands of Their Eviction***, your second collection of poetry, Robert Creeley writes that you see yourself "as a 'black and white' poet, for whom the principal* *agencies are foregrounding and shadow." Do you still define your poetry in these terms?*

Well, first of all, when Robert Creeley was writing about my work, he was writing about a collaboration with my father, a photographer.

ᵥ *Yes, the language is obviously couched in those terms.*

He's writing about works that I had written in the mid-1980s, and that book was published in 1987. Robert Creeley very graciously wrote a foreword. I think my work has probably evolved from that point, and yet essentially I think what he said is still true. Not that I see the world in black and white, as a matter of ideology, but I do think in terms of foregrounding and shadow when I create an image, especially, of course, a visual image. I'm also influenced by the great Brazilian photographer Sebastiao Salgado. So I'm really, to this day, affected by photography, and I find it influencing my work. Of course, it begins with my father's black-and-white images that were hanging on the wall when I was a kid. I think that over the years I have developed more of a handle on the use of color, so it's like taking black-and-white photographs for years and years and then trying color.

I certainly feel influenced these days by certain painters—Diego Rivera, for example. The Mexican muralists in general. I went to Mexico in the beginning of March, and I had the privilege of seeing Diego Rivera's great murals in the National Palace in Mexico City—one of the greatest phenomena I have ever witnessed. I can't even express what it did to me, looking at those paintings. So perhaps the presence of certain kinds of influences like that have enabled me to use color more and more, even frequently, now, in my poems. But that's how I interpret what he was saying about me.

ᵥ *You teach at a prestigious university, but you've also stated in one of your essays that not "every poetry reading occurs on a college campus, a bookstore or café." Do you feel that this is part of your role as an activist poet who happens to be an editor of anthologies as well as a teacher—to expose your students and others to the "poets of the kitchen" whom you mention?*

Yes, I think first of all that poetry should involve community service—whether that means doing a reading in the community or publishing poets from that community. And when I speak of "poets of the kitchen," certainly I have edited anthologies where I featured many poets whom I would define in that way. Poets who have emerged from poor or working-class backgrounds, poets who are not supposed to be educated, published, heard, or seen, and yet there they are.

I believe that the damned are not only a subject or audience, but also writers themselves. That manifests itself over and over again. I have encountered some of the most significant commitments to the act of writing in the most unlikely of places—prisons, for example. I can recall very clearly a reading in a juvenile detention center outside of Boston a couple of years ago. Following the reading, I was approached by a young man named Brandon. He showed me some of his poems, which were good. Afterward I got a ride to the bus station from the assistant warden, I believe that was his title. He said to me quite sternly, "We got a problem with Brandon. He's a poet." I said, "Oh really, how is that a problem?" As it turns out, this kid had been starting fights so that he could get thrown into solitary confinement, where he would have more time to write. The assistant warden went on to say, "We fixed Brandon; we stopped punishing him," which, of course, was difficult to explain to the other inmates. But I was really struck by this prisoner—how this young man could be so committed to the act of writing poetry that he would get into trouble deliberately so that he would be thrown into solitary confinement, which most of us would find a horrific experience; this young man was only adding time to his sentence and making his life there more difficult, and yet he could not stop writing, and he had to find a place to write where there was real quiet and real solitude. So he chose what they sometimes call "the box."

> ⌄ *You've described your teaching as this "English-professor phase*
> *of [your] existence." Is this teaching position temporary? Do you see*
> *it as one day becoming part of the work "résumé" you discuss in*
> *"Zapata's Disciple"?*

Well, my life has taken so many twists and turns that I hesitate to predict my future. I hesitate to assume that what I'm doing now, I will do for the rest of my life. Remember, I was a lawyer, and I had at the time a total focus on that. You know, I've had so many incarnations already that I am reluctant to say what is going to happen in five years or ten years. Lots can change, obviously. Now that I'm in my midforties, I have to start considering the whole question of mortality—

for myself, for my family, for those around me whom I love. That will change your life, of course, in a big hurry. As far as the question of my position here at the University of Massachusetts at Amherst, I am a tenured full professor. For the time being, that's fine; this is where I am. By the same token, you feel sometimes that you can be in a place and not of it. You can also feel that one day you have to move on. Those are things that do happen in the natural course of one's existence. I always see myself as a poet first, and no matter what else happens to me, I will continue to write poetry.

> ˅ *Actually, this work experience inspires much of your writing. Several poems in **Imagine the Angels of Bread** are influenced by one of the jobs you've held over the years, for example. Several poems from **Trumpets** and from **City of Coughing and Dead Radiators** also rely on this work experience. Can you talk about how you use this part of your life to convey a more communal message?*

Well, I am interested in my work experience as subject matter for poetry. I certainly could look back on it now and continue to write poem after poem based on the variety of jobs that I've held. I think there are some important reasons for that. First of all, I do come from a working-class background, and one of the ways to pay homage to that background is to write about the jobs that I've held. I also think that with the circumstances like that, if you have a particular kind of occupation where you use your hands, you are invisible to the people you work for. What happens is that those people will say or do anything right in front of you because you're not there. So you become a spy, a very good spy, because you cannot be seen. The people who hired me to do some of the things I did never envisioned that I would write poetry about that experience, poetry that might cast that situation in a less than glamorous light. When I was hired to work as a bouncer in a bar, who would anticipate that I would write a poem called "The Bouncer's Confession"? When I was working at a primate lab, would they anticipate that I would write a poem called "Do Not Put Dead Monkeys in the Freezer"? Probably not. The fact is, people standing before you will not see you in situations where you are literally covered in excrement, so they'll say and do absolutely anything right in front of you. They will give voice to unspoken bigotry and hidden prejudices. They reveal themselves in startling ways.

Even later on, when I became a lawyer and went into court wearing a suit, even then there were times when I was invisible because I represented people who were invisible. Sometimes I would be visible, and other times I would become as invisible as they were. And the judge—I think of this one judge, whom I despised, frankly—this particular judge never envisioned that I would write verse comparing his face with a fist. That's what it looked like, you know—you hold your fist out, and you press down so the lines of the skin run into the palm: that was what his face looked like. And certainly he treated my clients or any poor people as if he were a fist to bring down upon them. What a cruel man. So that made me a poet-spy. The whole list of jobs that I could enumerate—a janitor, a bouncer at a bar, a night desk clerk at a transient hotel, an encyclopedia salesman, a bindery worker at a printing plant. . . . Even in my day as an attorney, there were times when things would happen that I would turn into a poem.

> ⌄ *"Coca-Cola and Coca Frío" from* **City of Coughing and Dead**
> **Radiators** *is one of your most anthologized poems. You touched on*
> *this subject a little earlier, but do you feel that most publishers look*
> *only for the ethnic voice in the so-called ethnic poet and thus diminish*
> *the diversity these poets share with all other poets?*

Well, I certainly hope that a poem like "Coca-Cola and Coca Frío" is read for more than its cultural identity. It can be read that way. It can be read as a poem about a second-generation child returning to the homeland of the father and discovering something about himself in the process. It can be read as a poem about that first time in your father's homeland, and obviously that's a big part of the immigrant experience, when the next generation goes back. But it's about so much more than that. If people look at it closely, what they will see is a commentary on colonialism. It's very much about cultural imperialism. In fact, sometimes when I introduce that poem at readings, I call it "my cultural imperialism on vacation poem." It's very much about the colonized mind.

What I'm referring to here, of course, is that Puerto Rico has been a colony of the United States for more than a century, and one of the by-products of colonialism is a colonized mind. That's what happened to my family. They lived in a country with coconuts hanging from the trees, which to me was miraculous, but they were drinking Coca-Cola. And what's more, they insisted that I drink it because they wanted to give me the "best" that they had. Ironically, what the family defined as their best was this import from the United States, which to me was all too mundane. Coca-Cola, who cares? But the notion that you can drink out of a coconut—that was a miracle to me. In fact, until the first time I went to Puerto Rico, I had never seen a real coconut. I'd always see those little, brown, shriveled, hairy things in the market, but I'd never seen a coconut with its great big green shell. I had never seen a fresh coconut; I had never seen a coconut on a tree. And I'd certainly never seen anything like *coco frío*, where they cut the top of the coconut off, stick a straw in it, and you drink from it. That to me was miraculous because it was so damned resourceful, you know, and the resourcefulness of people who have little continues to amaze me. I couldn't believe that everybody around me was rejoicing over Coca-Cola. It was just surreal.

So I hope that there are people who can read it that way, but I also hope that there are people who can read it and appreciate it just for the language itself, just for what the images do. Just for what the metaphors and similes do. Because I take a great deal of care when I construct a poem and particularly when I construct metaphors and similes. I certainly hope that somebody notices once in a while that it isn't simply a matter of reading the poem for its content. I hope that people are also reading it for the way that it is structured, for the way that it is crafted.

> ⌄ At the same time, this realistic "ethnic" voice is the driving force
> behind some of your best poetry. When you're writing about Puerto
> Rico or the Nuyorican experience in New York or the aftermath
> of the Somoza regime or a killing in El Salvador or Chile, this ethnic
> voice creeps through. It's what, according to Amiri Baraka, "illuminates
> reality." Do you agree?

Well, it's interesting to note what we come to define as an ethnic voice because many people want to define my ethnic voice as being found only in the poems that deal with Puerto Rico and Puerto Ricans. I mean, that's the ethnic voice. I'm Puerto Rican, and that suggests the ethnic voice. There are those who feel that that's what the ethnic voice should be. I've always felt Latino in addition to being Puerto Rican. I don't see that as a contradiction in terms; I don't see that as a dilution. As far as I'm concerned, any human identity is multilayered, and my identity is multilayered. I am Latino and Puerto Rican, just the same way that I am a father and a husband. Those identities coexist. Why can't my identities as Latino and Puerto Rican coexist? Now, once you accept the notion that I am a Latino and I have a Latino identity as a writer, that opens certain doors. And I found myself thinking about and writing about certain topics that other Puerto Rican poets perhaps have not addressed or don't address as frequently. I write a great deal about Mexico. I write a great deal about the Chicano community. I write a great deal, as you pointed out, about Central America, about El Salvador and Nicaragua. I've written about Chile. I am a Latin Americanist. I've always felt that way. I've always felt that sort of Pan-Latin kind of impulse, and I've always believed, politically and aesthetically, that Puerto Ricans have to reach out to other Latino groups, creating bridges and bonds, because we are still small in number.

> ᴠ *I would like to finish by returning to* **The Immigrant Iceboy's Bolero**, *your first book of poetry. In one poem called "Heart of Hunger," you describe the Latino immigrant as "Fishermen wading into the North American gloom." Twenty years after the publication of this first book of poems, do you feel the situation of Latino immigrants is better or worse? What, in your opinion, is the biggest problem facing Latino immigrants today?*

Well, the biggest problem facing Latino immigrants today is the same problem Latino immigrants have always faced: racism. Racism is still the most important problem. The true borders of Latino experience are and always have been the borders of racism, and the fact that now we are greater in number, the fact that now we have the beginnings of a middle class in certain communities, and the fact that now we have more visibility in the media do not change the basic condition of most Latinos in this country, do not change the racism that keeps those Latinos in their place. The fact that Ricky Martin is a pop culture hero does not make the life of the average Puerto Rican any better. It has always been acceptable for Latinos to be entertainers. It was always okay for Carmen Miranda to do what she did. I for one am not going to join all the celebrants in the mainstream media who seem to think that everything is now okay for Latinos. I am only a few years removed from being a legal services lawyer working in the barrio of Chelsea, Massachusetts, and seeing the kinds of conditions in which Latino immigrants find themselves to this day. Until we can deal with immigration humanely, until we can do away with a system that can define any human being as "illegal," we will continue to have fundamental problems. And by "we," I don't just mean Latinos—I mean all of us.

Certainly things have gotten better in some limited ways. I would never argue that we are in the same place that we were twenty years ago. But if things have changed for the better, it is not because the U.S. government, in a fit of conscience or as a result of noblesse oblige, has decided that life should be better for Latinos. If conditions have improved for Latinos, it is because Latinos have improved them. One of the great Latino leaders of this century was César Chávez. When we talk about César Chávez, I think we should talk about how he was one of the essential civil rights leaders this country has produced and that César Chávez did make a difference in this world; he did help to improve conditions for farmworkers and Latinos in general. Having said that, I must point out that conditions for many farmworkers in this country, Latinos included, remain abominable. So let us not be deceived by the progress that has been made. Let's be inspired by the progress that's been made and try to build upon that.

Sandra María Esteves

Sandra María Esteves was born on May 10, 1948, in New York City. Her mother was Dominican, her father Puerto Rican. She learned early in life the restrictions placed on her Latina heritage, particularly in the strict Catholic boarding school she attended as a child. She eventually studied art at the Pratt Institute in New York. As a student, she discovered the value of words and started experimenting with writing. A few of these pieces are included in one of her best-known poetry collections, *Yerba Buena*. Esteves still lives in New York City, where she creates art, writes, and conducts writing workshops in the public schools.

This interview took place in New York, March 1, 2001. Esteves talks about the evolution of her work and about her unique heritage, which she traces back to the indigenous Taino and African blacks of the Caribbean. She also discusses the problems of publishing in a corporate industry that often discriminates against people of color, in particular Latina writers.

SUGGESTED READING

Yerba Buena
(New York: Greenfield
Review Press, 1980)

*Tropical Rains: A Bilingual
Downpour*
(New York: African Caribbean
Poetry Theater, 1984)

*Bluestown Mockingbird
Mambo*
(Houston: Arte Público Press,
1990)

Undelivered Love Poems
(New York: No Frills, 1997)

*Diving into the River of
Language: Sink or Swim?*
(New York: No Frills, 1998)

*Contrapunto in the Open
Field*
(New York: No Frills, 1998)

*Finding Your Way: Poems
for Young Folks*
(New York: No Frills, 1999)

ᵛ *You once wrote that you're "Puertorriqueña-Dominicana-Borinqueña-Quisqueyana-Taino-Africana." Can we start by having you
elaborate on this diverse background?*

My father's family is Puerto Rican, my mother's family is Dominican. I start with
Puerto Rican–Dominican, then I go to Borinqueña-Quisqueyana, because *Borinqueña* means I am a native of Borinquen, the Taino name for Puerto Rico, and
Quisqueyana means I am a native of Quisqueya, the Taino name for the Dominican Republic. The Tainos were the indigenous people who inhabited the islands of
the Caribbean before Columbus arrived and renamed their land. So if someone
calls you Borinqueño, Boricua, or Quisqueyana, they're saying that you're someone who identifies with your past and your culture. It's also a reference to nation-
hood. I'm making connections to my history by tagging that on. The *Africana*
identifies another part of my roots. I'm saying that I'm American, born in the
Bronx, but I'm also Taino and African. I disagree with the statements that all Tainos
were wiped out because many fled and hid in the mountains; they mixed and
married, so the Taino is still very present in our society. Recent DNA testing has
proved this to be true in spite of what the history books tell us. You know, you
can't always believe those accounts written in books. It depends on who is writing
it and why, what is the point they are getting at to try and convince whoever may
be the reader. The slaughter of the Indians started as soon as the colonists arrived,
but many survived by fleeing. Remember that Puerto Rico and the islands of the
Caribbean, which were home to the Tainos, are larger that we imagine, with many
effective places to hide, like lush mountains and obscure caves.

ᵛ *You started out as a painter, then switched to poetry. I was wondering
when and how you made this transition from one art form to the other.*

Well, I'm still a painter. I consider myself a painter who uses poetry as a different
way of painting. It wasn't until I was in college that I started experimenting with
words and language. It happened in one of my art classes. I had a Japanese sculptor-
teacher named Toshio Odata, who was one of my teachers at the Pratt Institute in
Brooklyn. He would create these giant sculptures out of tree trunks, and he had us
chiseling wood. Then one day we came into class, and he had sheets of typing paper
on the wall on which were two or three lines of conceptual sculptures that you

could not fabricate. You could only imagine them because they were megalithic in size. He'd have something like a sphere a hundred miles wide suspended fifty miles over a pink island in an orange ocean or something that you couldn't create except in your mind. He woke up the realization that words could be a different way of creating art because up until then I was not interested in experimenting with language. I had never considered that language could be a valid tool for creativity. Not for me. When I was young, I was placed in a boarding school where I was not allowed to speak my natural Spanish, which was all I spoke until I was five. Not being allowed to speak Spanish in school traumatized me with inhibitions about speaking. I'd always confused the English with the Spanish, not being sure which words belonged to which language. I knew the meanings of both of them, but sometimes I couldn't differentiate if a particular word was an English word or a Spanish word. I can remember being in the third grade, repeating words over and over, trying to feel the words in my being. I believed that Spanish was sweeter. Sometimes I could taste the languages, but I also made mistakes. When I would go home on weekends, my cousins would laugh at my mistakes, so I began to withdraw into silence. Not only that, I also ran the risk of being punished by the nuns if I didn't speak the correct language. The nuns had all kinds of clever ways of coming up with punishment for you—pulling your ears, spanking your hands with a ruler, hitting you on the butt with a plastic tennis racket, making you kneel on hard wooden pews until you passed out.

In boarding school, in the second grade I made the decision that I was going to be an artist because I wouldn't have to talk. I could express myself with colors, and it was safe. I was so good at drawing that the other little girls would give me their composition notebooks, and I'd fill them up with cutout dolls with elaborate wardrobes, for which they'd pay me ten cents. So I basically became a listener, an observer. My mother thought that something was wrong with me. I became an extreme introvert who wouldn't talk. You wouldn't believe that about me today because I'm very different, but back then I had a lot of fears about language.

It wasn't until that art class that I opened up to words. I started experimenting and incorporating words into some of my drawings. I actually have one drawing that's a continuous line, where I break from form into words, then back into form, then into words, until I filled up the whole page.

ⱽ *Earlier you told me something about attending a poetry reading or*
workshop that inspired you to begin expressing yourself through words.

The brother of one of my college friends was a member of the National Black Theater in Harlem, and he had been inviting me to come see one of their perform-
ances. Finally I decided I'd go, and the day I went was the one day out of the year
when they celebrated their "Community Day." There were about thirty people
there, and it seemed like everyone got up and recited one or two poems either
that they had written or that were written by someone else. Everyone except me.
I was the only one who did not recite, but I was in awe of the words I witnessed
that day. It was the first time that I heard the works of writers like Gwendolyn
Brooks, Nikki Giovanni, Langston Hughes, Amiri Baraka. I heard poetry that was
about me, that was very immediate. I connected to it in a visceral way. That experience moved me so profoundly that I went home and that night I wrote my first
batch of poems. It was like the floodgates opened. That reading empowered me
with a voice and gave me permission to express everything that had been fester-
ing in me for years. So I just started experimenting with language and writing all
kinds of things.

ⱽ *Have you thought about merging these two art forms, about*
including an illustration beside a poem to create a new aesthetic?

Not in those terms, but it sounds like a great idea. I have tried to put together illus-
trations with the poetry, but I haven't been able to do it successfully. They're separate, but not really, because I write visually. I'm a painter who uses words.

ⱽ *You also use paintings and painters in your poetry—sometimes*
to commemorate. You have "Raising Eyebrows" for Frida Kahlo and
"I Want to Paint."

Yes, that's right. But to add to that, I was not trained as a writer. I had writing
classes in college, sure, but I was trained as a visual artist. It's that training that
I apply to my writing. Those exercises in art are the foundation that fuels my
writing.

ⱽ *When you teach your poetry workshops, do you sometimes rely on*
this visual imagery? With children, for example?

I do stress visualization when I work with students. In every workshop, my students will hear me repeatedly talk about "word pictures." It's just another way of creating metaphors. When students write, they often generalize. I want them to be specific, so I ask them to imagine that they're creating a movie, that they're using a camera, and that they have to describe each shot for the listening audience. So I stress detail to overcome the hurdle of generalizing. Instead of the general "He feels bad," I tell them to describe how that looks—"His skin was as pale as twilight" or "His eyes are a river of tears."

> ∨ *Julia de Burgos is an obvious inspiration. Were there other women who helped you find your literary voice? In* **Diving into the River of Language: Sink or Swim?** *you list several poets from the "first wave of Nuyoricans," but only one of them is a woman.*

When I started writing, there were only two women writers that I knew: Lorraine Sutton and Margie Simmons. There were very few Latinas writing in English. You have to remember that Spanish kind of escaped me back then, so it was a while before I connected with Latina authors writing in Spanish. Even though some of the ways I use language has to do with Spanish, I'm not that familiar with poetry written in Spanish. So when I started, I was mainly surrounded by men—Pedro Pietri, Jesus Papoleto Melendez, Lucky Cienfuegos, Miguel Algarín, Miguel Piñero, Tato Laviera. Many of them had books already published. I was like a sponge, absorbing different things from these male contemporaries.

> ∨ *This was in the early 1970s?*

Yes, because I started writing in 1972, and a year later I was in the thick of it. I found that different devices would show up in my work, devices that my male colleagues were using, to the point that even their themes would become my themes. Then one day someone came up to me and said that the reason I write so well is that I write like a man. I didn't know how to take that. It hit me profoundly, and I had to think about it for a while. It made me realize that I wasn't really expressing my own voice. Even my style was very much like the men's style—strong and militant. Not to say that all men are strong and that all women are soft, but there were parts of myself that I just wasn't exploring or expressing by emulating these male voices.

ᴠ *So is there an evolution between your first and second collections?*
Do you feel that your first collection of poetry was inspired by what
you just described and that by the time you get to **Bluestown Mock-**
ingbird Mambo *you've finally come into your own authentic voice?*

I feel like I'm constantly evolving into my own voice. I'm getting closer every day, although I'm not sure what my "real" voice is. Some critics say they see my voice, but I don't always see that. The hardest person to see is your own self. I do know that my writing has changed in ways that I feel positive about. I see a process of development that has surfaced through the years.

ᴠ *Is it a more feminist voice or a voice focusing on women's concerns?*

I definitely think there's more awareness and consciousness of that than there was before. When I wrote "My Name Is Maria Cristina," that's the first time I tried to dialogue anything in a social context. Until then, I was writing poems like so many other poets—love poems and rejection poems. "Maria Cristina" was my first serious poem, but I was also very young, searching for my identity. I've grown over the years, and you still see some of those same themes in my poetry. It isn't just my female identity, but my social-political identity as well. I also see the bigger picture—how we are Latinos and Latinas struggling in a society that continues to marginalize us. Like the issue of Puerto Rico, as the island "mistress" of the United States, and how it plays itself out in a lot of different ways in our community. We know the projections about Latinos becoming the largest minority within the next few years, but you can go to Barnes and Noble across the street, where they have a department store of books, or any other franchise bookstore anywhere in the States, and you won't even find one aisle devoted to Latino literature. So what are they trying to tell us—that we don't have a literature? Or that we don't read or write or buy books? None of this is true. We are a community with a vibrant and extensive literature, but we are still a marginalized culture, even now in this new millennium.

ᴠ *Why do you think that is? Is it racism, or does it involve not knowing*
how to tap into the market?

I think it's both and more. They're also motivated by greed. It's not about cultivating a literature; it's about cultivating profit. That's the determining factor here.

One of the reasons I've used No Frills Publications as my self-publishing venue in the past is that I have complete control over my own writings. It's hard to grow your own oranges and then give them all away. You actually have to buy them back if you want them again when someone else is publishing your work. Of course, it's a two-way street. If I send my work out to get published, it gets visibility that I can't get when I publish it on my own. It gets distributed in places where I may never get to. But then if I do it myself, I maintain control over my work. I'm trying to find a balance. Most writers seem to experience an assortment of nightmares when dealing with publishers. I'm not saying not to, but you have to weigh how much to give away when you publish outside because that's what you do—you're giving away your work. There is also the argument, though, that anyone's writing is meant to be shared with the universe. I want to die knowing that my children are going to have some kind of legacy because this is all I have to give—my work. Then again, maybe I'm confused about the law on this. What exactly are my rights? What happens to my work when I hand it over?

> ∨ Let's return to the portrait of New York in **Yerba Buena**, your first
> collection of poetry. It isn't very flattering. You describe a city that
> "spits in my eyes," a "bleak / manhattan" where "no one escapes"
> and "people are dying in the streets." How have things changed for
> Latinos? Is it still such a grim picture?

I think the picture is still pretty grim, but I think that I've changed. Remember, I was a lot younger then, and I was still very angry about all the things that had happened from the time I was born. At that point, I'm only beginning to express myself. All that anger that had been building up for all those years was beginning to express itself in my poetry. So you find poems like those in that collection. I'm still angry, but I'm angry in a different way. I've released a lot of it. I'm still frustrated about a lot of things—about the marginalization that happens to us. It keeps showing its face. Like I'll go into the classroom, where most of my kids are Latino. In one school that I visit, it's 95 percent Latino, and as soon as I walk in, I imagine students subconsciously saying to themselves, "Oh, there she is. She's Latina, so we don't have to listen to her." This is conditioning. I don't ask them why they're treating me this way. I don't have to ask them. I know where it comes from, even if they can't comprehend what I understand. It shows itself in other ways as well. A few years back I directed a play. I gave directions to a particular Latina actress, but she didn't want to follow them. I asked her, "If I were Steven Spielberg, would you have the same reaction?" And she said, "Of course not!" Unfortunately, we also marginalize ourselves. That's the worst-case scenario. It's so prevalent, and to me it's absolutely frustrating. You have to fight for every little thing you get. Every little penny. Every shred of dignity.

> ⌄ *You also have poems in your first collection that are dedicated to men—Fidel Castro, Franz Fanon. And, in **Bluestown**, you have more portraits of women.*

That reflects my growth.

> ⌄ *What about the poem that is a tribute to Castro? How do you, as a Latina, view Castro and the revolution today?*

I wrote "For Fidel" at the beginning of my political awareness that I was a colonized woman in this society. I'm a child awakening in the late 1960s, at the tail of the civil rights movement, along with the acceptance of my blackness and a blossoming awareness of my cultural identity. I identified with the Cuban people struggling to stand on their own after years of victimization through colonization. So at first I embraced all of that. It's hard to take sides. I understand the pain and suffering of loss. And the older you become, the harder loss is to handle. I feel for those who have experienced loss. But when I look at Cuba, I also have to ask myself, Would I want to be exploited the way that Puerto Rico has been exploited in this century? And to me the answer is clear. We have only to look at the devastation reaped upon Vieques to understand why we have to demand our autonomy. I know exactly what I want. I don't want anyone telling me what to do. I want to determine for myself. I went to Cuba in 1984. And I have friends who are on the other side. Even in my family there is a split. That's one of the issues of great contention in my family. I have relatives who live in Miami who are against Castro, and I have family in New York who are pro-Castro.

My position is that people should be able to determine for themselves. I believe in the right of choice and self-determination. I also believe that people should not be exploited unless they agree to it. And who does? Even a woman who's a prostitute on the street is usually trying to support something. I believe it's not a choice, but a necessity, that causes women to do that. No one in their heart wants to be violated, not even for money. When I was in Cuba, I saw some things that really impressed me. When we arrived, on the way to the hotel we were driving through the streets late at night. I expressed concern when I saw a woman walking alone. Our chaperone told us that they don't have the same issues of sexual exploitation and rape like in the United States. And then I also saw that they had twenty-four-hour day care. That made sense. I saw free hospitalization and free education, even though I've heard criticism that the quality is not the same. Yet I question the criticism. I have friends who have gone to Cuba to receive medical treatment they were unable to get in the States, either because it was not available or it was just too expensive. What's important is that it's available.

   ˅ *Things obviously have changed since the fall of the Soviet Union as*
    well. Certainly life is a lot bleaker.

I think, though, that Cuban life would be somewhat normalized if the U.S. embargo were lifted, especially for humanitarian reasons. Something else I saw in Cuba was a musical, a play. What impressed me was that all the stars were black and Latino actors. It was as spectacular as any musical on Broadway. A play centered around Chocolate, the boxer. And I was elated to see a cast of dark people acting and starring. It was the same kind of Broadway sound, except that I wasn't on Broadway; I was in Cuba. I remember thinking that you'd never see this in New York. The closest we've come to that was *Zoot Suit* and *The Cape Man,* but ethnic actors are still being marginalized on Broadway.

   ˅ *Do you feel compelled to write in Spanish or English?*

I'm definitely English dominant. I've learned to think and feel in English, although on occasions Spanish comes back. I talked to my children in Spanish a lot when they were very young, as much as I could, because I wanted them to learn the language. Later I had to speak to them only in English because that's what they wanted, to "fit in." Now my children are rediscovering Spanish. My oldest daughter graduated from college with a degree in Spanish. She once rejected it. In high school, she didn't want her English-speaking friends to know that she was Latina. Sometimes, within the African American community, being Latina can be a liability rather than an asset. But then, that's why it's important to know our history, to know how we are connected, how we are victims of the diaspora that divided our families and plunged us into ideas of segregation and disunity. It's so important to know our history to overcome the misconceptions about race and culture.

⌄ *In your first book, you mention something about the "theft of your island heritage." In a more recent poem, "Puerto Rico Discovery #3: Not Neither," you deal with this same kind of theft. Do you still write about this subject, or is this kind of connection with the island something that came out in your earlier days, when, as you mentioned, you were angry?*

I think it's still there. The "theft of my island heritage" has to do with not having my original culture available to me. It goes back to the issues of marginalization. I didn't know anything about my Puerto Rican or Dominican culture until I was in my late twenties. This information was not taught or available in the schools. And it's still pretty much the case. I go into the schools today, and one of the first lessons I do with the children is to talk about the Taino Indians. You would think, with all the information available today, that students would know something. But the kids are amazed when they hear me talk about this. I ask them if they know the meaning of *Borinqueña* or *Quisqueyana*. Even in Washington Heights, in a school that is predominantly Dominican, they don't know where *Quisqueya* comes from, even though they've heard it a thousand times. They don't know that it's a Taino word. They don't know that it was the Indian name of their island. So this information is still missing, yet still terribly important.

To take it a step further, I was born here. I didn't go to Puerto Rico until I was seventeen, so I didn't get to know that part of myself until much later in my life. I feel somehow victimized by circumstances—not only the circumstances of having been born here and of not having any information about my identity available, but even my mother didn't seem to think it was important to pass along her heritage. Her thing was, "You're in America now; you have to know how to speak English well and be a good American." Even my mother was taught to devalue the worth of her own heritage, to marginalize herself. To this day, we argue about this. I want to learn about my past, my culture. She talks to me in broken English, reminding me how wonderful it is to be an American; I talk to her in broken Spanish, attempting to explain why I want to know more about our history and culture.

⌄ *Do you think the gap between parents and children is getting wider?*
Is this one of the reasons why the students that you were referring to
earlier don't know about their Taino past?

I don't know if the gap is getting larger. Sometimes I think the gap might even be getting smaller, at least at the college level. Now you have Latino studies departments in some of the universities. And even though some of these are still highly marginalized and no more than token gestures of integration, inclusion, and diversification, where you get only one or two classes, there's still a demand for it. People want this information. This is a multicultural society. People are tired and bored with exclusivity.

⌄ *It doesn't really reflect reality, does it?*

Of course not. It's an outdated, outmoded model. People just don't want that anymore. I think there are many people out there who are ready and want to embrace a multicultural ideology.

⌄ *Where do your "Puerto Rican" and "Affirmation" poems come from?*
I don't find a continuous theme to latch on to or a consistent
chronology. You'll skip from one to three to another number. Are
these testimonials?

They're like testimonials. Pedro Petri has a series of telephone booth poems I've been listening to since I've known him, and he was the inspiration for these. Mine are similar. They are also affirmations, celebrations, criticisms, mental landmarks about boundaries and identity. The idea for them evolved when I would get invited every year to about ten or more schools on the same day, to celebrate "Puerto Rico Discovery." And it was always the same thing—they'd have rice and beans, flan, *pava* hats, and *cuatro* guitars, and somebody would always play "En mi viejo San Juan." I found myself asking, Is this what it means to discover Puerto Rico? And I realized that discovering Puerto Rico and, more important, our identity has to mean more than this. It means us discovering each other, beyond the stereotypes, identifying other nuances of ourselves. So every time I made more observations about my Puerto Ricanness, I wrote these "Discovery" poems. I only have a few "Affirmation" poems. The Puerto Rican "Discovery" poems make more direct statements about what I'm thinking politically.

> ∨ Is **Undelivered Love Poems**, a more recent collection, a hopeful
> book? You end by "falling asleep writing love letters in the dark."

That was a moment in my personal life that has become a metaphor for how we live. I feel that everything I write is a different kind of love poem. Even the angry political poems are a kind of love poem. The "falling asleep" can be viewed in different ways: how we are marginalized, how whole communities are sedated with the new slavery of drugs, how we are easily offered various forms of addiction to cope with our situations, anything from drugs, alcohol, religion, sex, television, food, money—take your pick. A poet named Safiya said, "We all are addicted to something." But we still manage to dream in spite of it.

> ∨ Are the poems from this collection the most personal poems you've
> written, simply because they're "undelivered," as opposed to the more
> overtly political poems?

No. There are highly political poems included in this collection. The fact that they're "undelivered" has more to do with the plight of the poet. The poet is a truth bearer of reality and image. We live in a society of denial that doesn't want to see or hear these truth tales, so consequently poets are shunned to a great degree because people don't always want to hear the truth. I've had to learn to judge when and how to keep my observations to myself or how to exercise wisdom and better judgment in expressing them. Sometimes being a poet can be dangerous and unwelcome territory. If you look at the literary market, poetry is at the bottom, although I also know that's changing. In the past decade, poetry has been experiencing a blossoming, but teachers are still scared to teach poetry, mostly because they weren't exposed to it and never really learned how to explore their imaginations. So school kids know very little, if anything, about poems. I remember that in the old days poets used to go into the factories and the sugar and tobacco plantations and recite to the workers while they were doing their thing. No more. Perhaps it's a fear of intelligence, of language. A fear of self-realization. Part of the "undelivered" [in the title] has to do with poems that will never be delivered because people don't want to hear the truth, don't ever want to confront reality.

 ⌄ *You've experimented in other genres as well, haven't you?*

I've written for the theater; I've written a few plays, but they've had only minimal productions. I don't feel that I'm a playwright.

 ⌄ *And the essay?*

I do have essays that I've written, and I have essays that I still want to publish that have to do with my early years. I was raised by my mother, but around my father's family. She was alone. My father's family rejected my mother because she was too dark, and they were only a slight shade lighter. Their attitude was based on racist criteria of appearances that people had back then, when the hue of your skin defined who you were, where you were able to go, what you could learn, do, and achieve in life.

 ⌄ *Why don't we end with a few words about **Bluestown Mockingbird Mambo**. You celebrate music in this book.*

Part of it has to do with the oral tradition, but music has been a very important part of my life. My uncle, my father's brother, was a famous Latin Jazz musician named Joe Loco. He was a contemporary salsa musician of the 1940s and 1950s. I was young, but I knew him. I remember listening to my uncle playing the piano. My uncle told my mother that I had artists' hands. He told her that I should have piano lessons, but my mother couldn't afford them, so every night for seven years, while I was in boarding school, I'd sit in study hall listening to other classmates playing scales. We also lived a religious, contemplative, meditative kind of life. The nuns would take us to chapel every day. We used to sing all the hymns, and I learned to sight-read Gregorian Chant. So there were all these influences. As I got older, I realized that there was a lot that I did know through music. I was dancing merengue and *bomba* even before I had words for those things. In those days, I couldn't tell you that I was actually dancing a merengue. These were my very first history lessons, which endeared the music to me. The poems in *Bluestown* are an affirmation of being. I turned the music into poetry and poetry into music the same way I turned art into a written form.

Victor Hernández Cruz

Victor Hernández Cruz was born in Puerto Rico in 1949 but spent much of his youth picking up the "neighborhood jargon" and "stoop yap" of New York City. This ability to blend language and culture has always been one of his trademarks. A prolific writer of both poetry and prose, including "a couple of" unpublished novels, Hernández Cruz lives part of each year in Morocco and part in Puerto Rico, places he feels are "part of [his] exploratory migrations."

This interview took place via e-mail January 2001. Hernández Cruz discusses his position on the origins of the Spanish language, arguing that anyone who traces his or her roots back to Spain, which by extension includes parts of North Africa, is "swimming in olive oil." He also conveys his ideas on aesthetics and traces the evolution of his poetry, which was applauded by Ishmael Reed and some of the other early members of the Umbra Writers Workshop of the 1960s.

SUGGESTED READING

Papa Got His Gun!
(New York: Calle Once, 1966)

Snaps: Poems
(New York: Random House, 1969)

Stuff: A Collection of Poems, Visions, and Imaginative Happenings from Young Writers in Schools—Opened and Closed
coedited with Herbert Kohl
(New York: World, 1970)

Mainland: Poems
(New York: Random House, 1973)

Tropicalization
(New York: Reed, Cannon, and Johnson, 1976)

El Clutch y los Klinkies
(New York: # Magazine, 1981)

By Lingual Wholes
(San Francisco: Momo's Press, 1982)

Rhythm, Content, and Flavor
(Houston: Arte Público Press, 1989)

Red Beans: Poems
(Minneapolis: Coffee House Press, 1991)

Paper Dance: 55 Latino Poets
coedited with Leroy V. Quintana and Virgil Suárez (New York: Persea, 1995)

Panoramas
(Minneapolis: Coffee House Press, 1997)

⌄ *After a lot of crisscrossing and correspondence, I've finally tracked*
you down to this North African address. Why Morocco? Is this move
part of the "metamorphoses of regions and climate" you mention
in your essay "Home Is Where the Music Is"? Or the "personal
and landscape changes" you touch on in "The Bolero of the Red
Translation"? In that same essay, you write: "I am a body of migration,
an entity of constant change."

Well, let me start by saying that language is motion, that poetry especially is action. We are all verbs. I am somewhat nomadic or gypsyish. I see connections between various cultures and geographic zones. I am from Puerto Rico, which the last time I looked at the map was in the Caribbean, and the Caribbean is made up of international elements. It was created by Europe's imperialist games. The Spaniards who came to the Caribbean were fresh from overtaking Granada, the last Muslim stronghold in al-Andalus. So these waves of boats that started to leave the Huelva, Dos Puntos, and Cadiz ports must have been filled with the mixtures of the region. The Spanish of Puerto Rico is like the Spanish of the popular people of Cordoba and Cadiz. The European culture that came to the Spanish-speaking Americas was the Spanish culture of the Mediterranean coasts, and this culture had been under Islamic Moroccan influence for many centuries. So things we consider Spanish are really things that are North African, which by extension are either of Berber or Arabic origin or even sub-Saharan since this element has always been a factor in this region—the black African.

The main force that made up the invasion of Spain back in the year 711 was not Arabic, but recently converted tribal Berbers. There is flowing in Spanish veins much Berber blood, and there is flowing in Latin Americans this same substance. Spaniards from all the regions made it to the Americas, but the initial wave was from Andalusia, and that original impact was felt mostly in the Caribbean: Santo Domingo, Puerto Rico, and Cuba. What time has done to this brew in the Caribbean is mix it with African blood. In Morocco, which is where I live now, I feel I am looking at a branch of our cultural rhythm. There is here a similar *mestizaje* and *mulatez*. Yes, this is part of my exploratory migrations.

Poetry is always snappy. It is a dance. It is a force of great physical urging. My poetry is both a personal and a historical cultural inquiry. Fusion is one of the centers of my poetics. The two areas of acute fusion are the Mediterranean and the

Caribbean. It's not just fusion of two elements; it is a multiplicity of energies coming together. Language is not just description, you know, it is also metaphor, and metaphor is like fusion. It is a bridge between disparate forces. This fusion is one of the cornerstones where my poetic eye reposes.

Poets are involved in human events, personal and historical. I think this is true even of poems that minutely detail human life—Williams speaking about green broken glass, which he observes at his foot. To me, that has national applications— for the way he apprehends an image, the way he sees color, which comes through from his intense Latin side. The Spanish language is attached to color intensely.

All human life derives out of fusion. That is an operation that is going on in my work—that it is a cultural brew. Poetry is the center of life, you know. Think of the Taino *aryeto*. It was the singsong ceremony done in a round circle. It was their epics. Think of the Homeric hymns and bring it home to bolero lyrics and the blues, the language of expression. Poetry is the center of society, even when the social circumstances deteriorate and the people are not aware of it. The people who do not fuse will confuse, will isolate themselves into xenophobic cells. The task of the poet is to make descriptive and metaphoric bridges that create a constant fusion and highlight the geometric patterns of our daily life.

  ˅ *Let's go back to the beginning of your career. You write in "Home Is Where the Music Is" that it "was within the chin-chales of Aguas Buenas," where you spent your Puerto Rican childhood, "that [your] imagination first heard poetry declaimed." Walking around New York City in the early 1960s, you "picked up neighborhood jargon, stoop yap, and hallway vocabulary." I was wondering when you put all of these influences together, to write down your first poetry? You published* **Snaps,** *your first collection of poetry, when you were only nineteen.*

Yes, my grandfather was a tobacconist in the small mountain town of Aguas Buenas. I have been told that the *chin-chal*, tobacco workplace, was near my home and that I, as a toddler, was always around my grandfather. The workers sang and recited poems; my body heard songs, guitars, and oral poetry before my mind. The poems were almost chanted; they were dramatic; they belonged to the Spanish rhyming tradition of *decimas* and *coplas*. Later in New York, an uncle of mine continued to declaim in this tradition. When I came to New York, I spoke the popular Spanish of Puerto Rico. Spanish is my first language of listening and speaking. When I entered New York City schools, I learned to read and write in English, so that even till this day my English grammar is in advance of my Spanish, even though much of the sonance of my poems is Spanish. I have recuperated much Spanish by living in Puerto Rico for the past ten years, and I do produce work in Spanish, which is published, but my English is much more flexible. You must know how maverick and anarchistic American English is. It's easier. The English language has no system of accents like the Spanish and the French. American English, like American society, has less formation. There is no tradition of a king or a queen. The bourgeois is homemade and, like everywhere else, full of bad habits—morons with inherited money. So America is very loose and spontaneous. A place like California has some pockets we can consider barbarous. The savage manners of etiquette of a place like Los Angeles—it is not surprising that it is the capital of illusion entertainment. From there, minor characters like Sylvester Stallone and Arnold Schwarzenegger are projected toward the world. It's unfortunate that the Third World is eating this nonsense up. I live here in Morocco, which is not a democracy but a kingdom. I live in a kingdom, and the Islamic culture maintains breezes of medieval times, all within a very modern, up-to-the-times place. Moroccan cities are a mixture of Paris and traditional ideas. Morocco is both the present and an eternal style that stays always as an alternative for the future.

With my writing, my first manifestations seem to be impulses. I know that this instantaneity is a part of poetry, that it is, as Juan Ramón Jimenez has stated, made up of instincts.

The act of writing is full of surprises, guided as much as possible by a controlling intelligence. Poetry, like urges and desires, comes early in life, so I published when I was very young, as have many poets—García Lorca, Claude McKay. Most poets, actually.

> ∨ *How influential was the Umbra Workshop in helping you discover your poetic voice? How did working with these poets differ from later collaborations with writers of the Nuyorican Poets Cafe, whom you pay homage to in "Islandis: The Age of Seashells"?*

I came around the Umbra poets as a young man. They were a collective of mostly African American writers. I was a lone Puerto Rican among them. When I came onto the writing scene of Manhattan's Lower East Side, there seemed to be two writing camps: the white and the black. I grew up in a Puerto Rican and African American proletariat barrio near the Avenue D housing projects. The Puerto Ricans of my generation participated in a street culture of fusion with African American and other ethnic groups. Through my Caribbean background, which has a potent African element, I was drawn to the African American writers. Through Ishmael Reed and David Henderson, I was invited to the Umbra Workshop. I must note that I came after the workshop had been meeting for a few years, and my participation was mostly that of an observer. A few years later, David Henderson and I worked on a Latin soul issue of *Umbra,* which we did in the Bay Area of California. It was truly a workshop, for we would read poems back and forth to each other and discuss them; we would discuss politics and exchange information. I have great admiration for many of the Umbra poets and writers, like Clarence Major, Raymond Patterson, Calvin Herndon, Lorenzo Thomas, and the composer-singer Len Chandler.

The poets of the so-called Nuyorican Poets Cafe I came into contact with a few years later. By then, I was established in California. My association with them was minimal. I was able to communicate with Miguel Algarín and reserve much respect for his poetry and productive energy, which involves teaching, and also for his many years administering the Nuyorican Poets Cafe.

> ∨ In **By Lingual Wholes**, your third book of poetry, you include an epigraph by Chinua Achebe: "The African writer should aim to use English in a way that brings out his message best without altering the language to the extent that its value as a medium of international exchange will be lost. He should aim at fashioning out an English which is at once universal and able to carry his peculiar experience."
> Is this what you're doing in your own writing—composing an English that draws on several linguistic and artistic sources, yet an English that won't lose your audience?

To write is to use language, which is the mechanism of communication; writing, we might say, is an innovation. We cannot really say that it is experimentation. You should not be doing something upon a trial basis to see if it works or, in the case of poetry, to see if it is felt and understood, or vice versa, whichever comes first to the reader. Writing either communicates or it doesn't. It cannot be a failed experiment. You have to have lived the images and imagined the illusions. Whatever your penetration of experience through language, you have to recall it, conjure it for the readers, and make them live the instincts. I write in English or Spanish, and the words are all in the dictionary. The important thing is tone or accent, and I have an audible accent when I speak English—even when I speak Spanish because of my duality of languages. A writer's combination of words creates his or her tones and colors, a writer's tempo. But language should not be disfigured to the point that communication is lost, for then the very foundation of language and writing is destroyed; this most definitely would be a tragedy. In *By Lingual Wholes,* I was influenced by some Brazilian concrete poetry that I was looking at; the drawings are similar to the way the Tainos had of chiseling pictographs upon rocks; in Utuado, Puerto Rico, there is a whole ceremonial park intact, and it features these stones that form a rectangle within which is the ball park. Each of the stones has a different pictograph, and you look at each one, and it expresses something, something that perhaps we have lost. But just looking, we can imagine those pictural poems—what they mean in spirit.

> ⌄ *You turn to the prose poetry form in almost all of your poetry*
> *collections. When do you feel most compelled to write in this particular*
> *form instead of other, more traditional forms?*

Actually, I am vague about the prose poetry. I don't know if they work as well. I now tend to separate the two. Poetry is nomadic, instinctual—an impulse, nerves, bone. Prose is sedentary, relaxed. You move into prose from poetry. Poets eventually write prose. Prose writers almost never advance into producing poetry. Poetry remains the image, the rhythm, the essence. It could be written without a full control of grammar. Prose is details of patience and a much more total control. It is a knowledge and technical and can be obtained. That's why there is more narrative. Poetry is more difficult to balance or to step upon, though its rendering is quicker. At least, I see it that way. I have difficulty writing prose. It is torturous; it is not available to me. I have to obtain it. I have to sit very long periods of time just to produce three pages. That's why I wrote prose poetry some years back—as a way to enter into straight prose. Till this day, [writing] prose is laborious and full of insecurities.

˅ **Snaps** *has a harsh, often bleak landscape where "junkies rob their mothers," where there's "no place to run / no place to hide ... there is only ... a waiting / till the spirits / come ... to your funerals." Yet you also celebrate lighter moments in such poems as "A Day with Bo." I was wondering if you were conscious of some kind of balance when composing this first book of poetry, or were these poems actually realistic "snapshots" of people coming at you?*

Snaps was a raw book. The New York neighborhood I grew up in came out roaring in those poems. I don't know if there was a conscious balance. Situations were presented with a sharp street language as they actually were. You know, "tell it like it is." I am not totally happy with some of those harsh poems, but I had to clear my environment out of the way. Those poems jumped out of me on their own. There is in them, though, a quick, locomotive-subway speed. New York moves fast; it comes at you. *Mainland,* my second book, moves into different terrain. It's much more relaxed, as if someone else had written it.

˅ **By Lingual Wholes** *also includes a wonderful portrait of Don Arturo. You dedicate this book to Don Arturo Vincench, who now is "on the other side of the bridge." You also include this portrait in* **Red Beans.** *"Don Arturo: A Story of Migration" is one of my favorite pieces. Can you talk a little about this individual? Was he a real person? Was it people such as Don Arturo who kept you rooted to the Caribbean, even though you lived thousands of miles away?*

Yes, Arturo Vincench was a real person. He was Cuban and was close to my family. He was a friend of my aunt. He played all kinds of instruments—guitar, mandolin, harmonica, violin. He blew into whistlers. "Don Arturo: A Story of Migration" is a true story. Don Arturo was like a spiritual grandfather to me. He told me stories of the Cuba that he knew—the way the men and women were. He'd give me advice. At family baptisms and birth dates, he would play the guitar. I would play the maracas. Everyone would sing. That's the way I grew up.

˅ *You've written that poetry "lives between thought and music as a sonorous flickering bird." Music of all types informs your writing, doesn't it, including essays such as "Salsa as a Cultural Root"?*

Well, poetry is intelligence with sensuality, thought, and feeling. Do you have any other place to put it? It is not an essay. It is emotional research, thoughtful sentiment. Music is the constant organizing energy that informs much of the cadence of my poems.

> ⌄ *Do you feel you're more overtly political in some works, such as the section "Islandis: The Age of Seashells"? Poems such as "Problems with Colonialism," "Puerta Rica," "Is It Certain or Is It Not Certain Caso Maravilla," and "It's Miller Time" are more direct in their social and political criticism than some of your other poetry.*

Of course they are political. Art should always be an intense awareness of the social conditions that surround you. Poetry should be about everything: image and rhythm in language made beautiful with many levels of intent, to make someone conscious of the obvious that is hidden. So those poems are more of a direct hit on what you call "political criticism," but no matter what the subject matter of a poem, poetry is always about awareness of raw and blazing realities.

> ⌄ *In "Taos: The Poetry Bout Codrescu vs. Cruz," you write that "only in North America could poets engage in such leisurely activity, where two poets 'square off' in front of an audience. Most world poets are involved in questions of national identity and liberation." Yet twice you've been crowned World Heavyweight Poetry Champion in Taos. Do you, as someone partially rooted in North America, feel that the poet needs to find this balance—to explore "the center of spiritual and political existence," but also to approach everyday life "with a great sense of humor"?*

What I was trying to say is that North American poetry is so divorced from social function. Perhaps it is because the exact power of the word is not felt. In Latin America as well as in Spain, poets have been either imprisoned or made ambassadors. In the United States, people see poets as just playing word games, unimportant to the real operation of a materialistic society. In capitalism, there isn't a place for poetry. "The books don't sell," they would say. This doesn't change the function of the wordsmith in the society. The poet makes awareness available to the masses.

*v Your two collections of poetry from the 1990s, **Red Beans** (1991)
and **Panoramas** (1997), also include several essays. This writing is
more accessible than some of your earlier poetry. Are you searching
for other ways of expression the older you become? Are you reaching
out to a wider audience?*

I write in a whole lot of forms—poems, essays, short stories. I've actually written
a couple of novels, neither of which is published. They are in my archives. I live and
read and travel so that the poetic reach is constantly evolving. I don't know about
audience, but we must know the act of writing is not complete until there is a reader.
I've seen a lot go down since 1966, when I first published a chapbook and distributed it to the bookstores myself. A friend and I actually produced it—stencils,
mimeograph machine. Remember those toxic inks? I made the book with my
hands. Many young poets today don't want to do this. It's my suggestion to people
who want to get published: do the book yourselves and share it with colleagues and
neighbors. Start from scratch. Many poets today go into performance, producing
cassettes and CDs. They also go around in these bars slamming. All of that is after
my time. I am a poet-writer and a reader, a student of cultural history. I merge
geographies and poetics: the poetry of Spain, the poetry of Latin America, the
poetry of North America, with Islamic influences and Caribbean styles. I am outside of North America writing from Puerto Rico or Morocco. I write in English
and project it back to America. I feel influences from Ezra Pound, William Carlos
Williams, Ed Dorn, Amiri Baraka, Jay Wright, and many more writers. I can't mention them all. American jazz improvisation moves with me all the time. I've done
many things, and I always feel a new wave bringing me to new creative shores.

*v You've been publishing poetry for more than three decades. How
do you see your creative voice changing over the years? Is it always
evolving? Constantly developing?*

I see my poetic urges moving within a form of study, rather than random escapades.
For instance, I've done a whole series of poems that I call "Portraits." These are
poems about people who have had an influence upon me, such as Rumi or Miles
Davis, and many other poets, musicians, singers, writers, and historical figures. In
my book *Panoramas,* there are many landscape poems. It is a landscape painting.

I feel a long-term relationship with an inspiration for a poem. I also have a more relaxed approach than, for instance, the jolts of a book like *Snaps*. My poetic urges expand through my physical geographies; my journeys are cultural research. My urges go hand in hand with my poetic evolution. I am interested in the connections between Spain and Morocco and between southern Spain and the Caribbean. When I was in Cadiz, I saw how the old *casco* [husk] is similar to *el casco colonial de San Juan,* so that San Juan and La Habana are architectural replicas of Cadiz, this most American of Spanish cities. This is one of the ports from where the ships took off during the period of the conquest. Sailors coming back carried American things with them. The Islamic invasion of Spain was made from Morocco, so it interests me to know what rhythms were interchanged. Our mother country is not just Spain but also Morocco, North Africa. Our food and our rhythms from that side are from both coasts of the Mediterranean Sea. We all are swimming in olive oil. As I said earlier, my poetry is a historical, cultural illumination, and these are the roots of all my homes; in the Caribbean, we add the indigenous spices and the sub-Sahara Africans that came through slavery. Through it all, I recognize the personal gestures of pronounced individuality, which the kaleidoscopic stew has created. My poetry is a language of many coasts.

Carolina Hospital and Carlos Medina

*B*orn in Havana, Cuba, in 1957, Carolina Hospital was an early proponent of a Cuban American aesthetic. Her *Cuban American Writers: Los Atrevidos,* published in 1989, is a groundbreaking anthology of Cuban authors writing in English. She has published essays and poems in numerous magazines and anthologies, among them *Mid-American Review, Caribbean Review, Cuban Heritage Magazine,* and *Looking for Home: Women Writing about Exile.* Hospital is perhaps best known for the novel *A Little Love* (2000), which she coauthored with Carlos Medina, her husband, under the pen name C. C. Medina. A film based on the book is scheduled to be released in the near future. Hospital teaches writing and literature at Miami-Dade Community College.

Carlos Medina is a fiction writer and storyteller who teaches at Ransom-Everglades School in Miami, Florida. He coauthored with Hospital an instructor's manual for W. W. Norton as well as a chapter of the *New York Times* best-seller *Naked Came the Manatee,* a collaborative novel by thirteen South Florida writers.

This interview took place on November 25, 2000, at the Miami Book Fair International. The writers discuss their most recent work as well as their poetry, the

SUGGESTED READING

Cuban American Writers: Los Atrevidos
(Princeton, N.J.: Ediciones Ellas/Linden Lane Press, 1989)

A Century of Cuban Writers in Florida: Selected Prose and Poetry
coedited with Jorge Cantera (Sarasota, Fl.: Pineapple Press, 1996)

A Little Love
with Carlos Medina (New York: Warner Books, 2000)

challenges of cowriting fiction, the difficulty Latinos find publishing their material, Hollywood, and the cosmopolitan Latino community in South Florida.

> ⌄ *You were an early proponent of a Cuban American literary aesthetic. Can we start by having you talk about your groundbreaking anthology **Cuban American Writers: Los Atrevidos**, published in 1989?*

CH: In graduate school at the University of Florida, I wasn't actively writing, but I knew that somewhere down the line, I'd write. I'd always known that I wanted to write creatively. I was also curious about what other Cubans—people of my generation, younger people—were writing and if they were writing in English or Spanish, so I decided to do my thesis on the children of exile and their literature. It ended up being a major project. Actually, it could have been a Ph.D. dissertation; I compiled everything these young Cubans or Cuban Americans were writing. I wrote the thesis, graduated, and then the idea came up that, because I'd done all this work, all this research, and knew who all the writers were, why not put this work into an anthology?

I wanted to publish this anthology because the Cuban Americans writing in the mid-1980s were being excluded. Because they were writing in English, the Latino anthologies and magazines were not considering their work. On the other hand, a prejudice already existed against Latino writers in general, and the English mainstream certainly wasn't looking at Cubans writing in English, so they were in a void, where neither side was taking them seriously. That's why I decided, "Let's do something. Let's put an anthology together." Some of the writers included were a bit hesitant at first because they were trying to make it in the mainstream literary world and feared if they were part of an anthology of Cuban American writers, it might hinder them. They feared being ghettoized. My feeling, though, was that it would give them exposure and that if they were already being excluded, one of the ways to draw attention to them was as a group. As individuals, they were not being heard.

I remember, when *Los Atrevidos* first came out, nobody knew where to place these Cuban Americans writing in English. Even here, at the Miami Book Fair International, some thought we should read in the Spanish section, others the English. That was back in the late 1980s. They didn't know what to do with Cubans in English. And that's why the subtitle, *Los Atrevidos,* "the daring ones": a new generation daring to do it differently, writing in English, writing on different issues. That's how the anthology came to be. I think it helped launch the concept of a new generation of Cuban Americans writing in English, and it helped individual writers as well.

   v *What about today? How do you assess the current state of Cuban American literature? Do contemporary Cuban and Cuban American writers still have to "take risks"? Or is this idea of a literary aesthetic firmly entrenched in the reading public's mind?*

CH: Ten years later things have changed tremendously. But it's still not that easy to get published as a Cuban or Latino writer.

   v *But your new novel that you cowrote with Carlos was published by Warner Books, which isn't exactly a small-time publisher.*

CH: Yes, but I think we're one of the first to publish with a commercial venture like that. And we had to convince them. It wasn't easy. You still have to convince publishers that there will be a readership for your material. Their attitude is that "we have plenty of non-Hispanic authors writing out there, so why should we take a chance with a Hispanic one?" It's become easier in a way because certain individuals have succeeded, helping to open the doors for others. That's what we hope we're doing with *A Little Love*—opening doors for other Latino writers trying to get published.

   CM: Actually, there has been an increase in fiction publishing among Latinos. Poetry, though, is still not a likely possibility.

   CH: But Cuban American poets like Dionisio [Martínez] have published with Norton, and Ricardo [Pau-Llosa] has published with Carnegie-Mellon. If we look at this year in particular, there's certainly a major difference in how many people are being published.

   v *You also published another anthology of Cuban writers, didn't you?*

CH: Yes, *A Century of Cuban Writers in Florida,* which I coedited with Jorge Cantera. It is an anthology that takes the younger writers and puts them in the context of Florida history, all the way back to the 1700s. The introduction actually goes back even further. It covers the whole history of the Florida connection with Cuba. The book took six years to complete. I wanted to show that *los atrevidos* weren't a shot in the dark, that they were a part of a tradition, a connection that had been there between Florida and Cuba for two centuries.

CM: It used to be that the university presses, such as the University of Florida Press, published one-sided histories: like the English connection in Florida or the Spanish connection in Florida or the Indian connection—but never the Cuban connection.

CH: It was very difficult to find in Florida history books a chapter on Cuba's connection with Florida—at the most a couple of pages. Yet when we started researching the history and the literary contributions, we saw all kinds of connections with Cubans in Key West, Tampa, and other places, even Jacksonville. So we thought that with this anthology, we would bring in not just the literary but the historical elements as well. It was a labor of love.

  v That book came out in the early 1990s?

CH: Yes, with Pineapple Press.

  *v You were a scholar and a critic before you decided to try your
  own hand at writing creatively. I was wondering what influenced
  your decision? When were you first conscious that you, too, wanted
  to write in other genres? Were there major literary influences?
  Any Cuban writers?*

CH: I think one of the strongest, in fiction, was Guillermo Cabrera Infante. We really liked his use of language and the way that language almost becomes a protagonist in his text. He captures the flavor of the Cuban personality.

CM: And his novel *Three Trapped Tigers* has a very contemporary 1950s Havana lingo. It was a popular book that captured the then-present voice of that generation. His novel is still like high art. We both read it in graduate school. We also read a lot of Hemingway and other Anglo writers. You have to remember that Miami didn't become Latinized until after 1980.

CH: I didn't even think I was Cuban before I went to college. I thought I was an American. Then when I went to the university, everyone told me how Cuban I was. And my response was, "What are you talking about?" So then I said to myself, "If I'm Cuban, I better find out." I started taking every course I could on Cuba and Latin America. When I went to graduate school, I switched from my undergraduate interest in English, which was my major, to Latin American studies. But I loved literature. I would also say that all of the Latin American writers were influential, too, such as [Jorge Luis] Borges and Isabel Allende. In poetry, definitely Borges, but other writers, too, like Galway Kinnell and James Wright. So I think the influences are a mix of all backgrounds. Actually, I sought that out. I think it was inevitable, though, growing up here in Miami with a Latino background.

> v *Do you feel there's a major thread or idea that runs through your poetry? This theme of biculturalism seems to define a lot of your work. I'm thinking of poems such as "Sorting Miami," "Dear Tía," "Freedom," and several others. Can you elaborate?*

CH: Actually, despite the answer to your earlier question, I started writing when I was young, in high school. Then I stopped writing for ten years. I'll tell you why, which involves a little story with Carlos and me. We wrote some poems with no name on them, mixed them up, and then gave them to one of our college professors when we were attending the University of Miami. The professor thought he was being kind because half of the poems he was complimenting and half of the poems he was tearing down—tearing them to pieces. The ones he was tearing to pieces were mine. In a way, it traumatized both of us. I got traumatized because I was the one who was driven to write; Carlos was traumatized because he didn't care as much as I did, and his were the ones that were accepted.

Actually my poetry then *was* bad. But I stopped writing for ten years, and had I kept writing, I'd have had that many more years practicing. Finally, I got over that and decided to write again. That's when I seriously started writing, in 1984, after the birth of Nicole, our first daughter. I wrote "Dear Tía," which people must think is the only poem I ever wrote. It's the one that has been anthologized the most. Arte Público Press keeps giving that poem to anthologies. I think the big thing I was trying to explore at the time was my identity: What does it mean to be Cuban American? I published a lot of poems on that theme. I have found, however, that as I've synthesized my cultures—come to terms with who I am, culturally—I've moved on to other things, not just my "Cubanness." But since then I've had problems getting work published because it doesn't focus exclusively on my being Cuban. I think these new poems are better written and more mature, but the bottom line is, "Why should we publish this Cuban woman when she's not writing about being Cuban?" It's ironic. This is one of the reasons I haven't published a manuscript of my poetry. I've been told my poetry is not "sociopolitical" enough. The manuscript was sent out, but I kept getting rejections, even though 80 percent of the poetry has already been published in journals. So I got discouraged. I might send it out again one day.

ᵥ *What about Arte Público?*

CH: When I first started sending out the poetry manuscript, they weren't doing poetry books. I think that's changed now. They've been very supportive of individual poems. As a matter of fact, maybe one day I'll send them a manuscript. I basically, though, got fed up.

ᵥ *In your opinion, what is it that drives publishers to focus on the ethnic voice? The sociopolitical side instead of the "actual" or "real" voice of the poet?*

CH: I don't know if I can speak completely on that. I would guess that when they [the poets] have an issue on an ethnic theme, then they [the publishers] are interested. I guess, too, that the competition is so fierce, publishers think that since "we" get published in ethnic issues already, then what's the point?

CM: I think you're being too kind. Take the fiction side of all this. We've had experiences early on with major house editors—Farrar Strauss and so on. I think they still have a limited view of the world, and I think it's their burden to broaden their view, not ours. I think that the so-called ethnic writers are ahead of the time, ahead of the curve, and I think that the publishers are still thinking in terms of niche and compartmentalization. Of course, we suffer from their lack of foresight and from their prejudices, and there are prejudices out there. They're comfortable, ensconced in their ivory tower publishing houses.

CH: There's a grant that the state of Florida puts out every year. I applied for one for several years, but I never got one. I'm not crying sour grapes because I didn't get it. I just object to some of the comments that I received, such as "I can't relate to this."

CM: In the example with Warner and our recently published novel, our agent had to say it's a Latino *Waiting to Exhale.* That's what got their attention.

ᵛ *So you had to say that, then? You're the ones who made the comparison?*

CM: Not exactly. Some of the reviewers—*Kirkus, Library Journal*—have also made it, adding that our book has more depth to it than that. But that's the point of reference the publisher needed. You have to give them that lingo, especially in the Northeast. "You need a quick reference? Here's one." And then the other side of the story is the big-powered agent, who has obviously lost perspective. They'll take you if you can guarantee a certain return. But I understand also that the level she or he is trying to take these Hispanic writers to—that's the ball game. The agent really can't do "community service" anymore. There has to be a price tag, respect in the big circles. So it makes it difficult for Latino writers in general and for Cuban American writers in particular. The situation here in Miami is complex.

ᵛ *In what ways?*

CM: Take the Elián González case, for example. We had connected with Elián, but we hadn't done anything about it. We were busy teaching and writing. It was our sixteen-year-old daughter who kept saying, "You guys, I feel passionate about this." So, you see, it's complex, and it's generational. You would expect our parents to have told us that, not our daughters. Miami is an exciting city. That's why we set the novel here. We wanted an insider's view because there have been a lot of outsiders' stories—David Reiff and Joan Didion come to mind. Remember *Miami Vice*? Also, most of the Cuban American novelists don't live here. Pablo Medina, Cristina García, Oscar Hijuelos, for instance. And a lot of fiction writers have written coming-of-age stories or memoirlike works. Theirs is a different flavor. We wanted another flavor, a contemporary flavor, from an insider's perspective. We've lived here practically all our lives, and we think there's something that can be captured that hasn't been captured yet, especially for the English-speaking community, whether they are Latino or not.

ᵛ *How **did** the idea for this collaboration evolve? You've mentioned your one venture in college, writing poetry, which didn't sound too encouraging, let alone healthy, for a marriage. Did **Waiting to Exhale** actually set you in motion?*

CH: I was reading poetry for the Miami Book Fair International one year, and our agent, Janell Walden Agyeman, was on the fair's board. We didn't know she was a literary agent. She had invited me to participate in a sidewalk reading. While I was reading, she went up to Carlos and asked if he thought I knew how she could find some contemporary fiction about Latinas. "Something kind of like *Waiting to Exhale,* something contemporary, but I want something Latina." Carlos said he didn't know, but he'd ask me. Most of the literature we knew was, as Carlos mentioned, memoirlike. So we told her to let us think about it, mull it over on the way home, and we'd get back in touch with her. When we went home, though, we couldn't think of anyone. Then we looked at each other, and Carlos said, "You can do that!" And I said, "Wait a minute, wait a minute. *We* can do that!" I knew that Carlos was a great writer, and I had never decided to write a novel before, having little time for writing fiction, being a professor with children and all, so I said if we wrote this together, just for fun, we'd do it. That was the stipulation—that it had to be "fun." We wrote twenty pages, gave it to Janell, and she told us to keep going. Then we gave her fifty pages, and she said, "You know, if you give me just a little more, I think I could sell it." She actually wanted the whole thing.

CM: You have to remember that we had only these four Latina women, who came to life in a Jewish coffee shop, and we didn't know where we were going with them. It was arrogance—innocent arrogance!

CH: But it wasn't just arrogance or innocence. It was also consciously done. We needed an incentive. We knew it'd be a major sacrifice for the family. When you're writing a novel, you need big blocks of time, so we needed something at the start, dangling there.

CM: Two weeks passed. Janell called us and said, "I sold it!" She'd sold eighty pages to Warner Books. It was a large advance for such a small submission.

CH: But it was pressure after that. Then we were on a time table.

ᵛ *How long did it take to finish?*

CM: Two years. Two and a half.

ᵛ *The composition? How do you compose something with four characters and two writers?*

CH: Together we agreed on who the characters were and what they looked like. Really, literally, we had a pad, and we would decide on particulars. We even cut out pictures and made composites of what we thought one particular woman looked like. For the first third of the book, we sat together, side by side, with our laptop. We discussed the story, line by line.

CM: I want to make another comment about Janell's approaching us on the sidewalk and mentioning a *Waiting to Exhale* kind of novel. Some have said that the book was almost "made to order." I refute that argument totally. What it did was open our eyes to what was in our own front yard. We wanted writing that gets deep into what it's like to be Latino—not just Cuban, but Latino, in a major urban center like Miami. We decided to open up that Pandora's box, and that's the way I interpret that pure chance encounter with a New York literary agent who was sent here to Miami.

    ⌄ *Have you been able to voice that concern to the public? That you feel you've written something different from* **Waiting?**

CM: That's just it, no one has asked us for our response to that criticism, but that criticism is very subtle. It's one of the vestiges of prejudice.

CH: But you know, what I found amazing is that it was difficult for us, being that we came from that kind of highbrow, academic kind of writing. We had to maintain that line where it was a fun and entertaining and accessible book to write, but where it also had certain undercurrents of literary games, undercurrents of certain things being explored. That was difficult.

CM: It was a challenge because we wanted to write the kind of book that had provocative Latina kinds of women: intelligent, sensual, sexual, professional, confident, funny, and real. We wanted to make sure, too, that the characters were motivated by an authentic cultural experience. Most critics got that. Some of them really got it down pat.

CH: I'm rewarded, too, though, because we've been complimented by people who normally wouldn't be considered "book readers," including one of my sisters, who sat with the book at work and didn't put it down until she finished it. Then she asked, "Where is the second book? I'm dying to read the second book!" Other women readers have talked to us about the book and said things like they were a combination of this woman and that woman. Apparently people believe that they are authentic characters.

> ⌄ *One of the things I find interesting in the novel is the Latino commu-
> nity within the Latino community—the Chicana Julia, for example,
> embraced by the Latino Cuban community. Were you conscious of
> incorporating other Latinos into the book?*

CH: We were conscious that we wanted *not* to limit the book to Cubans because Cubans are not the only Latino experience in Miami or, obviously, in the United States. We see that mixing in our own social circle. It enriched the literature as well because it allowed us to explore other cultures and to travel to other cultures.

> ⌄ *Did you travel to conduct research for the novel?*

CH: To an extent. But we've always traveled to the Dominican Republic and to Mexico, so it was convenient that we'd already been to other places.

> ⌄ *Speaking of the Mexican influence, I'm curious about the
> homophobic television commentator and his point-blank question
> to Julia, when he asks her in front of millions of viewers if she is gay.
> Is he a vehicle to help make a larger statement?*

CM: It's Barbara Walters. When you look at the interviews she conducts, that's the person you get. I take insult to the question that man asks. There's no point in his asking Julia if she is "gay" or "married" or whatever. It's irrelevant to what it means to be human, and we wanted to bring that out. We chose that format because for all their so-called objectivity, commentators in that position want just one thing: whatever gives them attention. You're the first person who's seen that minor character as homophobic. Others typically see him as a user-journalist, someone who just wants to go for the person and get some kind of reaction from his audience. It's like Jennifer Lopez wearing her dress. That excitement lasted about three months. That's what a good PR person wants. A lot of people who read that section come out feeling sorry for Julia. "How could that man do that to Julia? What an unfair thing to do!" There is an element where we wanted to make Julia be such an attractive, nice person that even a person who's got resistance to that issue can't skewer her.

CH: So as Julia says, "labels hurt. What really matters is not whether you are gay or bi or hetero, but whether you are truly in love." That's the greater message we were getting at with that scene.

  ⌄ *You've mentioned a second novel. What's that entail? Have you started it yet?*

CH: It's also about four women, but they are younger. They're all born here, but they're all mixed up in terms of cultural backgrounds.

CM: There's an Anglo main character in the second novel. That's going to add a whole different dimension.

CH: She's married to a Cuban, and they're having problems based on cultural conflicts. It's kind of like what you said earlier today—that we didn't explore David's culture in *A Little Love,* only his wife's culture. This will be different. In this book, we want to explore what it means to be left for a culture. To explore how cultural tensions affect a marriage.

CM: We have another surprise character in the book, who is part of a current community in Miami, the Trinidadians.

  ⌄ *Has Warner shown an interest in this second novel?*

CH: Yes, plus they have the first right to look at the book. That's part of the contract. They can accept it or reject it. Our editor keeps asking us when we're going to let them see something.

  ⌄ *Has publishing with a commercial press like Warner differed from some of your work with other publishers?*

CM: They put out a lot of ads, but no tours.

CH: They have a different strategy, which is to put money into ads. The touring, they think, is not worth the investment. They think they might reach more people through ads.

CM: They ran ads for seven days in the *Miami Herald* when the first novel came out. They advertised in *Latina* magazine as well as in *People en Español.*

  ⌄ *Did you have a positive reaction in Miami? Did you become much better known here once the book was published?*

CH: I'd had a little bit of a following already with the Cuban community. They knew me from the anthologies. When *Naked Came the Manatee* came out, and my chapter associated with that book was published in the *Herald,* people knew me from that. When C. C. Medina published *A Little Love,* the public didn't know who that was, but then articles started appearing and people said, "Oh, that's you." There's something about fiction that people love as opposed to other writing; all of a sudden I'm a hero. It's strange because when I look back at some of my writer friends who have published three or four good books of poetry, they still aren't very well known. Then all of a sudden we publish this novel, and people are fascinated.

ᵥ *And now the book has been picked up by Hollywood?*

CH: Yes, we're very happy. The scriptwriter who's working on it is of Mexican background, Lisa Loomer. She did *Girl Interrupted.* We heard the producers, Harry and Mary Jane Ufland, of *Snow Falling on Cedar* and *One True Thing,* are in conversations with Latina actresses, such as Salma Hayek, Penelope Cruz, and others. I don't know if that will work out or not. They bought the option, and they have eighteen months to put it all together.

CM: One of the things they wanted was to tie it into this rising Latino pop culture kind of feel; they saw that the novel could have a good impact as a movie.

CH: They loved it. They usually have women themes in their movies. They loved our characters. When we talked to them on the phone, they'd ask us all kinds of questions about the women. "Oh, and Lucinda did this, and why did Isabel do that?" It's fun, and that's one of the interesting things we've discovered about fiction—how involved people get. With poetry, the folks you deal with are nice, but they don't interact as much as the fiction people. These people ask you questions like, "Why did you do that?" or "Why did that character feel that?"

ᵥ *Did you lose all of the rights when Hollywood bought it?*

CH: Oh, yes! We couldn't be that demanding since it was our first novel.

∨ It must satisfy you to see the book becoming a movie. There are so many references to film in the novel. You're obviously attracted to the movies yourselves.

CM: That's really part of our culture. We're a very visual culture. And I mean here, Americans in general. So when I write, there are a lot of visual reference points. I like to "see" what I'm writing. Actually, in my head I see it entirely as a series of scenes.

CH: What's amazing to me when I write fiction is that I become like a literary actor. You have to take on the voice of these people, these characters that you create. For fifteen years, I'd been talking from my own voice in essays and poetry. Then all of a sudden I had to become one of the four characters. Really, all of them. There were moments when Carlos would tell me that that's the wrong character coming out. He would ask, "Where is the right one?" I had to go back and find her. You really have to work at getting into another person's identity and then speaking like them. I tell him that we're masochists and ask why we had to have four protagonists because it really is like acting: every time you'd alternate, you'd have to readjust your mindset. And we're doing a second book!

CM: If they had been four Cuban women, that would have been easier, but you have four different nationalities, and they all go through their own Americanization experiences, having to take into consideration what they keep from their old heritage and how they adopt to a new one. So it was very hard, very challenging, but true to what we see around us. We loved it.

CH: At the same time, my experience with poetry was good for the novel because of the imagery associated with poetry. It's funny, one of the interviewers saw a connection between some of the work I'd published on identity and some of the stuff going on in the novel. I guess we're still doing the same thing, only this time it's in the fiction mode.

Demetria Martínez

*B*orn in Albuquerque, New Mexico, in 1960, Demetria Martínez is an internationally known writer. A columnist for the *National Catholic Reporter,* she is the author of three volumes of poetry: *Turning,* which is included in an anthology of Chicana poets called *Three Times a Woman* (1989); *Breathing Between the Lines* (1997); and *The Devil's Workshop* (2002). She also has published a novel, *Mother Tongue* (1994). She is currently at work on a collection of essays for the University of Oklahoma Press.

In 1987, Martínez was indicted by the federal government for aiding the entrance of Salvadorans into the United States. In a highly publicized case, the prosecution used one of her poems, "Nativity: For Two Salvadoran Women, 1986–1987" as evidence against her. Although charged with conspiracy and facing a twenty-five-year prison sentence, she eventually was acquitted on First Amendment grounds. The lengthy trial inspired her first novel as well as many of her poems.

In this interview, conducted after a poetry reading at Appalachian State University in Boone, North Carolina, on April 28, 2000, Martínez comments on her trial and subsequent publications. She also discusses

SUGGESTED READING

Turning, in *Three Times a Woman*
(Tempe, Ariz.: Bilingual Press/ Editorial Bilingüe, 1989)

Mother Tongue
(Tempe, Ariz.: Bilingual Press/ Editorial Bilingüe, 1994; rpt., New York: Ballantine, 1996)

Breathing Between the Lines
(Tucson: University of Arizona Press, 1997)

The Devil's Workshop
(Tucson: University of Arizona Press, 2002)

political activism, the U.S. Border Patrol, Elián González, spirituality, and artistic craft. She concludes by addressing her visit to a middle school in Durham, North Carolina, sponsored by Duke University's Center for Documentary Studies.

> ⌄ *After listening to your reading tonight, I'm curious as to what developed first—your political consciousness or your poetry?*

My grandmother tells me that when I was five or six years old, I'd make up poems on the spot. I'd say them out loud. I guess we call that rapping nowadays.

Meanwhile, I was growing up in a politically active family. My grandmother was county clerk and county commissioner. My father was the first Chicano ever elected to the Albuquerque School Board. My mother, an educator, worked on school reform issues. My aunt was county clerk. So I grew up in a family who assumed things could be changed—that one had an obligation to make the community a better place and that might just involve having to shake things up.

I began keeping a journal in junior high. I started by writing down lyrics of songs by popular composers—Joni Mitchell, for example, and I'd read them over and over again. In this copying down, in this reading and rereading and then branching out and describing a tree in my backyard or what I'd done that day, I found that I could write my way out of a depression. That's a very powerful thing to discover when you're in junior high and you're shy and fat. I had a very hard time speaking out loud, but I could speak to the blank page, and that's where I learned how to think. The lyrics were like training wheels. I took a melody from a Joni Mitchell song and wrote my own words. And I think that is what planted the seeds of poetry.

> ⌄ *In **Turning**, your first collection of poetry, there's a lot of pain and lament. Even your love poems are mournful.*

What poet doesn't start out writing lamentations? When I was writing that book, I was reading the feminist poets. At the time, I was developing a critique, if you will, of male/female relationships. I was tripping in and out of some crazy relationships. Some of the poems were written out of a broken heart, but they were also being written out of a head attempting to grasp society's role in structuring or determining how men and women look at each other. So my head was working on one project, and my heart was trying to heal.

v *Several of the poems are political, especially the ones about borders.*

The border section was important because at that time we began to see a lot of Central American refugees coming into Albuquerque, and I began to interview them. I went to churches and heard them speak. I wrote articles and poems. Art became a way of entering into the political milieu. A love poem became a vehicle for talking about political suffering.

In *Mother Tongue,* the love story is inseparable from the Salvadoran civil war and the U.S. funding of that war. This was the historical moment that I was living in. I was too young to remember Vietnam, but I knew that our government was sending more than a million dollars a day to El Salvador to prop up a bloody dictatorship. That period marked my political coming of age.

v *In several of your early poems, recasting one's life this side of the border is just as risky as fleeing oppression from one's homeland. As you see it, is the immigrant experience getting better or worse as we start the next decade?*

Huge numbers of Mexicans have died trying to cross the borders. The Border Patrol, because of its policy, has successfully sealed off traditional urban crossing areas all along the border, thus pushing desperate families into nightmare terrain. We heard all about Elián González and the tragic death of his mother at sea. Yet we hear nothing about little Elizama González, whose mother died of dehydration in the Arizona desert; the woman insisted on giving the last of her water to eighteen-month-old Elizama. The child survived and was shipped right back to Mexico.

We are looking at a failed border policy. The North American Free Trade Agreement [NAFTA] was supposed to create jobs here and in Mexico. Instead, it caused massive displacement of peoples from their lands, people who now come north looking for work. On the one hand, we want the workers. What U.S. citizen is willing to pay five dollars for a head of lettuce—or to pick the lettuce? On the other hand, we continue a massive buildup of agents and military equipment to stop immigrants. We've built a Berlin Wall.

If every undocumented worker were deported tomorrow, our economy would collapse; that's why even the *Wall Street Journal* has supported open borders. Yet racists continue to demonize the Mexican worker. They crow about Mexicans stealing American jobs, while remaining silent about the white man in the fancy suit and tie who shuts down a U.S. factory that a town has depended upon for jobs for decades and who then relocates the facility in Mexico or Vietnam. Who is the real thief? NAFTA has swelled the ranks of the hungry and fattened the wallets of the few wealthy elite.

> v In "Only Say the Word," the last poem in **Turning**, your character
> from Chimayo says, "Those who do not hold the gun are killed by the
> bullet / The rest look on, indifferent." Are you saying that there's still
> a lot of apathy out there?

It all has to do with how you name a group of people. If we as concerned citizens begin to see Mexicans for what they really are—as refugees instead of illegal immigrants—we might begin to see a change. They're not here so they can take a trip to Disneyland. It's a painful thing to leave your country, not to know when you're going to go back. More than three hundred people die a year trying to cross over the entire U.S.–Mexico border. That's like a plane crash a year. The good news is, the outcry and activism *is* growing among U.S. human rights groups, churches, labor, and other sectors.

> v Some of your poetry has multiple voices. When are you conscious
> of knowing you have to use more than one voice? Such as in "Blessed
> Are the Hungry" or "Only Say the Word"?

I was influenced by a Sylvia Plath poem that utilized several voices and the interplay between those voices. But also by *Oedipus Rex,* one of the great poetic dramas of all times. I wanted to see what I could do with voices that didn't sound like dialogue but sounded like poetry. The result was a very concise sort of language. I like "Only Say the Word" because it's a very religious poem in terms of New Mexican Catholicism.

> v In some of your poems, Catholicism doesn't meet the demands or
> needs of the people. The poor are ready to "burn the pews." One of your
> speakers tells Jesus to "come down off that cross" or "we'll call on our
> old Gods." You've also written that women like you have to kill their

"white God" if they're "to have any hope of finding God." Are you still searching for "priests of another order"? Is there a third force?

Revolution, spirituality, working one-on-one—all those go together. I don't want those to be falsely set apart. Sometimes we need a little more of this, a little less of that. Part of the journey is stripping away who we imagine God to be and allowing new images of God to emerge to speak to the times.

ˇ Do you find this is a prevalent theme in other Chicano and Chicana writing?

For the Latino writer, you're talking about roots in Catholicism, but also roots that predate Catholicism. We're all influenced by indigenous spirituality, by African religions, by Sephardic Judaism. One could argue that Catholicism never completely "took" in the New World, never entirely "took" in New Mexico. New Mexico was very isolated for a long time, and there were not any priests. Mostly women transmitted the faith, giving rise to popular expressions of spirituality. I think that's a vital source of inspiration for Latino writers. I think it's so much a part of us that sometimes we don't even realize we're playing with these rich worldviews. Religion is like the air we breathe, regardless of what our position is regarding the institutional church. That's another question altogether.

*ˇ One's reminded of the statement about your grandmother in the afterword to **Breathing Between the Lines**, where she learns more about Catholicism when she started searching for other religions.*

In those days, she desperately wanted to read the Bible, but she couldn't because only the priests could read it. She ended up leaving the church and joining the Assemblies of God. There she was free to read the Bible, to interpret it. Although she was a woman with a very limited education, she had that hunger for the Word and its multiple meanings. She was, in some ways, a mystic.

ˇ Have the Mexican ballads influenced any of your poems?

My grandfather was a poet in the days when political candidates would ask you to write a poem for a campaign. He wrote poems for various occasions; many were set to music. I follow in his footsteps by writing a poem at the birth of a new niece or nephew.

ᵥ *Let's talk about* **Mother Tongue,** *your novel. "North American Woman's Lament," one of your early poems, might be a preface to that book. You've stated that the novel was inspired by a voice, but did this poem or other works also inspire the narrative?*

I think the idea was always cooking in me. I've always been interested in what people do in response to trauma, how they deal with posttraumatic stress syndrome. The way I translated that metaphorically was to reflect on how we carry the conflict, the war, inside of us. You cross borders, and the war might be years behind you. But war is like a ticking bomb that can go off anytime. Just talking to refugees, I became profoundly aware of the human cost of war. Wars don't end. Nobody wins. They go into remission at best. That's why my character, Soledad, is so adamant when she says to María that it's not just enough to fall in love with José Luis and say that this great romance is somehow going to make us all better. We have to stop all wars in order for anyone to really heal.

ᵥ *You've called* **Mother Tongue** *a "long poem in disguise." Now that you've experimented in that genre, do you see yourself as a poet first and that everything else flows from that?*

Yes.

ᵥ *At the same time, in* **Mother Tongue** *you experiment with poetry, journal entries, letters, recipes, grocery lists, newspaper articles, prayers, and conventional narrative technique to help convey the story.*

And political fliers.

ᵥ *And political fliers.*

I didn't know how to write a novel. Every time I sat down to write, if I couldn't come up with a little block of writing, then I did a grocery list or a horoscope. I tried to imagine what it is people tape on their refrigerators. You can write a whole novel by paying attention to that alone. I thought in terms of the squares of a quilt. Writing a page or so a day was like assembling blocks; eventually I spread them out on the floor to see what order they wanted to be in. I didn't really order the book until close to the end. I wanted it to be written in such a way that the parts could be interchangeable. My hope was that my core meaning was so clear that no matter what order the pages landed in, if you threw them in the air, the book would still read well. I was thinking, too, about Ana Castillo and what she did with her "letters." I was intrigued by her saying to the reader that you can read the book in a different order. But again, it was such a magical kind of experience; a lot of it was not thought out.

> ⌄ *José Luis has the last statement in the book. Do you feel it's a hopeful ending?*

Yes, I do. I know that some people who've read the book thought that it had ended too positively, that I should have left him fashionably dead, so to speak. My feeling was that there were seventy-five thousand dead Salvadorans already, and I wasn't going to kill off one more.

> ⌄ *In **Breathing Between the Lines**, your world is broadening. You talk about Nicaragua, Vietnam, Rwanda—a lot more geography is brought in.*

This book came out of my teaching for two weeks at the William Joiner Center for the Study of War and Social Consequences at the University of Massachusetts in Boston. Each June I teach with Vietnam veterans, published authors. We bring in a delegation from Vietnam. We hold panels on war and literature. The book was written very quickly after my first summer of teaching there. Daisy Zamora, Nicaragua's great poet, was present that year and taught me a great deal.

> ⌄ *Rwanda was an obvious story in the news.*

Yes, and I was immersed in the stories of the [Vietnam] vet writers—like George Evans, the poet who was a medic radicalized by the war; Tim O'Brien; Larry Heinneman; Grace Paley; Kevin Bowen, the founder of the center and a great poet. When I was growing up, I listened to anchormen recite body counts. I saw the footage of body bags. I remember the fear I felt that a letter might arrive ordering my father off to war. He was in the Marine Corps Reserve, an officer. Kids are smart. They're intuitive. In fact, Dad later learned President Johnson was just minutes away from signing an order that would have sent him away. I and others my age, I'm sure, absorbed Vietnam in one way or another. It gave us an apocalyptic sensibility.

ᵥ *In **Breathing**, you're more conscious of language—of English, Spanish, Spanglish, of song and silences as languages. Can you talk about bilingualism in this country?*

It's been my observation that wealthy people, for good reasons, want their children to be bilingual; they'll often send their children to special language schools or after-school programs. But when poor families want to make sure their kids can speak two languages, to have this advantage, suddenly it becomes this political issue, where there's no money for school systems. We have to step back and look at the larger issue.

The truth is, we don't value education; we prefer to build prisons. If education were a priority, kids could learn English and Spanish, Russian and Arabic. It's a big world out there. We have to get off our island.

I'm interested in language, too, because I grew up speaking English in my immediate family. The next thing we knew, we were off to school immersed in English. Same thing in front of the TV.

It was only later in life that I had a chance to learn Spanish. I can hold my own in conversational Spanish, but I'm not totally fluent. I read a lot in Spanish. To do so is a cultural, political, spiritual act. I want to be able to influence my nieces and nephews, to encourage them to love languages.

We also have to commit ourselves to honoring our indigenous heritage. So many languages were wiped out during the conquest. My dream is that every Latino would one day speak an indigenous tongue. I'm living now among the Yaquis in Arizona. They speak Spanish, English, and their own tongue, Yoeme. I'd love one day to study it. I'd never be fluent, but that's not the point. Words are sacred. Merely to approach a new language is a blessed act.

ᵥ *When you were a child, was Spanish encouraged?*

My father was a Nixon appointee to the first Commission on Bilingual Education. Dad joined the fight early on for bilingual education. Dad insisted we take Spanish in school.

The first year of my life I lived with my grandparents. All four grandparents were fluent in Spanish and English. They were New Mexican, except my father's mother. She was the one person who crossed over as a little girl, with her father.

My grandfather, my father's father, was a court interpreter for the Spanish-speaking population in Albuquerque. He also interpreted for Diné clients. He couldn't speak Navajo, but he could understand it in order to interpret. Spanish was always in the air.

> ⌄ *Your trial with the federal government is now more than ten years behind you. When you write nowadays, are you conscious of self-censoring, or are you even more determined than before to expose the oppression you see around you?*

I love to connect with people as an activist. It's in the blood. After the trial, I wanted badly to retreat, but I have this big mouth and a pen to back it up! We're living in very exciting times. Look at what happened in Seattle with the World Trade Organization and in Washington. These are very dark times, but they're also hopeful times.

Sometimes I like to incite crowds. How can you get up in a poetry reading and talk about language and not have a dialogue about bilingual education? How can you write a poem about nature and not talk about the environment? Or a poem about spirituality and the creator and not talk about the mandate that we have as humans to repair the earth? To me, a poetry reading is as much about what is happening off the page as on it.

> ⌄ *You also were scheduled to meet the same middle school classes in Durham that poet Luis Rodríguez spoke to three months earlier. Was that experience engaging?*

In Durham, through a program offered by Duke's Center for Documentary Studies, I was able to work on a writing project with mostly African American fourth and fifth graders. We imagined what it would be like to be forced to leave your homeland to support your family, what it would be like to cross borders clandestinely, and, finally, what sorts of work would be available in the new country.

We focused on Mexicans. I was absolutely floored by the poems and narratives that were produced. These kids just got it immediately. Their capacity for moral imagination—for walking in someone else's moccasins—was stunning. They imagined hunger, they imagined backbreaking work. They drew, too, from close-to-home situations. They'd all seen Mexicans or heard of Mexicans working in construction in North Carolina, in tobacco, in slaughter houses, as hotel maids—you name it.

Above all, they drew from their own grasp of African American history. Without going into great detail about my own trial in connection with the Sanctuary Movement, I explained that some North Americans along the border have always offered a helping hand to people coming north. The students immediately started talking about the Underground Railroad. One girl wrote a piece about how she would disguise a Mexican in order to smuggle her to Durham—she'd dye the woman's hair blonde and put her in a Duke T-shirt! I bit my lip. What a statement about how she, as a black girl, perceives the Duke student body!

Finally, I had them write in the voice of a Border Patrol agent. In their own simple way, they elegantly covered the range of moral qualms many agents feel—but cannot voice publicly—about capturing and deporting Mexicans, about having to provide for their own families. What power in those young voices!

Pat Mora

$\mathcal{P}$at Mora is one of the best-known Latina writers in the United States. Born in El Paso, Texas, in 1942, she is the author of five collections of poetry, a critically acclaimed memoir, and at least fifteen books for children and adolescents. A former college professor and administrator, she speaks at conferences, universities, and public schools on a wide range of topics, among them bilingual and multicultural education, diversity, and writing. She often conducts poetry workshops when she speaks. When not traveling, she divides her time between New Mexico and the Cincinnati and northern Kentucky area.

This telephone interview took place on April 16, 2001. Mora discusses her success as a poet; the difficulty that Latino writers, in particular poets, have publishing their work; and the various themes that inform her poetry, including the desert, borders, the role of women in world societies, and Catholicism.

SUGGESTED READING

Chants
(Houston: Arte Público Press, 1984)

Borders
(Houston: Arte Público Press, 1986)

Communion
(Houston: Arte Público Press, 1991)

A Birthday Basket for Tía
(New York: Scholastic, 1992)

Nepantla: Essays from the Land in the Middle
(Albuquerque: University of New Mexico Press, 1993)

The Desert Is My Mother
(Houston: Piñata, 1994)

Listen to the Desert
(New York: Scholastic, 1994)

Pablo's Tree
(New York: Macmillan, 1994)

Agua Santa
(Boston: Beacon Press, 1995)

v *I'd like to start by asking you to talk
briefly about the evolution of your poetry.
How have you seen it change over the
years, since the publication of* **Chants,**
your first collection of poems, in 1984?

Always risky business, a writer talking about his or
her work. In part, we don't have the distance required,
which is why I'm always grateful to critics. I think in
many ways *Chants* was the beginning, on paper, for
me to express my fascination with my Mexican heritage. But in writing, there is a lot of unconscious
work going on. I've said before that the mystery of
writing interests me, which is always what makes me
a bit wary about intellectualizing what I do. So the
critical skills that I may have I like to apply to other
people's works, more than my own. Not speaking of
one's work somehow gives the work a veil of mystery,
if you will, that I think is both necessary and valuable. Having said that, I can see that *Chants* is very
much focused on the desert, on Mexico, on supersti-
tion, on the border. By the time I get to *Communion*
and *Agua Santa,* maybe there is a bit of a spiraling out.
Not that those themes don't keep reappearing, but by
the time of these other books I had done some international traveling and, I hope, deeper internal traveling. I had also begun thinking about a woman's
realities, about women's issues—on different borders,
in different cultures. In my later poetry, different ter-
rains begin to appear.

v *Were you conscious of wanting to
branch out from the region you had been
exploring in your earlier work, or did this
simply appear in your writing?*

Not at all. I did not force something to appear. When I'm talking to other writers, particularly at workshops, I tell them that it's important not to be strong-handed about one's work, that it's important to trust that your work will evolve as it should, that one should not be too pro-prescriptive or directive. I would never have said, "Well, you've done this; now you need to do something different," if it hadn't felt organic, natural. It was simply that my life experiences had taken me to India and Pakistan and some countries in Central America. Some of those experiences began to appear in my work. At the same time, there are other places I've visited that never appear in my writing. I think we experience psychological tugs that affect our core self, that are compelling sources that inspire writing.

> ∨ *Would you say that your later poems require more space? Although a few earlier poems such as "Oaxaca" are long, the poems in **Agua Santa,** your fourth collection of poetry, for example, are obviously longer than your earlier work. Are you conscious of that as an aesthetic choice, or is the length of these later poems coincidental?*

Well, it's a fascinating question since the book I'm working on now will require the most length, but length was not the impetus for the project. I am fascinated by issues of space—space on the page, geographical space, even the spaces in houses. Space intrigues me, especially the writer's power in that space. The book that I'm working on now is actually a book of odes, à la Pablo Neruda's odes, which will require—and I don't know if anybody will be interested in publishing the book— several pages per poem. Again, though, the decision goes back to my interest in following what intrigues me as a writer. At this point in my life, I'm intrigued by the things that I cherish, which is what the odes are about.

> ∨ *In an essay published about ten years ago called "A Poet for President," you write that the "work of the poet is for the people." Do you still hold true to this maxim?*

Absolutely! Absolutely! And to some extent it is a notion held by Neruda as well as by many contemporary poets—that the poet's work in the world is not that different from the carpenter's work in the world or the cook's work in the world and so on. Poetry is what we bring to the community, so my job is to do what I do as well as I can and to keep challenging myself. That's why I think the books change—

because there is almost a fear of repeating yourself. Poetry involves ways of creating situations or linguistic structures that will prompt me and maybe even force me to explore different things. And so *Aunt Carmen's Book of Practical Saints* becomes an example of that. I did make a conscious decision there that I was going to write a book of poetry in the voice of someone else, but the voice was going to be sustained throughout the whole book. I was going to explore form in a way that I hadn't before, but that form was going to be both coming out of traditions in English as well as traditions popular in Spanish as well as in New Mexican and Southwest history.

v *How much research went into this book?*

Quite a bit in the sense that I had the great opportunity to read a lot of books on the saints, which took me back to my early fascination with them. I also looked at research that chronicled some of the early literature of the Southwest. So I was very grateful to scholars who had done some of that work because I was able to read songs and prayers and texts and think about how I could take that form and adapt it into English. Sometimes the adapting meant that I was interested in the rhythmic pattern or the rhyme pattern. I wanted the poems to have a certain echoing quality. That notion has always interested me—the intersection of preservation and innovation, incorporating the past, yet doing it so that it is satisfying to me in a contemporary way.

v *Did the artwork you include in that book come later, or was that a conscious thought when you started writing the book?*

Well, it was certainly a dream fairly early on. Growing up a devout Roman Catholic, I collected holy cards the way kids collect baseball cards. I had albums of these things. I was used to connecting the image with a prayer, which is very common, certainly in Mexican and southwestern U.S. Catholicism. So when I actually worked on the poems, I would put images in front of me. I had a photograph of a woman who became Aunt Carmen to me. In fact, I actually saw this person at a place outside of Santa Fe. Her face really intrigued me. When it so happened that her face appeared in a magazine, I cut it out. I would put Aunt Carmen's photograph and the saint's picture that I was working on in front of me, and I would think, "What would Aunt Carmen say? What would her conversation be with this saint?" I was using those visual clues to create the book. When I spoke to my Beacon editor, Deborah Chasman—she was and has been wonderfully supportive—she was open to the possibility of including the art. In the beginning, though, the notion was that there was no way that the book would include full color. The images were going to be black and white. Some of my friends in the Santa Fe area, where the visual arts are so popular, would say to me, "Oh, no, you know you really have to get in there and argue for full color because it's going to be so essential to the book." Someone on the inside—I don't even know who it was—really argued that Beacon should publish the book with color. The power of staff, you know. It was a big risk, and I hope that the book, over its lifetime, sells well. It's the kind of book that needs attention to survive.

   v *It's a beautiful book.*

When the book arrived, I thought: "If I never write anything else, I at least have this."

   v *It's definitely not your most mainstream book, however. How has it been received so far?*

Well, I would say it gets some attention. Some of the audiences to which I read are unaware of the book, and when they become aware of it, they think that it would be a great gift, that they know exactly to whom they could give it. But it's hard to know how to get books noticed.

   v *You mentioned that you were a devout Roman Catholic. I really didn't see this side in the first two books I read. In **Chants**, you actually were writing on subjects one wouldn't necessarily associate with Catholicism—**brujas** [witches], **curanderas** [healers], the owl. It seemed like you were exploring another territory. You also wrote a poem called "To Big Mary from an Ex-Catholic."*

I knew you were going to say that.

   v *Right, and those references struck me as a contrast when I read the fifth book.*

Well, I think *Aunt Carmen's* really comes from a very specific geographical place
also. When I finished *House of Houses,* I had begun spending time in Santa Fe.
There is a very popular tradition there of saint carvings, which is not true where
I grew up in El Paso. The tradition was revitalized in the 1960s, at the time of the
Chicano movement. Traditionally, saint carvers had always been men called *san-
teros.* Now there are both women and men. There is an event in Santa Fe called
Spanish Market held at the end of every July, where the saint carvers display their
best works of the year. The images are displayed in the center of town, the plaza.
Seeing these images and studying about this carving tradition, I think, took me back
to an emotional-spiritual place. I became intrigued by the question, "What if I tried
to do that kind of shaping on the page?" That's really where that book came from.
It was the chance, then, to explore what we mean by holiness and who defines good-
ness and some of these issues that did and still do interest me.

> ˅ *You mentioned the research that went into this book. Did you also*
> *conduct research for your other books of poetry?*

Well, I liked your use of the word *explore* when you were referring to some of the
work in *Chants* and *Borders.* I like to read, period. Reading related to a writing project, then, is but another good excuse to read.

When I started writing, which was about twenty years ago, like most writers I
first had to explore personal issues, my complex feelings. Before bringing *Chants*
together, before I'd thought of a poetry collection, I was developing that faith in
the writing process that [William] Stafford talks about. I was writing to understand
my life—emphasis on *my.* In time, I began to expand my circle of interest. Of
course, my emotional knowledge and perspectives inform the poems, but I was
more and more intrigued by the realities and hopes and fears of others—as well
as of myself. I was fascinated by what I hadn't focused on: being Mexican. And so
"exploring" is exactly the right word. I was buying books about not only Mexican
history but Mexican folklore and Mexican superstitions, a mix of standard and
scholarly books. I would dip into them, and what I found intrigued me. It wasn't
that I was trying to amass a great deal of knowledge. It was more seeing this material as some kind of rich source. I think I've made the comparison before to clay.
It's like finding a great place where there is wonderful clay. That place and the clay

in it are going to lead you to interesting work because you're working with really good material.

> *Let's go back to an essay that you've written called "Bievenidos."*
> *You mention that you're "a child of the border." I was wondering if*
> *the longer you stay in Ohio, your writing will move away from this*
> *childhood border experience. Or does a poem such as "Braided" more*
> *accurately reflect your artistic inspirations? In that poem, you write,*
> *"here among Ohio maples and oaks / I hear those spirits return,*
> *gather." Do you find inspiration elsewhere, or do you still find yourself*
> *visited by those spirits from the past?*

I think if I get inspiration elsewhere, I'm not keenly aware of it, but I make that distinction because I feel there's so much we don't understand about ourselves. I believe that, so I can't speak definitively about what I do. I would be interested, for example, to hear what you would say about a book like *Chants* and a book like *Aunt Carmen's*. It's very hard for me to make those kinds of assessments. If I look at the work, I would probably say that I see only a few examples that deal with this Ohio and now the northern Kentucky terrain. And that is also true in my children's books. I'm asked that sometimes by children. They want to know if I write about places other than the desert. Again, I think we don't fully understand why certain things lure us. On a car trip that my husband and I were just taking, we were talking about how in many ways this is a beautiful terrain here [in northern Kentucky]—very green and lush, beautiful hills full of wonderful trees—but for whatever reason, this landscape doesn't fascinate me.

> *Haven't you written something about how the past is present?*

Well, if I may borrow the title of a current Chicago museum exhibit—"The Past Is the Present"—I have said that I feel like I carry the desert with me. I believe that. In other words, when I'm sitting in my little office here, I'm surrounded by images of the Southwest. When I get busy with my writing, that's where I am, in those images. I think for a Chicana—for this Chicana—writing about the Southwest comes naturally. It's my past, and it'll be the place where I'll spend the bulk of my life. I've spent half of the last five years in northern New Mexico. I'll probably be spending four to five months [each year] there from now on.

∨ *Do you work there? Do you give workshops and readings, or do you have a second home there?*

Well, actually we spent two full years in Santa Fe and a couple of summers. I also taught a semester at the University of New Mexico in Albuquerque. This is all in the last five years. I'm not even counting the speaking visits, and we now own a little house in Santa Fe.

∨ *You've written that the "desert persists in me ... compelling me to sing about her people, their roots and blooms and thorns." It seems that nature manifests itself in all of your work.*

Absolutely!

∨ *Can you elaborate?*

I'm interested in the whole notion of rejuvenation, and in such a complex world we need to stay renewed. So I often speak to audiences about the importance of finding what those sources of renewal are for ourselves, and for me the natural world is the key one. I have a very orderly side. That's what allows me to get work done. I focus on deadlines and goals and things like that. When I'm in the natural world, I feel like I'm able to let go and simply savor the present. I think that family is another source of renewal for me. And art. And, in a particular way, folk art.

∨ *I really enjoyed reading **Chants** and **Borders**, but **Communion**, your third book, has become my favorite.*

Really?

∨ *Maybe it's the international blend with the Southwest and the poems about your children. I was wondering where the title comes from.*

Sometimes it's hard to think back so far. At that point, though, I know I had decided that the book was going to be a one-word title. It made sense because of the other two books before *Communion*. Plus, I guess I've always been very interested in community and how we establish community.

∨ *Unlike the first two collections, only a handful of poems included in **Communion**, as you point out in the acknowledgments, were*

*published previously. Did you consider **Communion** more a "book"*
of poems instead of another collection?

I always feel, perhaps less with *Chants,* that I am working on a book. Of course, *Aunt Carmen's* has very discrete limits. I might have written other kinds of poems when composing *Aunt Carmen's,* but I knew those were not going to go into that book. The same thing is true for the book I'm writing now. The vision for such books precedes any of the writing. As far as the acknowledgments in *Aunt Carmen's,* there aren't any because the publisher wanted all the rights. And so the book was conceived as a project. Because the publisher had all the rights, I couldn't submit any poems beforehand.

ᵛ *You published your first three books with Arte Público Press. Why did*
you change to Beacon? You had success with Arte Público previously.

I did have success with Arte Público, and I continue to work with them on my children's books. They were doing less and less poetry, though. They do very little, if any, now.

ᵛ *There's a section in **Agua Santa** called "Where We Were Born."*
This part obviously differs from the other three.

Yes, again, that was conceived as a block.

ᵛ *And was there research there as well? You talk about . . .*

There was, and not only research in terms of facts, but a sort of visualizing was different for that part of the book, "Cuarteto Mexicano." I spent a lot of time try-ing to imagine these four women in Mexico's history: the Aztec goddess Coatlicue, Malinche, the Virgin of Guadalupe, and the folk figure La Llorona. And I imag-ined how they would walk onto a TV talk show format. It was a different type of thinking.

ᵛ *Earlier you said that family gives you inspiration. I've also noticed that*
several of your poems deal with aging. I'm thinking of "Pushing 100,"
"Rituals," "Stubborn Woman." Are the individuals you describe in these
poems connected to tradition? Are they links to stories from the past?

It's such a deep part of who I am—you know, right to my emotional core. Sometimes the sources for these ideas or poems on old age are unconscious. I was
recently working on a children's book, and it wasn't until after it had been sub-
mitted that I realized I had done it again—written about a relationship with an
older person. In this case, it was an older neighbor who plays a role with a young
child. But I grew up in a house with two older women. One was my aunt, whom we
called Lobo, and the other was my grandmother, Mamande. They had a very real,
physical presence in my life. They're still very much a part of who I am, and they
probably will be with me until I breathe my last breath. So it's an emotional attach-
ment more than an intellectual decision. My interest sort of naturally flows there.

> ⌄ *Another theme you touch on is class. Your poems centering around*
> *maids and exploited women are very effective.*

It is such a part of the reality in which I lived on the border—that is, seeing domes-
tic workers in homes. But it's still such a great part of the world in which I live
now, in the sense that the people who look like me at the conferences I attend are
often the ones serving the dinner or the ones cleaning up the room. The poems
often center around that sense of being part of that group and yet separate from
it. I want to make sure that these people are noticed. I'm working on a poem for
the book of odes on this topic, "Ode to Workers."

> ⌄ *Some of these kinds of poems appear in **Communion**, don't they?*
> *The ones set in Pakistan.*

Exactly. I was exploring issues of women's invisibility.

> ⌄ *I'd like to switch to your children's books. You've said in the essay*
> *"Endangered Species" that "my investment in the future, I suppose, is*
> *one of the many reasons why I write children's books." What are some*
> *of the other reasons you turn to this form of writing?*

I really love the form, and the connection between poetry and children's books is
a very close connection. In most cases, I'm dealing with very spare text, and I'm
trying to create strong and compelling images. In the case of children's books, it's
so that the illustrator can have a good time. Writing children's books has helped me

to write more visually. Writing for young readers is sort of like a secret pleasure for me. I find it very satisfying, though I have a lot of academic friends who can't understand why I do it. Even when I'm writing a relatively fun children's book or an alphabet book, I'm getting a certain kind of pleasure in thinking in that way. Like, "Oh, the illustrator's going to have a good time with this" or "I hope the illustrator is going to have a good time with that." So part of it is form itself. Picture-book writing is uncluttered by a lot of language. I also love the idea of language play and children's books, and poetry rewards language play. Almost half of the seventeen picture books are poetry books.

> ᵥ *I've noticed in your earlier books of poetry that the few poems*
> *for your children are playful as well.*

You're exactly right.

> ᵥ *I've also noticed that you turned one of your earlier poems into*
> *a children's book. I think it's "Poinsettia" in* **Chants.**

Right. I don't know if that happens often. It also happened with "The Desert Is My Mother." It had appeared in a slightly different form, I think in *Chants,* and then Arte Público Press decided to use that poem for what I think became their first children's book in their Piñata Books imprint. For the book, I went through and altered a few lines that I didn't think seemed natural in the voice of a child. With "Poinsettia," the poem definitely preceded the story. With Charles Ramírez Berg, I had written the story for a collection Arte Público was compiling. It eventually became a children's picture book.

> ᵥ *The Mora who illustrated one of your children's books—Is that*
> *person related to you?*

No, the illustrator Francisco X. Mora is from Mexico City.

> ᵥ *Let's switch to* **Nepantla**, *your collection of essays. Several of the*
> *pieces in this book include poetry as well. How does the poetry work*
> *here? Do you try writing an essay, then realize you've already written*
> *a poem on this subject, and later weave that poem into the essay?*
> *Or does the poem sometimes trigger the essay?*

Well, *Nepantla* in part, as I remember writing it, began as a way of taking a speech that I had given—because I was doing a lot of speaking at the time—and trying to get it down on paper. I would spend quite a bit of time on my talks, and I started thinking, if they were written down, they might be useful to people in different ways, including exposing them to poetry. Often when I speak, I include poetry in my talks. It doesn't matter if I'm doing a luncheon speech, a keynote address, or whatever. So it's crossing genres, which has always interested me. But I don't think the essays were ever really inspired by a poem that was woven in later. I had the talk in mind first, and then the poetry fit the speech. I'm keenly aware that not everyone reads poetry. I wish they did, and I wish they enjoyed it, but that's just not the case. And so *Nepantla* was a way of trying to reach a different audience. They could read the essays and at the same time read poetry, too. I wish that the book was promoted more effectively, I have to say. It's sort of like *Aunt Carmen's*. I feel that people who find the book find it helpful, but a lot of people just do not find this book of essays, so *Nepantla* just has not had the sales I wish it had.

˅ *Who published that?*

The University of New Mexico Press.

˅ *Could that be because it's a university press, and it doesn't have the same kind of influence with distributing as a larger publisher does?*

I don't know. How a book gets promoted is very complex. Personalities and budgets get involved.

˅ *You mention crossing genres. You've written poetry, children's books, essays, and a memoir. Have you ever thought about writing a novel?*

Well, you know, I wrote a short story that Arte Público Press published years ago. It was the only piece of fiction that I've ever published. I do have a number of books in mind for the future. I sort of maintain a steady pace so that I am always working on a number of manuscripts and have others that are in press. I am trying to finish up this book of odes this summer, and then I have thought about exploring a novella.

ᵥ *Any particular topic?*

It's about a teenager.

ᵥ *Set in the Southwest?*

Set in the Southwest.

ᵥ *I ask about the novel because your memoir has some of the same elements of fiction one finds in the novel—especially in the beginning, when you're introducing the characters and the settings. It's very fictionlike, don't you agree?*

Yes. I think one of the challenges will be how I will create that sustained time needed for fiction. I mean, I support myself in part by the speaking and school visits, which I find very satisfying. I might not have the time. I am very interested, though, in exploring longer fictional work. Right now I don't have that kind of space to work in.

ᵥ *You also mentioned earlier that you've been a teacher. You write about some of your experiences in your essays. Do you miss teaching?*

I don't miss grading.

ᵥ *I don't think anyone misses that.*

I say that very seriously, though—both the actual grading and the idea of assigning grades to people's creative work. I really dislike that. I understand why it's a necessary evil, but I think there is a negative aspect to that whole process as well. Assigning a grade affects the relationship of writer to writer, so I prefer workshops where I don't have to grade. There are aspects about campus life that I do miss—the excitement of ideas, learning, students. And it's possible that at some point in time in my life, I might decide to go back, but it'll have to be exactly what I want, the opportunity to teach and yet the necessary time needed for speaking and writing.

When I left university administration in 1989, I took a big risk. I believed—hoped—that I could be of greater use in the world as a writer.

Judith Ortiz Cofer

$\mathcal{B}$orn in 1952 in Hormigueros, Puerto Rico, Judith Ortiz Cofer spent her childhood moving back and forth between her native Caribbean island and New Jersey. After attending Florida Atlantic University, then doing further graduate studies at Oxford, Ortiz Cofer settled in the South. She is currently the Franklin Professor of English and Creative Writing at the University of Georgia.

As she explains in this interview, conducted in Athens, Georgia, on October 17, 2000, her experiences as a Puerto Rican woman in the deep South often differ from those of other Puerto Ricans in the United States, in particular Latinos who identify with a Nuyorican cultural aesthetic. Ortiz Cofer also discusses how language, memory, and folklore function in her writing, which includes novels, memoir, short fiction, essays, and poetry.

SUGGESTED READING

Peregrina
(Golden, Colo.: Riverstone Press, 1986)

Reaching for the Mainland,
in *Triple Crown: Chicano, Puerto Rican, and Cuban-American Poetry*
(Tempe, Ariz.: Bilingual Press/ Editorial Bilingüe, 1987)

Terms of Survival: Poems
(Houston: Arte Público Press, 1987)

The Line of the Sun
(Athens: University of Georgia Press, 1989)

Silent Dancing: A Remembrance of a Puerto Rican Childhood
(Houston: Arte Público Press, 1990)

The Latin Deli: Prose and Poetry
(Athens: University of Georgia Press, 1993)

ᵛ *You're an accomplished memoirist,
novelist, and writer of short fiction, but
you started your career writing poetry,
which you return to again and again.
I was wondering if you consider yourself
a poet first and that everything else flows
from that?*

Well, I would say that poetry is my first discipline. I felt that I did my internship with the word through poetry; I feel that it's easier to learn poetry first and then go to prose instead of the other way around. Poetry teaches us how to deal with the economy of language, the concentration of language, the cautious use of metaphor. So, yes, I was glad I did my apprenticeship as a poet. I am whatever the form I choose is first, though. When I'm a novelist, I give myself totally to that. That doesn't mean I don't work on poetry when I write fiction: I just become involved in a genre. But I always return to poetry. Even in the days when I can't find my way to the work, poetry always leads me back because poetry gives the material literature. Every great book contains matter that could be termed poetry. The Bible is a perfect example. So poetry, even if it's not what I'm doing, is my teacher.

ᵛ *You mention in your autobiographical
writings that you were an avid reader in
your youth. Were you also reading poetry
at this time?*

No, actually, I didn't have poetry around. My parents were always great readers. But my father, who was mechanically minded, read books on cars, machines, and that kind of thing. My mother read what would be considered Harlequin romance novels, but she also read the great Spanish novels. So we always had books around the house, but not poetry books. I discovered poetry in high school. My first real exposure, though, I received in college.

> ∨ *I'm curious about the construction of **Silent Dancing** and **The Latin Deli**. Many of the poems and prose pieces included in these works were published separately, before the release of both books. How do you compose the chronology of these texts? Is there a system that provides some sort of thematic continuity, or do you work much on this idea of ordering?*

If you're talking about *Silent Dancing,* then there is a chronology. It begins with my birth and ends when I'm fifteen. This book is a witnessing of a life. In the preface, I say that I got the concept for the type of remembrance, which I call a "partial remembrance," from Virginia Woolf, who believed that in order to reconstruct the events of her childhood, she had to follow the tracks left by strong emotions back to her moments of being. She said that's all an artist can do. We're not historians of our own life. We are not genealogists. What we're trying to do is reconstruct what made us who we are. With *Silent Dancing,* I figured that I had already experienced my moments of being because that's what poetry leads you to. But only if they're true poems, if they're not written for an audience but written because you need to write them, if they're written about the things that shaped you or the things that concerned you. So I took these poems and said, "They will lead me back." In many instances, they led me directly back; in some instances, they were just a trigger or an image out of the poem that I used. Every poem that follows a prose piece in *Silent Dancing* is not directly related; sometimes they are related at just a slant. One of my favorite quotations from Emily Dickinson is: "Tell all the truth / But tell it slant." So I remain true to the historical facts of those years. My father was in the military, and he was involved in the Cuban missile crisis, so I wasn't going to change that. What I needed to research, I researched. But in terms of reconstructing the past, I wanted a poet's truth to it, not so much claiming that I knew what I said to my grandmother at the age of three, but how what happened that day changed me.

ᵛ *Your mentioning Cuba reminds me of a poem you once wrote about your father, but I think I remember your father being supportive of the Castro regime.*

That was "A Legion of Dark Angels." I remember I was a little girl in first grade, and I was called to the television to watch the triumphant entrance of Castro into Cuba. Castro was a young man like my father. My parents remembered the awful days of the Batista dictatorship there, and they were rejoicing because one of their brothers was now going to lead their sister nation.

ᵛ *But your father was also involved in the crisis? In what capacity?*

He was involved in the Sixth Fleet, in the blockade of ships that were sent out around the island. We lost touch with him for about six months. We didn't know what had happened to him, although the navy assured us that he was alive. My father was involved because he thought Castro had lost the ideal of the Cuban Revolution.

ᵛ *Did your father ever speak to you about that experience?*

He became very bitter toward Castro. Before Castro, Cuba and Puerto Rico had been together. José Marti and the Puerto Ricans united in their rebellion against Spain. So our histories were very closely knit; they were considered sister islands. After the takeover of Puerto Rico by the United States and after the takeover of Cuba by Castro, our histories became more and more divided. My father would mention Castro only in terms of betraying the ideal.

ᵛ *In the acknowledgments to **The Latin Deli,** you mention that you've translated stories from Spanish to English; you write the same thing in your essay in the collected volume **Sleeping with One Eye Open.** Yet in some of your writing, you mention how, as a young girl, you "resisted" your mother's Spanish. Assimilating by learning English quickly seems to have been a big concern of yours during your early years in the States. How is your Spanish today? Do you feel comfortable writing in both English and Spanish?*

My speaking English was not a political choice. I went to school strictly in English, with only a few months' exception. I went to a school in Puerto Rico run by American nuns. As far as stamping out Spanish, I recall only one particular instance in *Silent Dancing,* where I had been brought to the United States as a little child, and my mother had taken me back to Puerto Rico and tried to put me in public school. I told her that I couldn't go to school there because I didn't speak Spanish. I was five or six. Then, later as an adolescent, I spoke Spanish at home, but in the streets I had to speak good English. In high school, too. So it was a difficult thing for a child growing up to remain fluent in two languages and to dwell in two completely different worlds at once. Of course, when I matured, I found out that having two languages was not a problem; it was a great gift. I understood two worlds, which not everybody can do. Later, as a scholar, I found out that I could translate. I don't speak perfect Spanish, nor do I write in perfect Spanish, but I can easily translate from Spanish to English. I found some Puerto Rican folktales, which I transcribed, and they have led me to all kinds of things. This new book I have, *Woman in Front of the Sun,* contains several pieces that began out of my translation of folktales, where I discovered kernels of wisdom and seeds of rebellion that I would never have been able to discover. They were part of my grandmother's world, without feminism, but there was a revolution in these folktales, as I reveal in "The Woman Who Slept with One Eye Open." Now, as a more mature person, I realize that keeping my Spanish was a great gift.

⌄ *When you mention speaking English in the streets, are you talking about the late 1950s?*

I was born in 1952, but for me my Paterson [New Jersey] years were really the 1960s. It's kind of a difficult chronology because I came to the United States when I was two, but, soon after, my father was stationed in Puerto Rico until I was in third grade. Next, we came back to Paterson, then returned to Puerto Rico. That's what *Silent Dancing* is all about. My actual conscious American life didn't really begin until about the eighth grade.

So that was the early to mid-1960s through 1970, when I was a preteen and a teenager, when I had two distinct worlds—the one with my parents at home, in Spanish, the other my world with my friends in high school, in English. The difference between both worlds is that I attended a Catholic high school, where there were only two or three Puerto Ricans. Everyone else was of Irish descent.

ᵥ *Can you talk about the title* **Silent Dancing***?*

It relates to the title essay, which begins with a home movie in which I describe these relatives who are involved in frantic New Year's Eve partying. I'm able to stop the movie and comment about each of them. "Silent dancing" to me is reminiscent of the immigrant or migrant situation, where you are trying desperately to live your life fully, but you're silenced many ways because you are not seen or heard. That to me was an appropriate way to see our lives then. We were part of a silent and invisible group of people.

ᵥ *Much of your prose and poetry reflects on the past, where you*
had to "struggle daily to consolidate . . . opposing cultural identities,"
where you "received an education in the art of cultural compromise."
Are those days of struggling and compromise behind you, or do you
still find yourself with some of the same problems?

It all depends on where I find myself. For example, in my role as a teacher, I know who I am. But, of course, I look very Latina; I have an accent, and sometimes when I go places, people don't automatically assume, "Oh, an American citizen, probably an English professor." The first question is, "Where are you from?" And they're not satisfied if I say, "Athens, Georgia." That happens with great frequency.

ᵥ *Do you find that happens more recently, over the past five years,*
when we've seen increased immigration from Latin America?

No, I've always looked foreign to people. It doesn't really bother me, but there's no way I can get around it. No matter how American I may feel—and I feel that culturally I'm more an American woman than a Puerto Rican woman, just having lived in this country for so long—I'm always reminded that people do not see me that way. And basically you are really not only a product of who you think you are but of how other people see you. So if you always have to trace your ancestry for other people, then you're not exactly feeling like part of the group. I don't see that as a problem, but I also see it as determining or defining the new race issue in the United States. When the Germans and the Irish first started coming to the United States, for one generation people asked about their accents. The next generation blended in. There is no way that I'm ever going to blend in, even if I start speaking English with a southern accent. So the color issue is always present there, for Asian Americans, for Native Americans, for blacks, for Latinos—there is no blending in, no melting into the melting pot.

> ∨ *I've recently read that there are more and more racist attacks against Latinos in North Carolina, including several unsolved murders. Do you feel we're seeing more prejudice as a result of what you're discussing?*

It's an interesting thing because when I was one of the few Latinas in the South, I did get the question "Where are you from?" a lot, but it was mainly a question of interest because I was "exotic." Now that they know I'm Latina and that there are a lot of Latinos everywhere, the prejudice is more likely to rise because a lot of problems are going to arise with population and that sort of thing.

I'll give you an example of how that happened. We lived in Miami for ten years, in the main Latino section where the affluent Cubans lived. There was no problem with being waited on when walking into a store. When the Marielito situation came into the picture, and there were a bunch of criminal elements and the kind of people that the merchants didn't want, all of a sudden the service changed. So the prejudice level rose for anyone looking Latino. I predict that it's going to happen again in the deep South. When you're an exotic and no threat, you're an interesting thing to have around; when there's a lot of you and you pose a problem, like "we don't want you in our neighborhood" or that sort of thing, the prejudice level rises. That's the basic thing I've learned in my lifetime.

> ∨ *I'm curious about something you once wrote in your poem "Exile." You stated, "I left my home behind me / but my past clings to my fingers / so that every word I write bears / the mark like a canceled postage stamp / of my birthplace." Does this idea of the past still motivate everything that you write?*

Well, I don't know about everything, but I don't know how one can stop being what one is, especially for me, where writing is a process of self-discovery, and looking into myself—the deeper I look, the more I find, and this affects everything that I do. But I want to differentiate that from what has become somewhat of a cliché now. I love *New Yorker* cartoons, and recently there was one where this musical group had changed its name from something like REM to Los Latinos del Momento, the Latins of the Moment. I never want to be that. I was writing long before any-one had an interest in my Latino heritage. Or whatever. In fact, one of my early novels got rejected numerous times because publishers didn't think there was a market out there. One publisher even said that Puerto Ricans don't read. And so I am not a Latina of the moment, just a Latina, any more than Flannery O'Con-nor could get rid of her Milledgeville, Georgia, sensibilities, even though she was able to look at the town and understand its foibles as well as acknowledge its pos-sibilities for grace. I can't ignore the fact that I was born on an island with an iden-tity crisis. It was a Spanish culture taken over by Americans. Then I went to the American North and had to experience that. So, yes, I think that all writers bear who they are like a canceled postage stamp. It's no longer currency, but it's there, fixed to you forever.

⌄ *When was your novel rejected? What years are we talking about?*

We're talking about the 1980s. It was finally published by the University of Georgia Press in 1989. But for two years the manuscript was circulating around New York, and my agent was getting rejections like, "It's beautifully written, but who wants to read about poor Puerto Ricans?"

⌄ *When did you notice this change with publishers—when they finally started publishing Latinos?*

I think it was a couple of years after Gabriel García Márquez won the Nobel Prize and the so-called Latino boom began. All of a sudden people said, "Hey, these guys may have something important to say."

⌄ *So you think that Latin American writers have had a lot to do with Latino American writers getting published?*

I'm not a business person, so I can't really back this up, but I really think the pub-lishing world is driven by the economy, by the marketability of something. So when a Latin American writer wins the Nobel Prize, and he's translated, and millions of copies of a book are sold, then publishers will start looking for another Latin Amer-ican writer to translate. It happens in cycles like that, so I think that opened the door enough. But it was years and years before American Latinos, the hyphenated group, started getting recognition. All of a sudden the schools started noticing that their student populations were becoming heavily Latino, so teachers started looking around for materials to use in the classroom. At first, no one would publish *Silent Dancing* because it had poetry in it. It's been my problem that I like to write in several genres in one book. But Arte Público eventually published it, and it's in its eighth or ninth printing. It's used in high schools and universities, and now there are quite a few other choices out there. But for a while, teachers were telling me that there were no books that reflected their students' background. I think that publishing is basically economically and demographically driven.

> ∨ *This idea of Puerto Rico as subject matter—sometimes the island is*
> *a place of yearning. Is this a correct assessment?*

No, I disagree with you. We talked earlier in the day about "The Idea of Islands," but to me that was sarcastic. It was an answer to someone asking me why I didn't go back to Puerto Rico, sit around in the sun, go swimming all the time. At this time, I'd been reading a lot on Puerto Rican history. I remember reading about one of the early American governors saying something like, "The Puerto Rican people are very lazy, but what would you expect? They lie around in their hammocks all day, and all they have to do is put a toe in the ground and up comes a yucca or reach up and pick a banana." I'm not quoting directly, but that was the essence of it. So this poem was written because I had been in Atlanta at a conference, and this one guy started saying something like, "Oh, you're an island girl? What is it like down there?" I answered sarcastically, "Well, I just wear hibiscus in my hair and sit around on the beach waiting to be rescued from life in paradise."

So my work is actually a response to the idea, like if you read my short story "Nada"—my mother's generation always had this idealized concept of the island as home and the only place where you could really be happy, like, "Oh, we were poor there, but at least we had the sun, or we had this and all this." Of course, I went back year after year, and of course I saw the sun, and it is a gorgeous island, but life was hard, difficult. So actually I don't have a nostalgic yearning for the island. I write about the dream of the island as opposed to the reality of the island. I think that many of my stories, like "Bad Influence," have to do with some of the beautiful aspects of the island, as a source of innocence that is still found, particularly in the older people or in the generosity and hospitality—that's not a stereotype, that's the truth. The harsh reality, though, is that MTV is everywhere and that people like to go to Kentucky Fried Chicken to eat and that sort of thing. My mother still says that the food is the greatest in the world, "but today we're just going to go to the mall." As far as the physical beauty of the place, it's gorgeous; it's like Hawaii. So—not to go on—this particular poem ["The Idea of the Islands"] is a satirical response to life as paradise in Puerto Rico.

> ⌄ *I know you can't account for other poets such as Victor Hernández*
> *Cruz, but how do you explain his returning to Puerto Rico?*

I'm not sure. With my mother and her generation, it was the immigrant idea of the eventual return: "We're going to make money and go back. The only thing the island doesn't have is money. It has everything else." But for me, that's not true. The island is an incredibly gorgeous place, but I can't live there on a permanent basis. There's some cultural things I can no longer adapt to. With Victor, I think he just had a deep and abiding need to get back to his Puerto Rican self, which he had experienced much more than I had. He didn't come to the United States as a baby. He came here as a young man, so his roots are deep there. But I tell you something that I happen to know—he has had to fight the prejudice. I talk about some of this in *Silent Dancing*. In the United States, I was considered a Puertorriqueña; on the island, I was considered a little *gringita*.

> ⌄ *There's a third category you seem to be identifying, too, when you*
> *say you're not Nuyorican and you're not Puerto Rican from the island.*
> *Are you a Puerto Rican writer from the South?*

I have an essay in my new book called "And Are You a Latina Writer?" And the question is, "What Are You?" The answer is, I'm a writer. If Cormac McCarthy decided to move to the Bronx, he'd still be a southern writer, right? And if I decided to move to Anchorage, Alaska, I'd still be an American writer of Puerto Rican heritage. So I don't want to belong to a school. I think the Nuyorican poets are willfully and willingly a very specialized group of people who have a vision, and it has to do with living in the universe of New York City. That particular sensibility. I didn't experience that, and for me to try to be a part of that would be ridiculous. I would be a fake. I happen to live in the South. Right now Martín Espada lives in Massachusetts. Does that make him less of a Nuyorican writer? He still identifies with that kind of school. And so being Puerto Rican is just who I am, but I could live in Connecticut, and I'd still be Judith Ortiz Cofer, the so-called Puerto Rican American writer. You can call me anything you want, but don't keep me from doing anything I want.

A lot of my poems and some of my other work have to do with being Puerto Rican, but I have a whole series of poems that have nothing to do with being Puerto Rican. I have a series of poems based on women in the Bible and literature that have been published in many journals, but when it comes to being anthologized, it's so much easier to categorize me. How could they publish a poem about Salome? How could they explain it? And that's a problem because, well, I don't mind categories, but these publications are keeping me from being seen as I really am, which is a student of world literature and interested in many countries.

> ⌄ What you're saying reminds me of poems such as "Room at the
> Empire" and "We Are All Carriers," which can't be so easily categorized.
> Are you conscious of this balance—of writing poems not only about
> Puerto Rico but about these other subjects?

I have poems about Magdalene, Salome, Helen of Troy, Hagar.

> ⌄ Where do these come from?

Well, one year I was teaching world literary masterpieces, and I was beginning to feel frustrated because everybody had a speaking part except the women. Salome was the one who, shall we say, changed the life of John the Baptist, but she didn't get to speak. Neither did Judith. And why? How did they feel? I wanted to know. In order to satisfy my own curiosity and my own desire to have a fuller story, I wrote a series of poems, trying to get Penelope out of the castle, to get her out of the house. They came out of, well, you could call it my feminist side. You could call it an exploration of voice. I wanted to hear myself think as Penelope. I wanted to hear what Salome had to say. They've been published in the *Kenyon Review* and all over the place, but they're never picked up and anthologized.

Actually, *The Norton Anthology of Poetry* has one of my poems, called "How to Get a Baby." That has nothing to do with Puerto Rico or being Latino. It has to do with my wide reading. I'd been reading the work of a white anthropologist, [Bronislaw] Malinowski, who had been studying the Trobriand Islanders. They had managed to convince him that they had no concept about how babies were made. Malinowski asked them how they got their babies, and they responded that they sent their women out to the oceans, and the women called the babies as spirits into their bodies. What he wasn't hearing is the other part of the story, which is, "This is the story that we tell, but we know where babies come from." That's my interpretation, of course, and I might get a lot of reaction to that, but I wrote this poem in which the women *do* go out to the ocean and call the spirits of the babies, but then the old woman narrating the poem says this is what you do: "You go out to the ocean, you call the spirits of your ancestors, then you go home and make love with your man; just make sure your baby knows that she's wanted." So what does this have to do with being Latina? It has to do with my eclectic reading, with my love of exploring all cultures. That's the problem with categories. Once you're labeled, you have a hard time breaking out.

> ᵛ *Do you see the Heath anthologies, then, that we were discussing at*
> *lunch, as those kinds of anthologies that **do** categorize, or are they a*
> *transition beyond that?*

It's a complicated issue. When I teach multicultural literature, I have to categorize. I say, "Okay, now we're going to do, um, Native American literature." And I think that's for an audience that has never been exposed to the diversity of the American literary experience. You have to be elementary; you have to say, "We're going to study African American writers now, and then Native American writers," and so on. I'm hoping that in another twenty years, the categories will be so widely available that they [nonmainstream writers] will be like the Jewish American writers are now. When I was a graduate student, Saul Bellow and Bernard Malamud were considered exotic, and now they're just men who happen to be Jews who write great stories. I don't think it will happen the same way, but at some point I'm hoping that it will transcend, and it will just be American Literature, but at this point we're at the beginning of an American revolution, and as with any revolution, you have to cover the elementary points. So I guess that categorizing is necessary, but only up to a certain level. I think that at the graduate level, for example, there's certainly nothing wrong with teaching *A House Made of Dawn* and a Faulkner novel in the same class. As far as regional, what's the difference between regional being the Southwest and regional being the South if the story is brilliant enough to be universal? Does it matter that Faulkner's universe was little? When he finished *Absalom, Absalom,* it wasn't about Mississippi; it was about the cosmos. So if a book like that is written by a Puerto Rican or a Native American, why should it continue to be taught as ethnic literature?

> ⌄ *I guess we can also point to something such as* **One Hundred Years of Solitude**, *which you alluded to earlier.*

Exactly.

> ⌄ *Your poem "Latin Women Pray" was your first poem published in a well-known journal. You also have an essay with the same title. Can you elaborate on both?*

The poem was about a time of frustration that had to do with language and marginality. My family has always been very Catholic, very faith oriented. The answer to them was *"si Dios quiere,"* "God willing," and that sort of thing. When I was growing up, I felt that when my mother asked me to say my prayers. The last lines of the poem are ironic because God is supposed to understand all languages. But it's like "silent dancing"—if everyone is acting like they don't understand you when you don't speak the language of the mainstream. Finally, I'm asking God to help me, but does he speak Spanish? Is he bilingual? It was published in the *New Mexico Humanities Review,* my first real publication, in 1978. It is a prayer that is supposed to say, "Is anyone out there listening?" I've written an essay with the same title, and it's about the frustration of the time when God spoke only English.

> ⌄ *You've also written a few poems influenced by your travels to Mexico. Do you give many readings outside the country?*

In the last few years, I went to Spain as a guest of the Foundation García Lorca, along with Victor Hernández Cruz and a couple of other poets. There's an interest there in New World poetry and Caribbean poetry. Two years ago I went to Germany, where several students are doing dissertations on my work. I visited three universities. I went to France in 1986. So there's a lot of interest, I think.

ᵥ *And Latin America?*

No, just Europe.

ᵥ *Sometimes you illuminate the social problems of our country,*
where our "indifference / . . . clings to us like the odor /of garlic."
Yet your poetry is not overtly political. Can you expand?

Perhaps not overtly political, but if you read even the early poems—"A Legion of
Dark Angels," for example, has to do with the disillusion of politics. "The Lesson of
the Sugar Cane" has to do with sexual politics. So I don't write poems that address
the social issues in a very overt or propaganda-driven way, but I feel every poem
that I write *is* political because if you write and you're engaged with life, where you
write about people who suffer as a result of societal problems, then in fact it is
political. I'm trying to think of a poem that is written that's not political. I write a
lot of poems about women. I never write a poem just to amuse myself. In fact, I
have always abstained from writing poems that are strictly pretty or only celebra-
tory. Even the poem I wrote for my daughter is a warning that to deny your heritage is to deny half of your humanity. All of my poetry makes a political statement
of some sort. You might say, "Well, 'Climate Changes,' how is that political?" It has
to do with the power of grief. Family politics, you know. The picture of my father is
on the mantel, and it's saying, "Don't forget me," and then I have to consider my
mother's life. Martín Espada is a political writer, maybe, in the sense you're referring
to. But I'm from the Emily Dickinson and Flannery O'Connor school of writing,
where you write about your Amherst backyard or about a farm in Milledgeville,
and then you're actually writing about everything it means to be human.

ᵥ *Earlier you mentioned "a poet's truth" to "reconstructing the past."*
Are you conscious of writing as memory and preserving the past?

Not as a family historian. I feel the poet does write on memory but . . . Wasn't it
Aristotle who said the historian keeps the factual record of mankind and the poet
writes the emotional history of mankind? I think you can read a history of Vietnam and know that so many men under the age of twenty were killed, or you can
read Tim O'Brien and you can "feel" those deaths. O'Brien is preserving the emotional history of Vietnam. A historian is preserving the facts.

> ⌄ *Do you think, then, that poetry is closer to the "truth" than fact?*
> *I mean, if you "feel" what O'Brien is writing as opposed to the*
> *historian's facts ...*

I don't think I would do without either one. I mean, I want to know the facts, but I don't just want to know that Joe González, who was nineteen, was killed on December 31, 1968; I want to know what Mrs. González feels after her son was killed in 1968.

> ⌄ *That's one of your stories, isn't it?*

Right, "Nada" has to do with the death of a Puerto Rican boy in Vietnam. In fact, that story has been anthologized in Vietnam. There's a reconciliation anthology in which Vietnamese writers and American writers write about their experiences. I was very honored to have it included there. In that story, I wanted to preserve the emotional history of a woman who lost a son in Vietnam. But, still, I want the historian's facts, too, to keep track of this war.

> ⌄ *Death is a recurring motif in a lot of your poetry. Can you elaborate*
> *on this image of death that appears in so much of your work?*

I don't know if you've read the new edition of *Reaching for the Mainland,* which ends with the death of my grandmother. Someone once said that all serious poetry is about death, and I think that doesn't mean the subject of death, but the acknowledgment of death. I guess I went from writing poetry as self-expression to writing poetry as self-discovery when I got a grasp of my own mortality. I think it may have to do with the death of my father, who died at a very early age. I have a poem called "Absolution in the New Year," where I talk about that, so a lot of my poetry has to do with death. But I think that poetry, in general, after a certain point in a poet's life, has to do with the acknowledgment of mortality. And even the most joyful poems have to do with, "Yes, let's not forget that life is brief." Once I started dealing with grief in poetry, I discovered that I had found my way to poetry. I think that so many young poets are only writing about the joy of love and that sort of thing and don't understand that the great poetry, like Dylan Thomas's "Do Not Go Gentle" and like [Wordsworth's] "Intimations" and "Tintern Abby," has all been a moment when the poet realizes that "this is my time to express what I have gathered in this brief life."

˅ *How old were you when your father died?*

My father was eighteen when I was born. He died in a car crash when he was forty-two, and I was twenty-three.

˅ *You've written many poems about your father. The tone of "Through Climate Changes" is different from the tone of some of these other poems. I was wondering if this poem—about your mother introducing you to another man in her life—was a difficult poem to write.*

Yes, it was, because I had a difficult and complicated relationship with my father, who was a military man, and he was also distant emotionally after a lifetime in the military; he suffered from depression. He was the complete opposite of my mother, who celebrates life. My father represents my dark side. He represents what I inherited and what leads me to poetry. I can't celebrate life without investigating it first. And he didn't live long enough for me to enjoy that. So when my mother went on and found someone else, I found it hard, and yet it was poetry and literature that led me to understand that to stifle someone else's emotional life is almost immoral, that you have to let people continue to live, and that grief is one of the great shackles. If you let grief hinder you, you can become trapped in it. So that poem is a working out of grief, where the memory of my father was so alive in me, and my mother knew that, and for her it must have been very frightening because she and I, even though we're culturally very different, we're very close. She was acting like I was an ambassador from another country. She was treating me very delicately because she wanted me to approve of her decision. And I had the power to say no. That was an interesting reversal of the daughter's role. I had to say "no," that I deny the power given to me by my grief, and let her go on. Writing that poem allowed me to be generous.

Ricardo Pau-Llosa

*B*orn in Havana, Cuba, in 1954, Ricardo Pau-Llosa moved to the United States in 1960, shortly after Fidel Castro came to power. His family eventually settled in Miami, where he lives and teaches in the Department of English at Miami-Dade Community College. As a young man, he met several prominent exile artists in South Florida who introduced him to "cultural images and artifacts." Since the 1970s, he has collected, curated, and written eight scholarly books on Latin American art.

Pau-Llosa's collection *Sorting Metaphors* (1983) won the national competition for the Anhinga Poetry Prize. His other collections have received critical acclaim as well. A staunch critic of the Castro regime, he feels it his duty as an artist to "keep the record straight, go back to what the facts are, and from there build a poetic assimilation of those facts."

This interview took place on November 26, 2001, in Miami, Florida. In it, Pau-Llosa discusses the Castro regime, which he calls "a horrible dictatorship," the problem of labeling writers, the visual arts, phenomenology, and the evolution of his poetry.

SUGGESTED READING

Venticino poemas
(Miami: Ediciones Universal, 1973)

Sorting Metaphors
(Tallahassee, Fla.: Anhinga, 1983)

Outside Cuba/Fuera de Cuba: Contemporary Cuban Visual Artists
coedited with Ileana Fuentes-Pérez and Graciella Cruz-Taura
(New Brunswick, N.J.: Office of Hispanic Arts at Rutgers University and University of Miami, 1989)

Bread of the Imagined
(Tempe, Ariz.: Bilingual Press/Editorial Bilingüe, 1992)

Cuba: Poems
(Pittsburgh, Pa.: Carnegie-Mellon University Press, 1993)

Vereda Tropical
(Pittsburgh, Pa.: Carnegie-Mellon University Press, 1999)

The Mastery Impulse
(Pittsburgh, Pa.: Carnegie-Mellon University Press, forthcoming)

*⌄ You published your second book of poetry, **Bread of the Imagined**,*
*in 1992, nine years after **Sorting Metaphors**, your first volume. Your*
*third book of poetry, **Cuba**, came out in 1993, a year after **Bread**. Were*
there distractions between the first and second books?

Yes, a lot of art writing. A lot of writing of poems, though, and publishing, but
there wasn't really a focus, no sense of a unifying theme. Although it took forever
to come up with some sort of manuscript sense for *Bread of the Imagined,* it's a
tight book. A lot of anthologies ask for poetry from that book. It was actually
ready for publication in 1989, although it came out right before *Cuba,* in 1992.

*⌄ Were you writing **Bread** and **Cuba** at the same time?*

No. *Cuba* was cathartic. I started writing *Cuba* in 1989, soon after *Bread* had been
accepted for publication. The famous year, 1989—all the convulsions, the collapse
of the Soviet Union, Tiananmen Square, the Berlin Wall, the Ochoa Trial in Cuba.
I guess those events triggered, for the first time, a sense, a clearing in the mind,
emotionally and psychologically, that enabled me to write about Cuba. I'd always
wanted to. And it's not that I hadn't been trying, but I'd end up throwing it away.
Occasionally I'd make some reference to Cuba, but I couldn't come up with a way
of doing it that I liked. I remember, though, one afternoon in September 1989,
when I was writing a letter in my studio. I had a framed, illustrated road map of
Cuba on the wall, from the 1950s, and I looked at it as if for the first time. So I
wrote a poem about it, and I realized that it had a conversational tone about this
Cuban reality that was new in my work. I knew then that I had to go through each
of the vignettes that illustrated this map—about sites and points of interest—and
circumnavigate Cuba, as it were, starting with Havana, going west first and going
completely around the island. I dealt with about twenty vignettes, depicting tropical fruit or waterfalls or tobacco fields, historical sites, things you would want to
see if you were driving around the island. The vignettes were like little works of
art inside this map. The whole multiplicity of map as a complex sign became
apparent. I had always admired C. S. Pierce, and I had dealt with his idea of a sign
being either a symbol, an icon, or an index in poems and art criticism. In this map,
all three kinds of signs were present and interacting, and this provided a frame to

enter Cuba from a personal level without ignoring the sense of historical juncture. All these levels of concerns that previously functioned as disparate forces suddenly became very cohesive rather than scattered elements of consciousness.

So I went into these vignettes as if they were windows into a personal and a collective memory. The map served not just as a catalyst, but as a way out of becoming too entrapped in this peculiar condition called Cuba. After the circumnavigation of the island on the map, there came a whole section of poems about Havana, as I remembered it and as I'd come to know it through study, through the testimony of those who lived in it when it was a great, modern city. The third part of the book deals with exile. But Cuban history and art, personal memory, and exile run through the poems in all three parts. That's how the book got written within the period of a year. I included in the book most of what I'd written and put the poems in the order in which they were composed.

⌄ *This must have been one of your most creative periods, considering the other work that came out the previous year.*

It was very productive. *Cuba* also took me into short-story writing, which I had never really done before. In that book, though, I wanted to deal with the epic dimension of Cuba and the personal dimension at the same time. I certainly didn't want it to be merely an ethnic book. I guess some people who complain about being pigeonholed as a Latino or Cuban writer fear being thought of as folklorists of a certain kind. Such writers appear in a very limited way to people outside their group, like an artifact. *Cuba* enters into the whole idea of Cuba as a history—not nostalgically, because I'm not interested in the lost palm trees of my parents' landscape. I do think of myself as an exile, though, a condition created by my rejection of totalitarianism and not just of one particular leader. Politically, exile is not something I shy away from, although being opposed to tyranny from the left earns one many enemies among the intellectual and cultural establishment in the United States. The Castro regime is a horrible dictatorship. It's my ethical and moral duty to denounce it—in the same way that if I'm a witness to a crime, I'm compelled to call the police and bear witness to what has occurred. So, on the one hand, when I write about Cuba, it is in an attempt to bring up into consciousness insights into a civilization, a whole attitude toward life that has been willfully and needlessly annihilated as a result of this tyrannical madness masquerading as "the Cuban Revolution."

And that sentiment gets carried over and developed further in the book that followed it, *Vereda Tropical,* which is much more a Miami book in that it deals with the cabarets, restaurants, and whatever public cultural life there is here that could be considered Cuban. There is an elegiac side of *Vereda Tropical,* which Eric Ormsby's comments on the book point out, and it has to do with the fact that Cuban culture did not survive in exile in any recognizable way, contrary to the widely held view of Miami as a "Cuban" city in the United States. *Vereda Tropical* is a hedonistic elegy for a very conflicted civilization that not only destroyed itself, but also killed the living memory of itself. So whatever references one finds to predebacle Cuba outside the island—in everything from media reports to novels, movies, and history books—are extremely distorted and very one-sided. The idiotic view held by many non-Cubans is that pre-1959 Cuba was the brothel of the world, a place of horrible dictatorship, unspeakable exploitation, with American gangsters controlling the streets, the whole *Godfather* image.

The Cuba I remember as a child—and the Cuba I know was there from the sheer fact of its enormous cultural output, its high standard of living, as well as from the fact of its enormous middle-class urban architecture—was not a country of only palaces and slums. It had those—what country doesn't?—but it also had a huge, modern middle class that created and identified itself with a dazzling high and popular culture that was original and eclectic. What's more, that culture, both high and popular, was alive in the hearts and minds of all Cubans and interconnected them to each other. The Cuba of the 1950s responded creatively to the music and culture it imported, blending it with its own rhythms, and it reveled in linking its painting, poetry, music, religions, humor, advertising, architecture and urban development, journalistic style—everything cultural informed everything else cultural. Amelia Pelaez, José Lezama Lima, Virgilio Piñera, Rafael Soriano, Orquesta Aragón, Cachao, Chocolate Armenteros, Beny Moré, Celia Cruz, Changó, Yemayá, classical ballet, Capablanca, a deluge of popular musical genres from *son* to rumba to mambo to bolero, five centuries of architectural splendor from the colonial to art nouveau, from castles to art deco and modernism.

As a poet, I feel that part of what I do is keep the record straight, go back to what the facts are, and from there build a poetic assimilation of those facts. Not simply to reduce, as is often the case in history, a civilization to data that fit some other culture's view of it. If all you know about ancient Egypt is Exodus—the evil pharaoh enslaving the Israelites and Moses liberating them—then you have an absurdly limited view of Egypt. It would be preposterous to say that an Exodus view of Egypt is complete, yet lots of supposedly intelligent people in the U.S. media and cultural establishment have a similarly caricaturesque view of pre-1959 Cuba, and hardly anyone questions what they say.

As an artist and simply as a thinking person, I feel an obligation to set the record straight as best I can, but it's not a joyless task. It's important that the artist finds his or her ground—to find it and to build on that—instead of attaching oneself to a trend that is politically viable and pleasant, and that whatever establishment forces at the moment are rewarding the artist, the writer or poet will find a way to make acceptable music to those ears. Currently in the United States, the so-called left or liberals are the establishment and function in exactly as dogmatic and arrogant a way as did the establishment they hated in their youth. My duty to myself as an artist is infinitely more complex than the requisites of careerism. I can't even consider what is correct or expected of me by the prevailing cultural establishment.

That is why considering myself a *Latino* in the current American context of that term is absurd. I am a "Latino" if that includes all Latin America, Iberia, and Italy. The Latino experience here is basically an immigrant experience of people who are descendants from Latin American economic or political exiles or who were annexed by the United States, and they have grievances against those who discriminate against them. I think of myself as more akin to a Minoan from Crete, a man hailing from a place that has evaporated or has been destroyed by forces that we don't understand or that are intentionally misrepresented to serve evil purposes. My origins left behind an indelible testimony—in stone, painting, sound, and words. I'm a Minoan survivor, and I want to put forward my explanation of what has happened to us, even though the other cultures that surround this bizarre extinction want to distort it so they can appropriate it for their own mythology, their own Exodus stories.

*∨ Don't we have to look at each country's experience independent of
the other's, though? Certainly there are different dynamics that separate one country from another—the Cuban experience as exile or the
Mexican as immigrant.*

Absolutely. The Palestinian writer Edward Said has written lucidly on the distinc-
tions between exiles, immigrants, and expatriates. I may not fit neatly into any of
those categories, but U.S. Latinos—Puerto Ricans living in the mainland as well as
Chicanos and others—do fit into the immigrant ethos with some exilic undertones.
The preservation of language is a bigger deal for Cubans than it was for Chicanos,
for example. I was stunned, though perhaps should not have been, in the 1980s,
when I cocurated a traveling exhibition of Latino art, to encounter Chicanos in
Los Angeles and Texas who appeared very nationalistic, very "Mexican," but didn't
speak a word of Spanish. I was the white, Anglo-looking curator with an international career and outlook, indistinguishable from the evil capitalist and so forth,
and they were the ethnic Latinos who dressed the part, but I spoke Spanish fluently,
and they could speak only the language of their supposed oppressors. Many generations had transpired in their experience, while only two had passed in this latest Cuban experience of exile, and our vision of "success" included fluent
bilingualism and dynamic simultaneity of cultural participation. Theirs had more
to do with being accepted as equals in America.

∨ How do you feel about the Nuyorican experience?

The Nuyorican experience is different from both the Cuban and Chicano experiences because there is a lot of traffic back and forth between the island and the
mainland. Puerto Ricans in New York think of themselves as Puerto Ricans in New
York. Puerto Ricans on the island do not see them as foreign, which is how Mexicans see Chicanos and, curiously, the way Cuban exiles see Cubans who emigrated
to the United States prior to 1959. Several Puerto Rican writers whom I know spend
time on the island and in the United States. What keeps the Chicanos and the
Nuyoricans together, though, is that they typically see themselves as a group within
the fabric of American culture, and they define themselves in those terms. As a
group, as "Latinos," they have this extended sense of identity provided by ethnic

American politics; it's a part of identity that is played out in terms of America. Some Cuban Americans, born here of Cuban parents, are entering into this mindset.

> ⌄ *Why have you made it your literary charge to correct this record, to portray the Cuba you remember and the one you say has been so horribly distorted by outside forces?*

It's not just simply because it's intellectually honest or for the same reason that African Americans want to correct the version of blacks in Tarzan movies—because it's insulting and ridiculous and inaccurate. I have to start with where I am. Obviously I can't change every mind, but I'm certainly not going to accept passively a series of distortions that foreign intellectuals and media people, out of malice or ignorance, use to shield or otherwise rationalize their collaboration with a Marxist totalitarian regime, because for them that's what this is all about—the ruthless advancement of personal and political interests by hypocrites who feign concern for the downtrodden. Those people who have collaborated with the Cuban regime and defended the revolution and screamed against the U.S. embargo, and who silence or ignore those who attack this regime—they call the shots in American and Western intellectual life and control much of the media. They operate under a movie Western ethos: the liberal or leftist always wears the white hat, and the villain is always bourgeois democratic capitalism.

I've lost count of the times when in universities and museums—that is, in the fora of American high culture and education—I've been grilled by sanctimonious leftists trying to determine if I can be believed or trusted on Cuba simply because I am an exile and must therefore be, to them, a fascist. No other people victimized by a dictatorship are systematically held up to such scrutiny and actually made out to be the victimizers. I find this state of affairs monstrous, incredibly outrageous, and a betrayal of everything the West stands for by those very people who are supposed to uphold Western values the most—the artists, journalists, intellectuals. I've even heard things like, "Oh, you can't really talk about Cuba because you're too close to it." That's like saying that African Americans can't talk about racism because they're too close to it or Jews can't talk about the Holocaust because they're too close to it or women can't talk about sexism because they're too close to it. No one uses this type of criteria on any other victimized or aggrieved group. Somehow I have to set out to defuse stereotypes and prejudices provoked by my temerity to oppose a dictatorship that is still the darling of liberals here. I have to overcome the vanity of liberals to get them to listen, never mind enlist their help in a cause that should be theirs as much as it is mine. For this, I'm the one who's called a fascist. It's lunacy. It's a frame of mind that I have run into many, many times.

Even some Cuban Americans have adopted this aberration. Just recently, the day of the [2000] presidential election, a Cuban American woman, who is older than I am and who works in the college where I teach but in another department, scoffingly asked me, "Since you're Cuban American, I guess you voted for Bush?" She asked this in front of my class—I'd never set eyes on her before; she'd come to work on a project there. Apparently, this Cuban American woman had assumed that bloc voting was a problem only when the votes were Cuban American, ignoring the far more homogenized voting statistics of other American ethnic groups. Facts are, 40 percent of Cuban Americans voted for Clinton, in both elections. In this race, in part as an Elián [González] backlash, Gore got 20 percent of the Cuban American vote. Contrast these statistics with the African American or Jewish vote for the Democrats. No one goes to African American intellectuals and in a ridiculing tone says, "Oh, you must have voted for the Democrats because you're African American." The vilification and perhaps the lawsuit would be immediate and overwhelming, and rightly so.

⌄ *Do you think this reaction has to do with the fact that Bush or Republicans in general are typically associated with anti-intellectualism?*

Yes, but I haven't found too many profound or truly intellectual Democrats or liberals either. In a recent article that came out in *Cigar Aficionado,* on Miami, I'm one of the people that Jonathan Kandell, a former correspondent for the *New York Times,* interviewed. Kandell is actually an extremely intelligent man and the most sophisticated, politically savvy, and worldly journalist that I've ever encountered. But even Kandell frames his representation of me in the article by referring to me as "the rarest of specimens"—and this because I'm a poet but also a "conservative" who's a fervent anticommunist. If I were talking about the kind of journalistic imbecile who typically writes for the *Miami Herald,* this kind of nonsense would be expected. But Kandell is fluent in Spanish and in Latin American culture; he also understands Marxism, in theory versus practice. Nonetheless, this is how even an informed and discerning journalist frames his perception of me. How bizarre, a poet who is also an anticommunist! Fact is, the only poets that I know who are leftists are those who have never lived under a Marxist regime. How different is my position from that of a Brodsky or that of any of the Russian or eastern European intellectuals who fled from those communist regimes? Name a single artist or intellectual who has lived under the communists, not as an official artist-leech but as a common citizen, and whose political position even remotely resembles that of the typical American left-wing or liberal academic or artist? Not one.

The new Julian Schnabel movie on the life of novelist Reinaldo Arenas, *Before Night Falls,* might shake a few of these American hypocrites up a bit. Once you've lived through the horseshit of socialism or even just been grazed by it, you understand that you're not dealing with just a theory; you're dealing with a psychopathic ideology. A conscionable person can no longer applaud such regimes in order to exploit his pose as a "progressive" because true progressives should be the first ones to denounce fascism in the name of their ideology. There should be no fashionable dictators. This is a moral and ethical plague that afflicts American intellectual life and journalism. Assimilating into America as an intellectual and artist means I have to subscribe to this supine ignorance of history or become a collaborator. I refuse.

Getting back to your question of why bother to reconstruct the record, I also believe that the model of Cuban civilization that was destroyed by the Marxists would have been a very useful one today. Precisely during the enormous convulsions of the 1960s, if there had not been a Fidel Castro in power and there had been a way to restore democracy, Cuba could have gotten its act together, and there would have been continuity from a cultural and economic and social perspective. Then Cuba could have been an example to follow—for many people here, Europe, and elsewhere—who were looking for an alternative to the kind of staid, complacent, hypocritical, country-club establishment that the rebellion of the 1960s wanted to overthrow. Middle-class, capitalist, modern, pre-1959 Cuba was revolutionary in that regard. We had a middle class that was very progressive, as contrasted with their counterparts here and elsewhere in Latin America.

ᵥ *What about race and how that figured into this successful economic
and social strata that you're referring to? What about racism in Cuba
before Castro?*

The notion that many Cuban exiles in particular want to try to sell us—that there
was no racism in Cuba—is false. There was racism in Cuba. But remember, Cuba in
that sense was still jelling from a second generation of immigrants. I was born in
Cuba in 1954. My mother is the daughter of Spanish immigrants. It takes a while
for people from diverse origins to come together as a nation—it still hasn't happened in the United States! The only color-blind society I've ever been in is
Venezuela. Throughout Latin America, there's racism, and certainly in Cuba there's
still racism. The Central Committee of the Communist Party has maybe two blacks
in it. Cuba is maybe 70 percent black and mulatto, yet all the leadership is white.
There is no racial sharing in Cuba—something that escapes most African American liberals like Jesse Jackson, Maxine Waters, Charles Rangel, who admire Castro.
Now Afro-Cuban religions are permitted to a point, but only because they can be
"sold" as an exotic show to foreign tourists who bring hard currency. It wasn't long
ago that *santeros* caught worshiping their gods were imprisoned.

Cuba was a modern, capitalist, entrepeneurally alive Hispanic Latin American
country, which, at the time, didn't have any of these Protestant hang-ups over sex
and pleasure; it made money and had a very modern worldview. And culturally
Cuba was much more open about racial integration than the United States. Cuba
was not some cowering, pathetic, banana republic run by idiot generals with fat
rolling off the top of their tight belts, surrounded by head-twitching priests of dubi-
ous sexuality. Cuba was a totally modern country. The Catholic Church, thank-
fully, played a minor role in Cuban life, more like it is in France as opposed to the
way it is in Mexico. This culture was overrun, annihilated, at the point of a gun. The
firing squads took over the moment Castro descended on Cuba, and they haven't
stopped since. So it's not just a sense, then, of correcting the stereotypes that are
convenient among my colleagues in the American intellectual world. It's also a way
of understanding other ways of conceiving a collective, where you don't have the
kinds of hypocrisies that we associate with pre-1960s American life. Recovering the
historical Cuba is an ethical duty that can still enlighten Americans on how to
resolve their own conflicts, teach them lessons on real multicultural life, and suggest ways of overcoming their own cultural prejudices.

v *I think you touch on this dilemma in one of your short stories,*
"Martes."

Yes. There are a number of exiles that believe that going back to a free Cuba means recovering property our parents left behind. I am exasperated by this Cuban exile habit of envisioning Cuba in terms of the lost house of the grandfather, the one that had a huge backyard with a big mango tree, and they had a swing. Or these idiot visions of parental palaces or maybe a lost shoe store somewhere. I tell them, "Imagine you were a Venetian, and suddenly your city was overrun and burned to the ground and sunk into the sea, but all you're worried about was your grandmother's bistro on the Grand Canal. You've lost Venice! Who the fuck cares about your grandmother's bistro! You've lost something far greater than some property. Even if you say that your mother or your father got shot by the revolutionaries, and even though that personal tragedy is horrible, we're talking about something far greater, above and beyond even that. You've lost an entire unique, modern culture that was an undervalued glory of its time and that you could have been a participant in or contributor to. That is a far greater loss than all the plantations in Cuba multiplied by a hundred."

It's this sense of epic loss that I try to bring home to a lot of exiles and Cuban Americans. My suspicion is that the loss of Cuba as a civilization, as a culture, was so enormous that it's hard to deal with it without starting to go haywire. To confront that loss, it's better to think of your grandmother's little store. Synecdoche comes to the rescue when the horizon of painful memory threatens to engulf us.

v *Is that what your story's about? The cow and the shoes as your*
grandmother's bistro?

The story grapples with this. For the protagonist, all of Cuba was reduced to this cow that his father had left behind. Recovering the cow would have meant recovering Cuba, but the cow's been butchered and turned into several things years ago, including the shoes. So the protagonist wants the shoes—he wants some kind of physical recovery. What's astonishing is that he's dealing with this woman who is a collaborator of the government. She watches other people, denounces them to the state, and all he wants to talk to her about is the shoes she's wearing. He can't really think about this new Cuba that he's looking at. This is the new Cuba, and a lot of people in Cuba are like that. It's a people who have been reduced to totalitarian complicity. And that's also one of the great crimes about Cuba because Cuba was not a place of political fanaticism. Cuba never had a right wing. There were a lot of communists in Cuba, but they were very corrupt and notoriously bourgeois. The bloody political gangsterism of the 1940s and 1950s was motivated by greed, not ideology. There's a saying, "This is Cuba, Chagito," meaning, leave all those rigid parameters behind. There was a bizarre softness to social and other categories in Cuba. Fidel Castro installed a very draconian, fascistic state, based on either being with him fanatically or being against him. No in-between, and they're going to watch to see who stands where. This had never occurred in Cuba before 1959.

> *I'd like to switch to art. You've been a curator for many years, a*
> *collector, and a critic with some eight books to your credit. Can you*
> *talk about how you became interested in painting and how this*
> *interest informs your poetry?*

The visual arts have interested me since I was a child. I was much more drawn to painting than to music when I was a child. In Miami, in the late 1960s, the Freedom Flights had broadened the Cuban population in Miami, and consequently an economic base was created, attracting exiles living in New Jersey, Chicago, Tampa, and elsewhere. Like a lot of other Cuban families that had come before and settled elsewhere in the United States, we moved to Miami in 1968. It was around this time that many Cuban intellectuals—most of whom had supported Castro despite his willingness to imprison or shoot anyone who dissented from his directives—started having problems with the regime and began abandoning Cuba. Cuba always became a tyranny ten seconds before the exile in question decided to leave it, which helps explain the longevity of this tyranny. It didn't matter that the regime had been murdering tens of thousands of people all along—part of that lack of national cohesion and the lack of a national consciousness I spoke about earlier. It's the major flaw in Cuban civilization—that fragmentation, the inability to see what's happening to the guy across the street as important to me and to everyone else.

The intellectuals started coming in the 1960s. All the writers went elsewhere— New York, Madrid, Caracas, wherever newspapers or universities could ensure a living wage. Miami was not a welcoming place for writers, but the painters were able to make a living here. Some had come with reputations they had had before 1959. A painter can work in his house and sell his paintings, unlike a writer, who needs an infrastructure to survive. So painters became the first cultural unit or focus to emerge in Miami as an expression of the Cuba that was being derailed ninety miles away. And as a young man, eighteen or nineteen, I went regularly to these painters' houses, and it was not just a way of connecting with my parents' friends, but of connecting with cultural images and artifacts. Art was connected with this artistic tradition that's still in Cuba, although there it is imprisoned or forced to serve the state. It was exciting to visit artists, go to their houses, and see their work. It was a very physical and tangible expression of Cuba as a living culture, which up until that point I'd only thought of in terms of narrative. Cuba was now a painting that I was looking at. The painters were very lively, colorful, bohemian, full of wonderful stories. They provided me with a Cuba that wasn't made up of nightmares, tortures, prisons, firing squads, neighborhood watchdog committees. They had another narrative—the narrative of the arts. These were the people who were actually the protagonists, the builders of cultural imagery. It was intoxicating, so I began trying my hand at writing about their work.

٧ *Was there a certain style or school of thought that these artists followed?*

The scene was very diverse, very European, deeply influenced by surrealism and constructivism. The School of Havana since the 1920s had been one of the pioneers of modernism in the Western Hemisphere. Havana had been producing artists who were influencing or impacting American artists and writers. Havana and Mexico and Buenos Aires and, to a lesser extent, Rio were centers of modernist art before any American city. In Miami, I was apprenticing, you could say, with the second or third generation of Cuban artists, who were real cultural protagonists. Rafael Soriano, José Mijares, Enrique Riverón, and many who went to Puerto Rico but would travel to Miami often: Cundo Bermúdez, Rolando López Dirube, Alfredo Lozano, and others. These artists knew the poets and writers of Cuba: José Lezama Lima, Virgilio Piñera, and others. Some writers eventually moved here, including the ethnographer Lydia Cabrera, and novelist Enrique Labrador Ruíz.

For me, these painters and writers were cultural heroes because they were the creators of a Cuba of the imagination, which I could inhabit and would never be expelled from. And I could talk to them about how they created art. It was a very physical experience—you could smell it, you could taste it. Dealing with artists became a very normal event in my life, as it rarely is for an average working-class American young adult who is not related to an artist. I remember the first painting my parents bought in 1970 for twenty-five dollars—a watercolor by Mijares. And now, here we are, some 250 works of art later. My own proclivities toward the visual arts were magnified many times over by that experience.

> ᵛ *How does this appreciation of the visual arts influence your*
> *own poetry?*

It influences my work enormously. But even when I'm not writing directly about painting or writing a poem that's inspired by painting, being around painters and being around art educated my eyes—educated me to see formal and symbolic correspondences in the visual world, so that painting and sculpture have trained me to look at the world the way an artist would. Painting also gives me an appreciation for context and the scenario in which a poem occurs. In some poems, it's very clear—the persona is in a restaurant or a bar and interacting with other people. In others, it's not so obvious, but it's implied—that sense of a context where the reader is walking into a painting and the painting is his or her universe. In most of my poems, I aspire to that painterly sense of context that interests me more than simply having the persona spinning off opinions or ideas or memories. Often the context functioning as a scenario undermines or conditions what the persona is "saying." That theatrical presence or context of a poem I got from exposure to Latin American art. North American painting rarely has that same sense of oneiric, enveloping context.

In the case of "The Map," which I alluded to earlier, there are those Piercian divisions between signs. One is the icon, which is an image that signifies by means of resemblance—e.g., a portrait. The second is a symbol, such as a word or number, which means by virtue of social agreement. The third is the index, where signification occurs through the physical impact of reality on the signifying element—for example, a thermometer reading, a fingerprint, something very physical that leaves a mark, and that impact is the meaning. So the map operates at all three levels. Obviously, it is an icon of the Cuban archipelago with its topography and roads, and it is covered in symbols that are the names of cities, etcetera. The wrinkles and folds I ignored as playing the role of index. Instead, I took the map in essentially, in a Husserlian sense, and let the index of this act of the mind be the poem itself. So I'm playing with all those Piercian designations of signs and how they're interacting with the imagination, using Pierce to engage what Husserl would call transcendental consciousness or awareness of awareness itself. I've digested what I could from these thinkers and detest the parading of erudite epigraphs, so a reader is not likely to retrace these steps. Artists are the digestive tracks of the imagination, absorbing what culture, history, and immediate experience offer up.

From Husserl, I learned there is a clear discipline and method to the way painters envision ideas or think the world we see. The Husserlian phenomenological suspension, the mechanics of intentionality, and many other ideas helped me reflect on the whole act of consciousness, on how the mind registers and therefore imposes certain realities on reality. These are the ideas Wallace Stevens talked about, without crediting Husserl. I wanted to enact them, put them into practice in the creation of contextually conceived poems where the voice was theatrical and personal, historical and immediate, all at the same time. Only then can the poem control, somewhat, the reading act, envelop it, serve as a world for the reading act.

The whole dynamics of intentionality and how that's also working in a different way, internally, through memory, are also in play in these poems. How the mind is like this double-sided machine that is altering the outside world and the internal world simultaneously, and the intersection of those two manipulations is thought, idea, image, poem, act of the mind. So I'm very interested in those things when I'm writing and as I'm writing. It's not just simply a nostalgic trip laced with references to a pained, exotic place. It's a phenomenologically informed study of the way in which images of the physical world set up the mind at a certain moment to produce this tangible expression of these things that otherwise would be mysteries.

*v And for you as a poet, the "image" of this "physical world" is most
often Cuba under Castro, and your "tangible expression" is that which
exposes a reality that you feel, quite strongly, is not accurately
portrayed by the media?*

I don't know why thinking Americans have so much trouble with the moral challenges posed by the Cuban regime. They don't have any trouble with condemning
abuses and oppressions in South Africa and El Salvador and Chile or seeing through
propaganda and manipulations coming from their own government. But when it
comes to Cuba, the ethical guard is dropped, and everybody is happy, like Jack
Nicholson, who goes to Havana and smokes a few stogies with Fidel and comes
back saying, "It's a paradise." I don't know why that is, but it has to be examined,
and it has to be examined by Americans who are so good at condemning others.
Nothing that I say can be taken seriously because I'm a Cuban exile, remember?
The rules are set up so that the people who can speak about this can't. During the
Elián crisis, for instance, even someone as intelligent as Charlie Rose had, on one
occasion, four people, all of them American journalists, not one of them a Cuban
exile embodying that position, talking about the Cuban exile community in Miami.
It was simply outrageous. Can you imagine a group of four straight marines being
interviewed and holding forth on gay life? Or four men talking about women's
issues? Or four African Americans talking about Chinese issues and being taken
seriously? Without any equivocation? Without anyone in the media saying, "Wait
a minute!"

Silence about atrocities in Cuba is the scandal that defines American intellectual
and moral emptiness at this time, and it also condemns the pope and the Catholic
Church, whose complicity with the regime is absolute. I could understand it if it
happened with other issues and with other people—if the stupidity was general and
not selective. As I mentioned earlier, part of my duty as an artist and especially as
a man of conscience is to refute this scandalous view, in all its manifestations, of
the country in which I was born.

Gustavo Pérez Firmat

*B*orn in Havana, Cuba, in 1949, Gustavo Pérez
Firmat moved to the United States shortly after Fidel
Castro came to power. Described as "one of the most
intellectual of those who are writing about the Cuban
condition" (Nicolá Kanellos, ed., *The Hispanic Literary Companion* [Detroit: Visible Ink Press, 1997], 237),
Pérez Firmat has published five books of criticism on
Latino literature. He is also a novelist and a memoirist. The autobiographical *Next Year in Cuba* (1995)
captures many of the tensions he and other exiles feel
when living between two cultures.

Pérez Firmat also has published five collections of
poetry. In this interview, which took place via e-mail
December 15, 2000, he discusses his career as a poet,
which started in his thirties; his run-ins with other
faculty at Duke University, where he used to teach;
his new teaching position at Columbia University;
bilingualism, biculturalism, and "life on the hyphen";
and love.

SUGGESTED READING

*Idle Fictions: The Hispanic
Vanguard Novel, 1926–1934*
(Durham, N.C.: Duke University
Press, 1982)

*Literature and Liminality:
Festive Readings in the
Hispanic Tradition*
(Durham, N.C.: Duke University
Press, 1986)

Carolina Cuban, in *Triple
Crown: Chicano, Puerto
Rican, and Cuban-American
Poetry*
(Tempe, Ariz.: Bilingual Press/
Editorial Bilingüe, 1987)

*The Cuban Condition:
Translation and Identity in
Modern Cuban Literature*
(Cambridge and New York:
Cambridge University Press, 1989)

Equivocaciones
(Madrid: Betania, 1989)

*Do the Americas Have a
Common Literature?*
(Durham, N.C.: Duke University
Press, 1990)

Suggested Reading
(CONT.)

*Life on the Hyphen: The
Cuban-American Way*
(Austin: University of Texas Press,
1994)

*Bilingual Blues: Poems,
1981–1994*
(Tempe, Ariz.: Bilingual Press/
Editorial Bilingüe, 1994)

*Next Year in Cuba:
A Cubano's Coming-of-Age
in America*
(New York: Anchor/Doubleday,
1995; rev. ed., Scrivener, 2000)

*My Own Private Cuba:
Essays on Cuban Literature
and Culture*
(Boulder, Colo.: Society of
Spanish-American Studies, 1999)

*Cincuenta lecciones de exilio
y desexilio*
(Miami: Ediciones Universal, 2000)

Anything but Love
(Houston: Arte Público Press,
2000).

ᵥ *You've published a memoir, a novel,
five books of criticism, and at least fifty
scholarly articles. One wonders when you
find the time to write poetry.*

I guess the answer is twofold: (1) poetry, for me,
doesn't take a lot of time; and (2) sometimes I go for
long stretches, months or even years, when I don't
write a single line.

I didn't begin writing poetry until I was in my thirties. The first poem I ever wrote, "Carolina Cuban,"
was written the night my son was born. I used to
carry around a little pocket notebook where I would
jot down quotations, ideas for critical essays, book
titles, new words. While Rosa was in labor with
David, I took out the notebook and, out of the blue,
the Carolina blue, scribbled the poem (I use the word
loosely). So for me poetry and fatherhood, creation
and procreation, seem to go hand in hand. After that
night, I continued to write "poems," sometimes in
Spanish and other times in English. Many of them, I
now see, had to do with my astonishment at being a
parent. No, not a parent, a *father* (I hate the whole
"parenting" business: a parent is nobody's mother and
nobody's dad). As the father of two children—my
daughter came along a couple of years later—who
were born not only in the States but in the South, I
began to worry in a more deliberate way about issues
of identity, culture, choice of languages, and that led
to more poems. But I'll always be an "occasional"
poet, not only because my poems are triggered by
specific, usually trivial, occasions, but also because I
write them very occasionally.

⌄ *Most of your poetry appeared the same year as your longer, critical work—**Equivocaciones** and **The Cuban Condition** in 1989, **Bilingual Blues** and **Life on the Hyphen** in 1994. Does one kind of writing inspire the other? Or, as you've questioned in the past, is there really little difference between your critical writing and your creative writing?*

That some of my books of poetry and of criticism have appeared at the same time is only coincidence. I'm not sure how much of a connection there is between the poetry and the scholarship. At least overtly, very little, but then again everything one writes, whether it's a laundry list or *War and Peace,* bears one's signature in some way. So it may be that the collection *Carolina Cuban* is *Literature and Liminality* by other means, and that inside *The Cuban Condition* there's a bunch of *Equivocaciones* trying to get out. The repetition of phrases or sentences is sometimes deliberate—I couldn't think of a better way of saying it the second time around—but at other times inadvertent. The advantage of not having a good memory is that you can quote yourself (and others), convinced that you are inventing something.

I do think that if I hadn't written so much criticism, I'd be a more consistent poet, and that if I didn't have the choice of languages, I'd be a more complete writer. Last year, when I turned fifty (fifty in Cuban years; in American years I'm thirty-nine, even if they are light years)—I decided to drop English (the way one drops a lover perhaps) and return to Spanish, my mother and father's tongue. I found that I had to learn how to write in Spanish all over again for the first time. So I wrote a book of poems, *Cincuenta lecciones de exilio y desexilio,* about the process of relearning. But I wish I could just write rather than always seeming to be writing about being or not being able to write in this or the other language. It's the critic in me that makes me think twice.

There are dumb writers, and there are smart writers. I'm a smart writer, but that doesn't necessarily make me a better writer; just the opposite, I think—there I go again. Hemingway was a dumb writer, and his work is the better for it. Scott Fitzgerald was a smart writer, and his intelligence ruined him.

Friends of mine tell me that I'm striking a pose when I say that I'm not a writer but only a man who writes, but it's not a pose. I'm not comfortable being—or being called—a writer. It doesn't seem like what I was cut out for. It's vaguely embarrassing. I can't explain it to my father. In spite of my success, I have the abiding sense that I've ended up in a place where I wasn't meant to be. Two roads diverged in a wood, and the one I took was the garden path. These feelings of vocational mis-placement—*vocación* as *equivocación*—haunt me, and they arise as much from my career as a professor as from my career as a writer—I mean, as a man who writes. Sometimes I'm angry at myself for not having made more conscious and consci-entious decisions when I was young. You're twenty years old, in college, feeling worthless; you don't know what to do after you graduate; all you want to do is hide, and so you find a hiding place in an M.A. program in Spanish, not realizing that you've just signed over your life to literature. Then, thirty years later, still hiding, you sit in front of a computer making a living from literature by bitching about it. Even though my writerly signature is Firmat, I'm really *un Pérez cualquiera,* Span-ish for an average *yo.*

> ᵥ *I just finished reading **Anything but Love**, your recently published first novel. I was wondering why the anger resurfaces? It seems you'd exorcized a lot of your anger in some of your earlier writing, including your poetry.*

Anger can be relieved, but I'm not sure it is ever exorcized, unless the conditions that feed it change, and normally they don't. I wrote much of *Anything but Love* in the aftermath of a very stressful period in my life. The basic story had originally been a chapter in *Next Year in Cuba,* but my publishers refused to include it in the memoir because they found it offensive. So I turned it into an independent nar-rative and called it fiction because everything in it is true. People who know me and who've read the book are made uncomfortable because they see the links to my own life. I'm not quite sure how to react to this. Others have been bothered by the "machismo" in the book. I'm not sure how to react to this either (what Amer-icans call "machismo" is to me only manliness.) Since writing is done alone, it seems like a completely private act at the time I am doing it, though of course in the back of your mind you know that what you're writing will eventually be read by others, including friends and family perhaps. But apparently my need or compulsion to make a record outweighs any potential embarrassment I might feel (or cause) upon publication.

Also, I'm not very good at gauging how others will react to what I write. I've written some things that I thought were fairly harmless, yet others regarded them as scandalous. Years ago I wrote a couple of poems, "A Sensitive Male's Mea Culpa" and "The Poet Discusseth the Opposite Sex," generally on the subject of the gender wars. I liked the poems and thought one of them in particular was very funny, but when I sent them to a friend of mine he wrote back: "Don't *ever* publish this!" Of course, I went ahead and published the poems, and perhaps I've paid a price for having done so, but not to have published them would have been an act of cowardice. My tacit compact with the reader is: I don't have to please you; you don't have to read me. This way, I am free to say whatever I want, and he or she is free to disregard it.

This doesn't mean, obviously, that I write without any awareness of an audience, and I know that at different times I have been concerned about what my children will think of what I write—I mean, what they will think of me as a result of reading those "sexist" poems and whatever else I have written (including poems I have written about them). But even in this situation, I generally end up giving myself and them the benefit of the doubt and betting that if they read me fairly, they will not love me any less than they do—and maybe they will love me more.

> ∨ In **Next Year in Cuba**, when discussing one of the classes you
> taught at Duke University, you state that "writing poems is something
> done by a real human being in response to concrete, often banal
> circumstances," that "a head cold is sometimes just as good as the
> Trojan War." You've written about head colds, but you've also explored
> larger subjects, such as "life on the hyphen." Can you respond?

The remark about the head cold is a reference to A. E. Housman, who wrote *A Shropshire Lad* when he was laid up with the flu or some other similar affliction. It's true that I've written about "larger subjects," but always from a personal and even idiosyncratic angle. In fact, I'm still trying to learn how to speak ex cathedra (*catedrático* in Spanish), a useful talent when one is a professor. Some of my colleagues do it wonderfully well—so well, in fact, that they've forgotten how to speak any other way. But since I'm not Hegel, and since I'm generally clueless about general schemes, I tend to stick to details and leave the phenomenology of the spirit to others.

It's true that the notion of a "life of the hyphen" has become something of a rallying cry for a generation of Cuban exiles—the Cuban American baby boomers, those of my peers born between the end of World War II and the Bay of Pigs—

but I didn't set out to write a manifesto. *Life on the Hyphen* is basically a 250-page valentine to my wife, Mary Anne. I got the idea for the book when I fell in love with her, and I wrote it during the first couple of years of our marriage. It's my happiest book and, for that reason, maybe my best.

> ⌄ *All of your writing celebrates verbal and linguistic play, but do you feel more freedom taking chances when writing poetry? Freedom to experiment more with both English and Spanish?*

In prose, it's easier to play because the margin of error is larger. Whereas in a short poem one misstep can ruin the whole thing, in prose you always get a second paragraph. But the "verbal and linguistic play" is not something that I set out to do; it happens. Some of it goes back to anger: puns are nasty; puns are instruments of aggression. (Have pun will travel.) They are a way of blowing off steam and settling scores with yourself and your languages. They're also indices of uprootedness, words unmoored from their meanings, exile in language.

In the most recent things I've written, I've tried to avoid going for the jocular (it's hard, as you can see) because to make a joke is a way of not facing up to the unfunny facts of life on the hyphen, a kind of cop-out. Given the choice, I'd rather make you cry than make you laugh. But the angst or anger that drives my language engine sometimes can find release only in word play.

It's also the case that the nature of the languages makes it easier to play with words in English than in Spanish. Puns don't work very well in Spanish, for example, because the language has very few homophones. So if you fall through a window, you can't say in Spanish, "I have a pane in the ass." In addition, Spanish has almost no nouns or verbs that are monosyllabic—the word for *pun* in Spanish is *equivoco,* four syllables instead of one—and this also hampers play because it slows you down; it imparts a certain stateliness and even solemnity to the language.

Every language has its distinctive voice print. The sounds of a language compose a kind of melody incommensurable with that of any other language. And since every sound has an affective correlate, the melody of a language—its collection of bright or blue "notes"—imposes upon its users a gamut of nongrammatical moods. I believe that you can learn a lot about the temperament of a people merely by listening to the *sound* of what they say, provided that you don't understand a word they're saying. I like to watch broadcasts on SCOLA in languages I know nothing about—Croatian, Chinese, Russian—and see what I can glean from their music. I put myself in the shoes of the pretty news anchor from North Korea, and I ask myself: "Now, what would *you* be like if you sounded like that?"

So to get back to your question about linguistic play, with me it's less genre specific than language specific. I'm fascinated by the sounds of words and the music of sentences, in English or Spanish, but I find that English lends itself a little better to the prosodic hide-and-seek that we call "linguistic play." What I like best, though, in prose or poetry, is interlingualism, where I can take advantage of the happy accidents that occur when my two languages bump into each other.

> ⌄ *In one of your poems from* **Bilingual Blues**, *you write, "I would recant that poem, if I could / except I never throw out text." Having stated this, has there ever been a time when you regretted publishing something you wrote? I was wondering, for example, how some of your colleagues might have felt about a poem like "The Poet Discusseth the Opposite Sex."*

I touched on some of this question earlier. I'm not sure how my colleagues at Duke reacted to some of my poems because we didn't talk much (maybe that was their reaction). But *je ne regrette rien*. As I said, I have this urge to leave a record, an urge that I don't quite understand but that I know is deeper than mere exhibitionism. So the things I've written are an account, good or bad, deft or artless, of whatever was bothering or bewitching me at the time.

Regarding the autobiographical nature of much of my work: as a reader, I tend to take everything literally. I prefer nonfiction to fiction; and even when I read a novel for pleasure, I choose novels that place me in what I take to be a real world. That's why I have never been interested in science fiction or fantasy literature; naive as it sounds, I don't want to waste my time with stuff that's not true. When I was in college and everybody was reading *The Hobbit,* I couldn't get past the first page of the book. This literalist bent or bias extends to my writing. I don't like to make things up. What's the point of writing about it if it didn't happen? If it's too good to be true, leave it alone. I remember that years ago I had a colleague who also wrote poetry. One day I came across a poem by her that I liked very much; the poem talked about the differences between her and her sister. When I mentioned to her how much I had liked the description of her sister, she replied that she was an only child. I felt totally defrauded and thereafter thought less of my colleague (and of her poems).

> ⌄ *In the poem "Carolina Cuban," you write, "I'm not mixed, just mixed up." Having lived in the United States for almost forty years now, do you still feel "mixed up"?*

I take the fifth. I don't think I want to answer this question. I'm tired of being mixed up and even more of writing about being mixed up. Wholeness. Wholeness. Wholeness. Wholeness.

> ⌄ *Well, stated a little differently: Exile from Cuba has provided you an "ambivalent cultural and linguistic positioning," a topic you continue to explore in your writing. You've lived in the United States a lot longer now than you ever lived in Cuba. Do you think there'll ever be a day when this "ambivalence" disappears, when your position will be clearer and more predictable?*

OK, since you insist, I'll answer. I don't believe the ambivalence will ever disappear; it's become part of my core/*corazón*. Long-term exiles are damaged goods: the wrapping is torn and the contents are tarnished (*ojo:* I may be quoting myself again). I wish it weren't so, but I don't see what I can do about it. If it's broken, you can't fix it. But I'm not sure this makes me and others like me unpredictable, as you suggest. The pendulum is mightier than the sword—and how is a pendulum unpredictable? It's the monotony of my Cuban mood swings that tires me. No matter what I write, I always seem to return to the same issues: language, exile, family. Kafka once said that sometimes he had nothing in common with himself. I wish! No weird metamorphoses for me. I wake up in the morning, look in the mirror, and see the same *gusano* [exile worm] that I was the night before.

> ⌄ *Someone once described your writing as "wickedly funny." Having read most of it, I agree. But there's also a tragic element that creeps through—in your poetry, in your fiction, and in your recollections of Cuba. In one poem, you write, "It may be that happiness is no longer / a relevant category of experience." Are you speaking mainly for*

the poet and at a particular time in your life or for one particular
individual? Or is this a condition you see as universally human?

I'd say that the mood is more melancholic than tragic. And I think it comes through especially in the Spanish-language poems, which, as I said, tend to be less "playful" than the English-language ones. I blame (and credit) my melancholy on exile, of course, but that could well be my own sustaining fiction—the belief that things would have been different in Cuba. The poem you refer to began as a reaction to some news about a friend who never seemed to be able to get her life together. I do think that as you get older, "happiness" becomes less important. You learn to settle for safety, comfort, companionship—all of which may add up to contentment, a more stable condition, rather than happiness.

Someone once remarked that the word that appears most often in my books is *Cuba.* This is understandable, given my status as an exile, but every time I write *Cuba,* I cringe a little. Even as I delight in the name, I realize that my obsessive repetition of it is a symptom of dispossession. Cubans in Cuba can take Cuba for granted; we exiles cannot. Naming is a poor substitute for having, but it's a substitute nonetheless. This naming what you don't have breeds melancholy. The task for me is not to let melancholy sour into bitterness.

   ᵥ *One has to wonder how painful some of your writing must be*
   for those who read it. **Next Year in Cuba**, *for example, has appeared*
   in both Spanish and English, which would allow your father, mother,
   and other relatives to read it. Carlos, your brother, too. Did you ever
   have that kind of audience in mind when you wrote, or were you
   bent on showing how exile affected you and your family in so many
   different ways, shapes, and forms—no matter the consequences
   or emotional expense?

The latter. In *Next Year in Cuba,* I was trying to tell not only my story but that of my family and my tribe (Miami Cubans), a story that I don't think is sufficiently known. I wrote that book very fast; in a way, I had been writing it ever since we arrived in this country in October 1960, but some parts of it were wrenching to get down on paper. My family didn't know anything about the book until after it came out, and although I wrote it out of love and respect and sorrow, they didn't take it that way. My mother in particular was very upset. She read the book as an attack on our family. She hated that I wrote about my strained relations with my brothers. The chapter on my father, which was the hardest to write, she took as an indictment of him, though I certainly didn't mean it that way. And not long ago she informed me that one of my uncles had gotten Alzheimer's when he read and found out that his daughter—my cousin—was a lesbian. "He hasn't been the same since, Gustavito." So you can see why I have mixed feelings about being a writer. But would I write the book all over again? Yes. Why? Because it happened.

> ˅ You write about popular music in all of your work. I was wondering how you feel about recent CD releases such as **Buena Vista Social Club** or **Afro-Cuban All Stars**? Any comments on the film **Buena Vista Social Club**?

I find the whole Buena Vista phenomenon exploitative, and so I've refused to see the documentary. Ry Cooder is a contemporary version of the Great White Hunter who travels to the tropics in search of Exotic Wildlife. Spare me! The exoticization of Cuba is not a good thing for Cubans. Ultimately it strips us of part of our humanity, our like-everybody-elseness. As for the band, my impression is that they are well-meaning but second-rate musicians.

By the way, I write so much about popular music because it has been such an intimate part of my life. A *son* by Lost Matamoros moves [me] much more deeply than a sonnet by Shakespeare. I was not raised with poems or symphonies or paintings; I was raised listening to popular music, Cuban and American. Songs speak to me in a way that great literature does not. What others find maudlin, I find profound. What others dismiss, I treasure. I have spent half of my life daydreaming to the tune of one or another popular song—from Doris Day's "Que será será" to Luis Miguel's "No me platiques más." My writing, poetry as well as prose, is full of echoes of lyrics by little-known (to the general public) Cuban singers: Willy Chirino, Hansel and Raul, Clouds, Carlos Oliva. I've told Mary Anne that when I die, I want to be buried with two things: my c.v. and Willy Chirino's *Greatest Hits*.

> ˅ You're now teaching at Columbia. Do you care to discuss why you left Duke?

Sure. Although I liked the university and the students very much, I left Duke because the atmosphere in my department was asphyxiating. The Cuban writer Virgilio Piñera says: *"La literatura no es estilo sino respiración"* (literature is not style but respiration). I found it difficult to breathe at Duke. In New York City, the air is dirtier but the breathing is easier, and my Columbia colleagues, unlike some people I know at Duke, actually *like* literature. But I still live in Chapel Hill because my children are here. Life on the hyphen now means spending most of my time between airports.

> ∨ *Do you have any immediate predictions concerning Cuba once the*
> *Castro regime finally does come to an end?*

No, no predictions, though I am reminded of what Flaubert said after the outbreak of the Franco-Prussian War: Whatever else happens, we shall remain stupid. I try to live as if Cuba didn't matter, but I'm obviously not very good at it.

> ∨ *How do you feel about being labeled Latino? You're on record as*
> *stating that you're Cuban, not Latino or Hispanic. Do you agree that*
> *some kind of label is necessary when referring to different peoples*
> *from Latin America now living in the United States?*

For years, I've been saying and writing that "Latino" is a statistical fiction. But that is less true now than it was when I began saying it. Teaching a lot of "Latino" students at Columbia, I see that the label does apply to some of them, second- or third-generation Puerto Ricans, Dominicans, Colombians, or Cubans, who call themselves "Latino" somewhat in the way other Americans call themselves "Republican" or "Democrat." But, for me, nationality is way more important than ethnicity, and the term *Latino* erases my nationality.

Years ago I read a filler story in the *Miami Herald* about a man who had been left paralyzed as a result of a stroke. He would spend his days in his wheelchair by the window of his Miami Beach condominium, looking south and mumbling to himself the only word he was still able to pronounce: *Cuba.* Sometimes I think I am like that man.

Leroy Quintana

*B*orn in Albuquerque, New Mexico, in 1944, Leroy Quintana was raised by his grandparents, who introduced him to the traditional Mexican folktales characteristic of the American Southwest. From 1967 to 1969, he served in the U.S. Army in Vietnam. After his return, he received a B.A. from the University of New Mexico in 1971, an M.A. in English from New Mexico State University in 1974, and an M.A. in counseling from Western New Mexico University in 1984. He started writing poetry soon after his return from Vietnam.

In this interview, conducted by telephone October 17, 2000, Quintana discusses the influences on his writing, including the *cuentos* or stories he heard as a young child; other poets and writers; and the Vietnam War. The war in particular helped shape some of his best poetry, including *Interrogations* (1990), which, according to one critic, exemplified "the capacity of a human being to transcend the experience of war" (*Contemporary Authors,* New Revision Series, 65 [1998], 249). Quintana's first collection of short stories, based in part on his Vietnam experience, is forthcoming.

SUGGESTED READING

Hijo del Pueblo
(Las Cruces, N.Mex.: Puerto Del Sol Press, 1976)

Sangre
(Las Cruces, N.Mex.: Prima Agua Press, 1981)

Interrogations
(Chevy Chase, Md.: Burning Cities Press, 1990)

The History of Home
(Tempe, Ariz.: Bilingual Press/ Editorial Bilingüe, 1993)

Paper Dance: 55 Latino Poets
coedited with Victor Hernández Cruz and Virgil Suárez (New York: Persea Books, 1995)

My Hair Turning Gray among Strangers
(Tempe, Ariz.: Bilingual Press/ Editorial Bilingüe, 1996)

The Great Whirl of Exile
(Willimantic, Conn.: Curbstone Press, 1999)

*∨ The old cuentos you heard as a child from your grandparents have
obviously influenced your poetry. I was wondering when you made a
conscious leap from hearing these stories to putting them into poetry.
Did you learn your craft as a student at the university, or had you
started writing poetry at a much earlier age?*

First, I am not a rational or "conscious" type of person or writer. I am completely intuitive. This is not to say that I do not make conscious decisions when I'm working on a short story or a poem, but this occurs when I'm working on successive drafts, long after the story or poem "visits" me, "suggests" itself to me, introduces itself. So I did not make a conscious leap from hearing the cuentos that influence my poetry to setting them down on paper. No doubt they were there, churning, preparing themselves to come out, but first of all I had to learn my craft, which began with taking workshops under Keith Wilson at New Mexico State University while working on an M.A. in English. My problem then, as I suspect with most young writers and graduate students, was that I *was* writing poems consciously— that is, for all practical purposes, forcibly. Yes, I had tried to write poems previous to that, but it was purely experimental, though I didn't intend it to be. Everybody has to start somewhere, and you cannot avoid writing fifty pounds of drivel and another one hundred of doggerel. I think I wrote rough drafts of Vietnam poems, but mainly I struggled with trying to write, which was really learning how to write—quite a long way off from finding my voice. Once I learned my meter, my format, once I had read and listened to many, many poems, the old cuentos were ready to meet me at the crossroads. I had my topic, and now I had to learn to wrestle forever with making language say what I wanted it to say and in the form I wanted to use. And to wait for new poems to tug at my sleeve.

I guess I worked on the Vietnam book, *Interrogations,* when I got back from the war. Actually, I ended up working on that book for twenty years, off and on. Of course, I didn't know what I was doing and perhaps had a vague—very vague—idea of what I wanted. But at the University of New Mexico as an undergrad, I took an introduction to poetry class. Though the professor was cantankerous and not very popular, he did his job, introducing us to Dylan Thomas, e. e. cummings, and many others—a good and necessary education for me. When we got to William Carlos Williams, the heavens opened. I wanted to write like that—concise, practical, and yet very understandable. I wanted to write poems that everybody could understand. Later, I learned to like Williams even more when I saw he could write about a plain old woman eating a plum.

It was at New Mexico State that Keith Wilson, the dean of the Southwest Writers, began working with the graduate students. We'd have long workshops, but it was incredible how much we learned from that process. He had several books out and was a great inspiration to us. He truly was a father to us, a literary father, and we always went to him for answers. We were a bunch of young prima donnas, but he was patient and, most of all, loving. It is because of that love that I became a writer. We never know how many lives we influence and save. It was from Keith that I began to see he was writing about the life I had lived. He was an Anglo who had gravitated toward the Hispanic side of town, and so he knew the people and the customs well, the joys and the sorrows. He understood the people. That's when I knew what the content of my poetry would be. Prior to that, I didn't know you could write about your *vecinos* [neighbors], *tíos* and *tías* [uncles and aunts], and any other people around you, in your backyard, so to speak. It was a great discovery. I was learning what to write about; I was learning how to write it.

> ⌄ *The theme of home has also influenced much of your poetry. In one poem, you write "a place called home, I think about / now and then, often, today." In fact, many of your poems yearn for the yesterday of your youth. One wonders why you ever left New Mexico.*

Leaving home, leaving New Mexico, has always been difficult because of our ties to the land. Very difficult. Our quaint Spanish, our special foods—such as green or red chile, piñon nuts—and friends and family and their *tontierias* [foolishness] that contribute constantly to our writing. I miss it because I know I'm missing out on a lot of foolishness—and seriousness. But it's just as difficult to return home.

I left home to go to Vietnam, which may be the toughest thing I ever did. I guess the smart thing would've been to cross the border into Canada. But I felt that if I did escape to Canada, I would be dishonoring my family, especially my mother, who held soldiers in such high esteem because of their heroic action in winning World War II. When I was young, she gave me *The Boys' Book of Famous Soldiers* one Christmas.

Then [after the war] I left, complete with family, to attend graduate school, first in Denver and then in Las Cruces, at New Mexico State. That was difficult because we had a house and were settled. Uprooted again. After graduation, I taught there a year, then moved to El Paso, where I taught at the community college for five years. But I gave up tenure because I hated it so much. It was good to return to Albuquerque to the familiar. Southern New Mexico has a different type of Spanish, different food. The culture is different. El Paso is, of course, completely different as far as culture, language, and food are concerned. After a year and because I had been away so much, it was terribly difficult to move to Silver City, New Mexico, where I earned a second master's—in counseling. Then we moved even farther away from home, to San Diego, with the hopes of working on a Ph.D., where we've been for about fifteen years. So, as one can see, I left New Mexico—home—mostly out of necessity, to attend school to better myself or to work.

I don't go back too much any more, though I know I should, because it's so terribly difficult to leave, even though it's changed so much—the New Agers, the rich Anglos driving the prices up, the loss of kindness, the high crime rate. People are no longer helpful. The old ways are eroding. Your neighbor will not hesitate to rip you off.

I don't know if I will write about home ever again. It doesn't seem to pull me the way it once did. Perhaps I've become a Californian. As for home, I've left more often than returned, but I suppose I can always go back; it will always be mine. Perhaps the closing lines from my "Poem for Grandmother" sums up my feelings: "Grandmother, how the days pass, how quickly / the days pass. And the road between here and home / seems longer with each passing weary year. / Longer with each passing weary year. / If I am not careful / and I am not a careful man, soon and that seems very, / I too will be a stranger here."

ᵥ *Do you still have connections there?*

My mother and stepfather are there. I don't see them enough. I have other relatives I haven't seen in years. You see, in northern New Mexico, an injury goes a long way. People remember the exact date and time that you offended them or that your grandfather insulted their grandfather. So we are vindictive in any way possible. People just don't forget or forgive. Your own family can and will be treacherous. I'll admit I did my share of offending, or my mother did. But there will be members of the same family, our family, whom I treasured as relatives, who also turned and joined their clan. The result is I haven't seen or talked to them for years. I've come to realize that I never will—not in this lifetime. I have friends who have been more loyal than family. For a while, each summer I would go visit my grandparents' grave in northern New Mexico and stop to visit a cantankerous uncle, but I haven't gone back in quite a while. So it seems that I am from there. Supposedly we are the descendants of the original colonizers, five hundred years of history coursing through our veins, but I don't belong there.

> v *The oral tradition that you celebrate in much of your poetry,*
> *especially those poems centering on your grandparents—Do you feel*
> *this tradition is still an important part of Chicano culture, or are we*
> *seeing more and more Chicano and other Latino cultures blending in*
> *with popular American culture? In music or the movies, for example?*

That's both an easy and a difficult question to answer. I think there will always be *abuelitos* [grandparents] telling their story, the old stories, especially here in Califas, where you have a great number of people who are first and second generation. But you also have the battles raging between the parents, particularly the fathers, who have lost their authority, their roots, their culture, their point of view, but who insist on inflicting that point of view on their children, especially their daughters who want to wear lipstick and jeans and to date.

Do these young people really care about their ancestry? They want to become Americanized as soon as possible—go to the movies, listen to rap music, get a car, and dress cool. Not all of them, of course, but I would say most of them. They may be introduced and learn to appreciate some of their history at school, which will serve as a stamp of approval to certify their lives. On the other hand, a lot of these people live their culture in addition to living life American style. Maria Mazzioti Gillan, the head of the Paterson Poetry Center [in New Jersey], once said that once she stepped out of her house to go to school, etcetera, she was American; when she came home and closed the door behind her, she was Italian. I think this is true for all minorities—you learn to live two lives. It can get confusing and dangerous. You've got to know who you are—learn how to go through life as a split personality. It isn't easy being us.

I also think that we need to make movies, though, whenever the Man gives us a chance, that vary from the standard device of a man and his woman fleeing the *revolución* and crossing the Río Grande into the Promised Land, where one son will become a marine, the other a professional gangbanger, where the girl will resent the father forever because she couldn't wear makeup or go to dances, so she gets pregnant just to show him he really isn't such a *chingón* [cool fucker] here in the good old U.S. of A. as he was in Sinaloa.

It's important to know that this experience of crossing the Río Grande into a new life is quite foreign to people from northern New Mexico, who have no connection to Mexico. Students will ask me what state [in Mexico] I or my parents are from, and I have no answer for them. New Mexico was settled long before the *Mayflower,* and people have lived there for many, many generations. So it's strange for us to conceive of people being there for two generations. We lost contact with Mexico a long time ago because of the distance between northern New Mexico and Mexico City, so we kept our quaint, fifteenth-century Spanish. People look at us as if we're pretentious snobs because "being Mexican" is completely foreign to us. As for the films depicting the trial of people fleeing the revolución—I think they're a good start, but we seem to be handcuffed by Hollywood. We need to make our films in our own way. To do that, we need to raise money and put an end to internecine war.

We also have to stop making prison movies. African Americans can always make slave movies, but when will they be allowed to make a movie about some positive role model, such as Frederick Douglass? That's freedom. When can we get away from drug dealers and wife beaters, who, incidentally, are served to white audiences—who think that's the way ALL of us act—by Chicana writers who capitalize heavily on this. I'm gonna get more than a boatload of crap for saying that, but it's true. In the end, there will be those who will listen and keep the traditions and culture alive, and we can hope and perhaps bank on the fact that some or a few or many will love literature and film and theater and will retell the stories and that the rest of their generation will learn and appreciate their heritage. As far as New Mexico is concerned, I'm *certain* the old stories are being passed on. It's simply a way of life there. But I worry. Last time I was going north, I noticed that a lot of people had moved from the family home—perhaps rightly so, they were quite old—into trailers, and every one of the trailers had a satellite dish on the roof.

v *Even if some of what you're talking about is generational or*
concerns living in a more modern society, you still include many
references to American popular culture in your poetry—Hopalong
Cassidy, rock 'n' roll, Jerry Lee Lewis, Groucho Marx. You even mention
that you "fought Mexicans at the Alamo to make America free"—
a reference to the old John Wayne/Davy Crockett movie. Were there
no popular Chicano figures for a Chicano kid growing up in 1950s
New Mexico? Did these folks come later, in the 1960s?

Absolutely none. None whatsoever. So we had to identify with folk heroes like Fess
Parker, whom I met in Vietnam many, many years later. We had been smoking the
wild weed and acting like complete fools, and he stood there, Dan'l Boone, big as
a b'ar, trying to figure why American GIs engaged in a war against communism
could not stand at attention and stop laughing, prepared to meet another of Santa
Ana's charges, ready to die defending the Alamo.

When I visited my grandparents in the summer, the minute I arrived, Grandma
would pull down the old wind-up Victrola from the closet. She had only a few
records—78s. My favorite was Pedro Infante, the idol of Mexico. He truly had a
golden voice. When he died in a plane crash, the entire world seemed to mourn.
He was handsome—a captivating movie star. The women didn't love him—they
adored him. I listened over and over and over to a song titled "Juan Char-
rasqueado"—a ballad about a ladies' man who is killed by an angry husband, a
ladies' man who fathered many a child but thought he was invincible. I think I
learned a lot about poetry from that record, from that and singing the hymns in
my catechism after school. I had to have learned a lot about rhythm and rhyme.

But he was Mexican. Not New Mexican. So we had Dean Martin and Jerry Lewis,
Francis the Talking Mule, Gene Autry, Rex Allen, and, of course, Roy Rogers. Years
later Roy Rogers rode around the State Fair Coliseum, and all the kids ran down
to shake his hand, except me. He looked at me strangely as I sat there, as if I were
some sort of commie. I guess I didn't run down 'cause everybody else was; perhaps
I secretly wanted to zap him, show him he was not such a hot tamale after all.

One person we had and with a quiet dignity admired was Tonto, the Lone
Ranger's trusty companion. But deep down inside we knew he *had* to play Tonto
or "the Tonto," which means "fool" in Spanish. My mother's generation suffered

even more from such terrible discrimination. We had movies and some false heroes; they were so poor they could afford nothing. They had no heroes, except for the Mexican film stars and Art Aragón, an Albuquerque boxer who hit the big time, even Hollywood. But he was a rarity.

⌄ *Was the 1950s then a decade of cultural transition for Chicanos?*

I hardly think so. These were the Eisenhower/Nixon years. There was a code of decency—for movies, for everything. And everybody was trying to be a good American. That was all that counted. But it was because of my cantankerous uncle that I learned about politics, about the necessity of a social conscience. Every summer in that small New Mexico town, everybody celebrated the Kearny Entrada. There was a parade honoring Stephen Watts Kearny, and it was quite an honor to be selected to play Kearney. But my uncle refused to go downtown. He saw Kearney for the colonizer he was. Kearney led a contingent of mounted troops to claim the state as part of the United States. Thus began the Anglo period and the rest. My uncle refused to honor him. He claimed the Anglos were pulling the wool over our eyes—having us honor the very man who had conquered us.

⌄ *This was the 1950s?*

Yes, my uncle, who had very little education to speak of, figured it all out. He would talk about discrimination, and so would my mother. So there was not a cultural transition in the 1950s for Chicanos. The 1950s was good because it was the decade of the future, but I don't think people saw Chicanos very much differently than they had before.

⌄ *If we can, I'd like to switch to your Vietnam poetry. In one of your Vietnam poems, you write, "Twenty years after Viet Nam / I still walk the jungle in camouflage . . . I'm still on recon patrol . . . It's an M-16 world." You return to Vietnam in your latest book of poetry, **The Great Whirl of Exile.** I'm wondering if a Vietnam vet who's also a writer is always "at the trigger / of an electric typewriter," as you state in one of your poems?*

Always. Whether you're trying to pull poems out of yourself, when you're reading, when you travel—always. I haven't written seriously for two years. I don't know what happened. I used to write as much as possible, almost daily, and managed to publish a book a year for four years. Then I went blank. Perhaps it's burnout. I also had my gall bladder removed, so that added to my woes. I don't look at the world the way I once did, though. I don't have that wild enthusiasm for poetry. I once lived for poetry. Now I read biographies and nonfiction. I am interested in reading novels. The University of Oklahoma Press recently notified me that they are going to publish my book of short fiction. I'm no longer hungry; I'm complacent, indifferent. But I still want and intend to be a poet. People think that writing gets easier as you grow older and publish books, but the complete opposite is true. You have to outdo yourself, delve deeper. You have to learn humility, overcome your ego, and it's hard to bust through that. It's far easier to remain comfortable, high on yourself. You've got to get back to walking around with your M-16 on rock 'n' roll [full automatic] and an itchy trigger finger.

> ⌄ In **Interrogations**, you expose the racism you and some of your
> Chicano friends experienced in the military. In "Jump School—Detail,"
> for example, "The Sgt. handed out / swing rakes / Mexican lawnmowers
> he called them / chuckling." Was racism one more problem you, as a
> Latino American in Vietnam, had to contend with? Was it common?

Racism is always common. What was surprising was that it was common in Vietnam, where we were all Americans supposedly with a common goal: to stay alive and to fight communism. Of course, it was subtle. There's nothing worse than for an American to be called or labeled a racist. People had to be very careful because the Black Power movement was going strong; nevertheless, racism was alive, in subtle ways, and disguised in humor. Also, it was open season on the Vietnamese—a.k.a. "chinks," "slopes," and "gooks." Of course, when you're in a line outfit or in recon, where people need each other, you can't afford to be racist. That's for when you get back to the world—home, the United States of America; when Charlie [from Victor Charlie, VC, or Vietcong, taken from the military alphabet] is trying to blow your shit away.

> ⌄ Were any of these bouts with racism ever reported?

It's hard to say, probably not. What happened is, there would be a physical confrontation, and then somebody, usually blacks, were sent to "LBJ City"—Long Binh

Jail. Interesting that the president's initials would be used for the slang of the notorious jail. Mostly the way racism was dealt with would be by some black GI saying, "It don't mean nuthin." And the war went on.

> ∨ *The poem "Interrogations" from the collection we're talking about is one of your most powerful poems. I'm wondering if the kinds of atrocities that you describe here—"The last I heard of him / he was sporting a large necklace of rotting ears"—really occurred? Or are this line and others like it simply metaphors for the horrors of war?*

My philosophy about writing poetry has always been that everything I write has to come from real life, must be true. The United States committed some horrible atrocities over there. We're lucky if we'll ever be forgiven. It was the Wild West, and there was a new kind of Indian to abuse. I only recently began to read about Vietnam. What a beautiful history! I also took a Vietnamese language class. I only in the past few years began to recognize them as people.

> ∨ *Having spoken of popular culture, in your opinion, are any of the Vietnam films accurate?*

To some extent. But as a veteran, it's hard to watch some of these Hollywood guys trying to portray GIs. They don't know what they're doing, and it shows. It's hard to take Charlie Sheen and Michael J. Fox seriously. And Sean Penn, as bad as he's supposed to be, looks like he's been an FNG [fucking new guy] for as long as he's been in the Nam. M. J. Fox looks like a punk. He'd probably get fragged [hit by a fragmentation grenade] a half-hour after he landed in the country. Not hardened at all. The VC would have a great old time skinning him alive. That would make a film accurate. Teach him to make a Vietnam film again. *Deer Hunter* had parts that looked accurate, but the Russian roulette scenes seemed a bit overblown. For accuracy, there's a film titled *64 Charlie Mopic* [for "motion picture"], where a handheld camera follows a recon team. America still does not want to deal with Vietnam, so Hollywood can't either. Now we're getting superhyped films that look like World War II movies, only played out in the jungle.

> ∨ *One more Vietnam question. You've talked about this comparison of Latino and African American films. Some reports indicate that there*

were a disproportionate number of Latinos killed in Vietnam, similar
to the reports on the number of African Americans killed. Is this
something you witnessed as well? That Chicanos and other Latinos
were killed because, typically, they were involved in some of the
worst fighting?

Remember, I was in recon, so there was no wholesale killing. Our mission was to go quietly, check out the enemy, and return quietly with the information. To this day, I have a problem with noise. You needed to live quietly out there. When you had confrontations, it was usually a recon team—six GIS—against however many Vietcong happened to be passing by, from fifteen to a much larger number. I prayed that if my recon team ran into the VC, not everybody would get dusted. I didn't want to be the only one left alive, holding Charlie off until I ran out of ammo with no chopper in sight to exfil [evacuate] you. If the VC got to you, you were gonna suffer. There was a dude in headquarters company who had been the only one of his recon team to survive. He looked like he had seen hell, and I'm sure he had.

ᵛ *Another subject you've explored from the past is the Catholic*
Church. These poems haven't been too flattering.

I hated the Catholics I went to school with. They were the biggest hypocrites around. They believed they were so holy. They'd smile at you and then put a knife in your back. Smug. They owned Jesus. Therefore, they could bury a knife in your back. It seems that having religion, owning God, entitles some people to gossip about you, slander you, snub you, and commit a hundred other sins, which they don't see or recognize as sins mainly because they are the ones committing them. Catholic school was exactly like that. The nuns had their pets who could do no wrong. They got to sit in the first row to mark their intelligence. Some of these people were pretty dumb. Dumb but holy.

ᵛ *But in "Sangre 19," you write about your Vietnam experience: "But I*
never prayed / until that day / in Viet Nam / when death walked by /
(saw his sallow face, / the slanted eyes)." What did you pray to?
Certainly not a Catholic god?

Hell yes, it was a Catholic God, which is the only one I know, by the way. You'd pray, too, if a column of VC passed within arm's reach. War will convert anybody.

I promised God so many things as I lay in the road, teeth chattering, shivering from fear. I was so scared I regressed to the point where I was silently crying out for my mother. I know I do in my poems, but one shouldn't blame God for creating the types of Christians, mainly Catholics, that he does. Yeah, I prayed. And I continue to pray when I'm in a tight spot or my life is in danger.

> ˅ *You're also a trained psychologist. Has your study of psychology influenced any of your poetry?*

I write mostly about people, so psychology taught me to examine motives, to evaluate and diagnose, and to see the problem behind the problem. My poems are short, but my characters have been worked out. I've learned to develop, to give characters depth.

> ˅ *You're also a teacher. You've been teaching for...*

Forever.

> ˅ *And at a community college, where the teaching load is very demanding. Do you feel that this other profession cuts into your time as a writer?*

It demands a lot of your time and energy. But I'm not one for socializing, so I used to work a lot—all the time, really. As I mentioned, I haven't written seriously for about two years, though. I don't know if I burned out, got complacent because I had published a book a year—plus published a lot in journals—gave a lot of readings around the country, slowed down because of physical ailments, or all of the above. I'm gonna make a comeback, but that will be decided for me, not the other way around.

Aleida Rodríguez

Born in rural Cuba in 1953, Aleida Rodríguez moved to the United States when she was nine years old. One of approximately fifteen thousand children airlifted out of Cuba in the early 1960s under a covert mission called Operation Peter Pan, she settled with a foster family in Springfield, Illinois. She and her older sister were joined two years later by their parents. After living in the Midwest for five years, the family moved to Los Angeles, where Rodríguez has lived for more than thirty-five years.

Rodríguez became fascinated with language at an early age, when she learned to switch back and forth from Spanish to English. "I learned to scrutinize language . . . to search for the roots of words as a way to get a deeper hold," she states. She started writing in her teens. In 1998, poet Marilyn Hacker selected Rodríguez's first book of poems, *Garden of Exile* (1999), for the Kathryn A. Morton Prize in Poetry. Her first collection of essays, *Desire Lines,* is forthcoming.

In this interview, conducted at the Miami Book Fair International on November 25, 2000, Rodríguez discusses her role as an artist, which she feels should "inhabit as many identities as possible." She also talks

SUGGESTED READING

Garden of Exile: Poems
(Louisville, Ky.: Sarabande, 1999)

about her past in Cuba as well as her life in Los Angeles, which is far removed from the larger, "constricting" Cuban community in South Florida.

> ⌄ *I have difficulty separating your essay "The Glass Cage" from*
> ***Garden of Exile***, *your recently published collection of poems. I can't*
> *read the essay without thinking about the poetry, the poetry without*
> *thinking about the essay. Both are expressing the same concern,*
> *aren't they? That, as an artist, you're not "a three-note piano," and you*
> *won't accept "the ghetto of ideas assigned" to you by other people?*

Yes, they're connected—the essay being an expression of my core beliefs, my manifesto, if you will, while my poems are the proof of the pudding, the ideas made manifest. What's happened is that I have been cross-pollinated like crazy, and it would be unauthentic for me to express anything other than what I've lived. I've also always thought my writing should reflect my imagination, not my identity, per se, and expressing an imagination without borders has been my lifelong goal— fields without fences. Openness.

> ⌄ *In the foreword to* ***Garden of Exile***, *Marilyn Hacker writes that*
> *your book has "remarkable range." I was wondering if you're conscious*
> *of this range when you write? That is, because so many people want*
> *to "identify" you—Cuban American writer, Latina writer, exile,*
> *lesbian—do you purposely seek out subjects that make it impossible*
> *to pigeonhole you?*

No. I simply write about what I'm drawn to and can't stop myself from loving in the form of words. In fact, I thought last night before going to sleep about the meaning of this *range*. What do people mean by *range*, anyway? What does it really mean? Are they saying that I have no focus? That there's nothing I do well? That I attempt a lot of things? I'd like an explanation of what this *range* really means. So, no, I don't seek range consciously. Because I came from a repressive government, one of the things I feel I've learned the hard way, and that other people would do well to understand, is the importance of personal freedom. That's what's absent there, in my native country. Leaving there was an opportunity to expand, to inhabit my authentic self in every possible way, in every area of my life. So it's mostly that—

satisfying myself first and foremost, choosing my own path, self-determination. That's what my work reflects, and maybe it accounts for that pesky range.

> *Do you think this ability to "cross-pollinate," as you've said, might have something to do with your having lived for more than thirty years in Los Angeles, far away from the larger and historically more "reactionary" Cuban American community in South Florida?*

Yes, it is simply who I am, who I was allowed to become outside that constricting ghetto. It's important to me to express who I am at the core of my being and turn a blind eye to normative and mainstream values. Actually, though, I didn't become aware of this penchant of mine until someone interviewed me a while back for a short essay on my work. And this is a way I think writers can learn from critics, from the perspective of people commenting from the outside—that is, when they see you clearly and can reflect you back to yourself and phrase something that you've felt but hadn't quite articulated for yourself. The woman writing the essay observed that my work doesn't acknowledge normative values, that it acts out of its own impulses and makes its own rules. This is part of the problem I have with the majority of today's multicultural writers. The oppressor, or white society, is forever sitting heavily on their mind, and they are forever writing in opposition to it, but this also keeps a kind of umbilical connection, and that force is always in the room with them when they write. I just don't want it in the room with me. I want whatever my world is, whatever my aesthetic happens to be, to exist apart and separate from what is expected of me in that one-trick-pony way that happens with so many minority writers.

> *How, then, do you feel about labeling writers? How do you feel about being called a "lesbian writer" or a "Latina"?*

I don't mind the label as long as I can say what I want to say and how I want to say it within that designation. I'm not reactionary—like Elizabeth Bishop, who didn't want to be "identified." I'm happy to be there, visible, audible, as long as whoever I am is accepted as another way of being "Latina" or "exile" or "lesbian." As long as the definition gets expanded to include all the things I am. When the label allows for only two or three "colorful" qualities and a cupful of subject matter, it's simply too constricting for me.

‿ *Did this consciousness develop because you did not grow up in Miami? You actually spent your first few years of exile in Springfield, Illinois, didn't you? This experience must have been quite different for you, surrounded by millions of people speaking English?*

Living in the Midwest at the time when I did was a very valuable thing for me; I lived there for five years, from the ages nine to fourteen. I think I was a very hungry, curious kid, and I absorbed everything greedily. This is why I don't harp on things like, "Oh, that's so tragic. You came from Cuba without your parents. You were put down where there were no Latinos. Plus, there was all that snow!" That's the sad song most people sing in front of me—and expect me to join in—when they find out my trajectory. Yes, it had its tragic elements, but I'm thankful for all those things because I think the more varied my experience, the more varied I am. And that's why I think I can address wider territory with more confidence than many U.S. Latinos—because I have inhabited it widely, traveled through it, had my passport stamped in many places. Explored. My favorite word as a child was *exploration;* my father still remembers my asking him to go exploring with me the city dump that was behind our house in Springfield, Illinois. Creative people can go in and out of all sorts of places. My whole purpose as an artist is to inhabit as many identities as possible and to express those identities, too.

‿ *You arrived without your parents? Can you talk a little about that transition?*

We, my sister and I, came to the United States on July 23, 1962. It was very sudden and shocking because it's only a forty-five-minute plane ride from Havana to Miami. I had lived in a rural town, with dirt streets, and we had to get a friend to drive us into Havana. I had no idea where I was going. When we arrived, I sat with my sister in the baggage area in Miami, and no one was around to claim us—we had apparently fallen through the cracks of the system. The Cuban government had tried to staunch the mass exodus that was making the revolution look bad by holding back visas. In reaction to that, a Catholic priest and the CIA collaborated on a covert mission called Operation Peter Pan, which airlifted about fifteen thousand children out of Cuba and placed them in homes in the United States during the early 1960s. We were placed with a Presbyterian family in Springfield, Illinois. I remember arriving at the airport. It was around midnight by then, and I remember thinking to myself that that couldn't be them, our new family. We started walking in a different direction. But there was a translator with them, and he called after us. I remember going home that night and the family trying to feed us a snack—cold milk, with nothing in it—no coffee or chocolate like I was used to—and green grapes. I was really frightened. I mean, we'd never had plain, cold milk before, and we'd certainly never seen green grapes. It was like Martian food. I thought the grapes were unripe, that they were poisonous. What a weird combination of things to feed new visitors!

We thought our parents were going to come right away, but we were there for two years. The family really wanted us to adapt, so they separated us into different age groups. Practically the only time my sister and I saw each other was at dinner. My foster parents wouldn't allow me to speak Spanish because they wanted me to learn English. No one put in the batteries. How was I going to communicate when my parents arrived? My sister was old enough—she was fifteen—so she retained her Spanish. There were also Colombian students at her high school, so she was able to speak Spanish every day. I was simply plopped down in a third-grade classroom, not knowing what the hell was going on. When the others went to art class, I was sent to a speech teacher, which, in the end, turned out to be a great thing. I got one-on-one attention. I had always been interested in language, and I think I refined my curiosity about the secret nuances below language, then.

∨ *How is your Spanish today?*

I had to relearn it, so I'm fluent now, but with some insecurities. When my parents finally came, I understood everything they said, but I couldn't make anything come out of my mouth. I even forgot how to say *doll* in Spanish. When I began living with my parents again, in the beginning I was always asking, "Cómo se dice?" and pointing at something, just to regain my vocabulary. Unfortunately, this experience also made me insecure about my ability to speak because I'd had that two-year break with my first language. It's especially difficult when I'm talking to educated people in Spanish. I get nervous, and my brain freezes up, and I can't get anything to come out. I'm back there again, stammering, being that eleven-year-old kid trying to speak. Like in Truffaut's *Wild Child.*

ᵛ *That's a similar story for so many immigrants.*

Yes, that's true, but it was still a very good experience, as difficult as it was. I learned to scrutinize language—not only English but Spanish. I'd ask my mother, "Why is it called that?" And I learned to do the same thing in English—to search for the roots of words as a way to get a deeper hold. *Vaso,* which was like *vessel,* just had to be connected somehow. When I lived with my parents, we had an intense Spanish-language world inside the house, and I was afraid that this private world was going to leap out of me suddenly in the cloakroom, in that transitional space between home and the English-language classroom.

> ᵛ *It's ironic that publishers in the past have rejected your poetry that doesn't focus on exile, family, and childhood in Cuba. To me, some of your strongest poems are the ones that delight in visual art. In your book, for example, you have a section called "Why I Would Rather Be a Painter." You're creating a new aesthetic appreciation for visual art—discovering painting through written words, not sensory perception. Can you elaborate?*

I'm just sublimating. I'm not one of those people who can be a Sunday painter—I'd be too judgmental. If I can't do what my eye has been trained to see or am simply ill-equipped to do that, then I just wouldn't attempt it. So I say, "Maybe I'll take up painting when I'm eighty-three." By then, I hope, the prickly, critical side of me will have subsided. Instead, I'm left to render my vision in words because I have no other medium. People say to me what you've just said—that I'm creating a new way of appreciating, even apprehending, art, but I never thought about any of that while I wrote the poems. I simply had a need, so I went down into the basement and invented something to satisfy me.

Did I tell you the first thing I ever wanted to be was an inventor? I read, obsessively and methodically, those little biographies they have for children; I went down the shelf alphabetically every Saturday morning in the library, checking out Alexander Graham Bell, then Thomas Edison, etcetera. I really resonated with the whole notion of necessity being the mother of invention. So, since I am visually hungry, I try to craft what will please me. I haven't had as much of a plan in mind as people seem to think; it's been more of a gut attraction—like that Annie Dillard quote: "You were made and put here to give voice to this, your own astonishment." That's why I love and have used as a breaker page in *Garden of Exile* that quote by Fairfield Porter: "The most important thing is the quality of love. Love means paying very close attention to something, and you can only pay close attention to something because you can't help doing so." It's practically my mantra or my rudder; it's what directs me. I hate to bring up spirituality, but it's how the spiritual manifests in my work. When I'm struck to the core with the beauty of something—most often it's visual, but music also does this to me—I'm so filled with love that my writing is what spills out in appreciation.

> ⌄ *Are these poems also influenced by visual artists that surround you?*

I lived with a visual artist for four years. But what I'm talking about goes back before that. You know how far back it goes? From the start, visual art struck a chord with me as a child. I've always gravitated to it with great admiration and longing. Then I discovered this right before my mother died. At the age of eight, Mother had been farmed out to work for an aunt. Her cousin, who lived in the same household, would sit in her room and paint all day, while my mother did all the housework and cleaned out pigsties and all that messy stuff. She never, during my entire life— and I knew my mother for forty-seven years—never mentioned anything about wanting to paint—that is, until right before she died. But I'm convinced that there had always been this longing in her to paint, which in turn became my longing, subterraneanly, like roots that meet and intertwine. Her unexpressed desire became my desire, which, though unexpressed visually, is abundantly expressed in my writing. Years before I learned about this painting connection with my mother, I went to the Squaw Valley Writers Workshop, where I had a dream that became the first poem I wrote there, "My Mother's Art," in which she's sitting on the floor, having painted these really beautiful landscapes of Los Angeles. This reminds me of that Susan Griffin book, *A Chorus of Stones,* where a repressed element rears its head in a subsequent generation.

> ⌄ *Much of your poetry celebrates verbal play. I'm thinking of "Parts of Speech," "Lexicon of Exile," "The First Woman." Do you feel your linguistic insight and ability to turn a phrase results from your being bilingual?*

Yes, but more than that—I think it has to do with the abruptness with which my first language was completely uprooted from its natural soil, then plopped down in another language. Then having to learn the etiquette of that language, worrying about how I was going to make myself understood. There was that initial bit of anxiety, which made me focus, detective-like, on the nuances. And everything was so regimented in my foster home—charts in the kitchen, scheduled visits to the library, planned activities—which helped anchor me in a kind of grid of activity when everything else in my life was so chaotic. The fact that I had foster siblings my own age helped me to learn English quickly—almost through osmosis. In five months, between July and December, I was fluent.

> ˅ *At the same time, only a few of your poems switch back and forth from English to Spanish. "The Rosario Beach House" is an obvious exception. Can you talk about the construction of this poem and why you write almost every other line in either Spanish or English?*

I wrote it when I was about twenty-four, half my life ago—which I guess speaks again to that issue of range, of the places I've wandered over to in my life. At the time, the mid-1970s, there was a form going around called the "pocho form," meaning a melding of the two languages in a single poem. I was starting to delve back into my Cuban childhood as subject matter for the first time, and I thought that form would be the perfect structure. But how would I choose what would go in Spanish, what in English? Luckily, the answer was embedded in what I chose to render—an emblematic day at the beach house where I was sent to live with my grandmother to recover from chronic bronchitis. The poem follows the structure of a single day, beginning with waking to the sound of the sea lapping gently. And it was that lapping sound, that soft back and forth that, once I became aware of it, provided the musical foundation—an organic movement from one language to the other.

Also, since I've been largely educated in English, I think in English, while I feel that my emotions are in Spanish. In other words, my mind's in English, and my heart's in Spanish, so I let each part speak its native tongue. I have always disliked bilingual poetry that repeats the same phrase, first in one language, then the next. That just seemed dumb to me, saying the same thing twice. That's something that's gotten focused on in reviews of *Garden;* one reviewer even said that I "refuse to translate for us," which I find funny. It's not a refusal; it's just unnecessary. Look at all that French or Latin or German that appears untranslated all over the place.

The assumption is that one can refer to a dictionary, if necessary. I consciously thought about the English/Spanish split within me when I chose the form, but then I let it unconsciously spill and seek its own shape—that is, let it choose for itself what parts would be in English and which in Spanish. I knew that if I wrote it entirely in Spanish, it would limit those who could understand it. With the bilingual form, though, people who don't speak Spanish have told me that they feel like they got it all, subliminally, that the experience felt unified to them, without experiencing those speed bumps between languages. My life is like a piece of marble cake, I say—anyplace you cut into it, you're going to get a mixture of flavors. For better or worse, I can convey only what I've experienced.

ᵛ *I think it was Charles Wright who said during a recent poetry reading that everything he wrote about he had in his own backyard. Considering the poems you include in the section you call "The Garden," I guess you'd agree?*

Yes, I always joke at my readings that whenever I feel like I've run out of things to say, I just stand out in the backyard for a few minutes, and a metaphor will pop up. And I don't have to wait long. Right now it's some pesky squirrels that are trying to wriggle into a poem.

ᵛ *You also have an amazing eye for detail. I'm thinking about the "drops of water" that flick onto your "white patent leather shoes, where they bead but roll off whenever the jeep hits a bump." Or in "Little Cuba Stories/Cuentos de Cuba: III": "A piano stands against the left wall, facing a couple of caned chairs that raise perfect little circles on my thighs when I sit for too long in shorts." Where do these lines come from? A poet's obsession with close observation? Memory? The imagination?*

Memory, first of all, which is a powerful thing for me. But you could also say "all of the above" because memory is two parts loving observation and one part imagination. When I thought about my childhood, when I thought of anything from the age of nine back, the memories came as a series of these little pools of yellow light surrounded by immense darkness. Then, when I returned to Cuba for the first time in 1979, with my parents, I discovered that the streetlights of my tiny, rural hometown physically reconstruct that mental image: spaced very far apart and focusing weak yellow light only at their base, they made a corridor of darkness punctuated every once in a while by a yellow spot. Walking below them late one balmy night, all alone on the street, I had the sudden flash that I was physically inhabiting the metaphor I had always used to describe my memories. I find it interesting that I wasn't able to write about my childhood again after that. It's like the realization broke my ability to dream-imagine it the way one has to do when rendering memories. No doubt, I had stored that sensation of walking between alternating patches of dark and light from my childhood; it had sunk into my skin and surfaced years later as a metaphor.

v *What was it that motivated your parents to leave Cuba?*

First of all, we have always been poor. And this is one fallacy that I always want to point out—that not all people who left Cuba in the first exodus of the 1960s were professional people who owned property. Of course, there were many doctors and lawyers and other professionals who left Cuba then, but there were also many so-called ordinary people, peasants like us. My father had worked trading cattle out in the country; he went to work on a horse every day. After my birth, my father started a little butcher shop in town, right at the corner of our street. This was the first time he'd had a business. Life was going to change. And then the revolution came, and all dreams of controlling one's destiny went to hell. If you knew my father now and knew his life, you'd see that he's never asserted anything; my mother was always the one who took action. He always forced her to make decisions, then promptly disapproved of them—that kind of thing. But the revolution was the only time he took the lead.

I was in second grade. I'd gone to the Presbyterian school, not the Catholic one, because my mom had been abused by nuns. And our family never practiced a religion. Some representatives of the government came into our classroom one day and said to us, "Pray to God for a dish of ice cream." We put our hands together, but nothing appeared. Then they said, "Pray to Fidel Castro for some ice cream," and while we had our heads bowed and eyes closed, they went around and put little dishes of ice cream on our desks. My parents pulled me right out of school when I came home with that story and applied for visas.

ᵛ *And then you returned to Cuba in 1979. What was that like?*

I was afraid to return. I thought everything was going to make me cry. And it did. From that point on, after I'd seen Cuba through adult eyes, I couldn't write about it in the same way. Memory, with its hazy, cobwebby corners, had allowed me to write about it, but after my return, after I saw the devastation in the blanching light of the tropics, it was never the same. I could never reenter that childhood world; it was the second time I got kicked out of Eden—this time, imaginatively. In 1979, there was much more of a military presence—soldiers with guns everywhere, and at the airport they searched our suitcases and removed things for the hell of it, just to be sadistic. It's still like that, but much more subtle because they want to encourage tourism.

ᵛ *Despite the criticism you level in "The Glass Cage," you still write some powerful poems about your memory of Cuba. Is Cuba an impossible subject to avoid? You write in your poem "Exile" that "you begin to feel intimate with the missing part." Or is Cuba simply another one of the "lenses" that you alluded to earlier?*

I don't know if this is my personality or if it's the result of my being uprooted from my birthplace, but I have an active relationship with longing and loss, with absence. I have a Cuban friend who lives in New York but who's still really mad about living in exile. Her family had been well off and owned a lot in Cuba, and here she has to struggle. My father was a simple neighborhood butcher; we never had much in Cuba. I always came from nothing, so I didn't have anything to lose in that respect, certainly no life of luxury. When I read Anne Carson's *Eros the Bittersweet*, I suddenly went, "Yes, yes, I get it!" I write about this in more detail in an essay called "Walking," which appeared in *ZYZZYVA* and is in my next book, a book of short, creative prose called *Desire Lines*. But I don't know if I'm configured like this from birth; I suspect that I am and that it has little to do with the historical events I've been a pawn of, only that those events have emphasized it. Cuba, that lost-forever place, has become a metaphor even for romantic relationships—that is, for the idyllic place that can't be accessed.

∨ *Do you think you're different from your friend in New York because of where you grew up? Again, getting a different perspective because of living in Los Angeles instead of Miami or somewhere else?*

Had I stayed in Illinois, who knows what would have happened to me, though I seriously doubt I would've ever stayed there long. But certainly that experience shaped me, that immersion in Middle America, away from both coasts and from ghettoes. The only other working-class friend I have is my Cuban friend who lives in Miami. She was my best friend when I was a child in Cuba; she lived right around the corner, and her *bohio* [thatch hut] was one of the first places I walked to, as if in a trance, when I first went back. So when she came over on the Mariel boatlift, naturally I claimed her. She lived with me in Los Angeles for a while, but she missed being immersed in the stew of Cuban culture. In Miami, she can speak Spanish everywhere, including the hospital where she works, and eat Cuban food any time of the day. There's another Cuban woman I know who has liberal politics like me, and two years ago we returned to Cuba together because she hadn't been back since the age of six. She, too, lived in a small rural town, but at the other end of the island. When we arrived, everything was dilapidated and mildewed. Her father had been a doctor, as well as her grandfather, so there had been some privilege, but tropical rot is the great equalizer.

∨ *Why do you save the prose poem for the "Cuentos de Cuba" section in your book? Is it that prose lends itself to story? That it better fits the oral tradition?*

You have to remember that this first book is comprised of work that spans a couple of decades, at least—maybe we finally have an explanation for the so-called range. Those poems came at a time when I was writing prose poetry almost exclusively, exploring narrative, yes, but more than that. I also saw the prose poems as little physical "rooms"—those solid, margin-to-margin squares—and it fit nicely with my idea of conveying my childhood, my memories, via a series of rooms in the last house I lived in. You first see the whole house as if from across the street, from the widest perspective, before you stand on the porch, which holds—and releases—its own memory, and then each room after that delivers up its own memory. It was a structure that fit the subject—the sequencing of the rooms creating a narrative.

ˇ *You're very conscious of form in this book, aren't you?*

I go after form when I think the subject matter calls for it. For "The First Woman," for example, I was attracted to the terza rima because the tercets let me think of it, playfully, as a ménage à trois—me and Adam and Eve. Then the envelope rhymes—the ABA BCB CDC, etcetera—made me picture a series of little nested valises that were being drawn out one from the other—like nested Russian dolls, but also like a magician's trick, and finally I liked the sense of "unpacking." I chose the terza rima form consciously because the scaffolding, though invisible to most people, could convey the "journey" subject matter on top, an idea riding the crest of a wave. Nobody sees this kind of thing, but I don't care. I only care that I was able to find the right structure for it. The sweet thing about the terza rima, after all the fortuitous associations I've already made, is that in its most formal form it ends in a couplet—which I saw as my two feet landing in the new world—which is both the United States and the loss of innocence.

ˇ *You've mentioned before that journals avoid publishing your "psychological and spiritual" poems. Do you think this might be because not that many people know about the writings of James Hillman, someone you allude to in "Parts of Speech" and a writer who obviously has influenced you? Or Carl Jung, who came before Hillman?*

I grew up interested in Jung. I've admired his ideas all my life. I related to his work because it gave me a way to relate to the world—plenty of metaphors! I think there are many people out there who know about Hillman and Jung and who are influenced by both. It goes back to what we were talking about earlier, about publishers wanting to publish only certain kinds of poetry from me because of my identity. "What the hell is this chick writing about this stuff for? What is this reference to James Hillman all about?" They think it's pretentious and want to know why this chick, being Latina, isn't referring to someone with a Latin name, as if that's the only well I should draw from—like race-specific drinking fountains.

ˇ *Earlier you referred to the new book of prose you've just compiled. Can you talk a little about this work?*

It's called *Desire Lines,* from the landscape-design term for those worn footpaths people make when veering off the planned paths through a garden. Here we have another example of range! It's a loose collection of my mostly published prose that uses Los Angeles as its backdrop but wanders all around within it, literally in different neighborhoods. A friend calls it a "connect-the-dots without any of the dots connected"—in other words, a kind of constellation of ideas. It captures, in a meandering way, my explorations in prose. There's a kind of "through line," but a very, very subterranean one, as usual. I'm writing more prose right now, for some reason, including a small piece for the *Los Angeles Times* about the hill I see across from my desk, which has often made cameo appearances in my poems. Maybe I'm feeling more comfortable with taking up a bit more room. Either that or I'm getting more verbose in my old age. Seriously, though, I'm feeling increasingly attracted to more expansive forms, widening my territory even further.

Luis Rodríguez

*B*orn in 1954 in El Paso, Texas, Luis Rodríguez is best known for his vivid memoir *Always Running: La Vida Loca, Gang Days in L.A.,* published in 1993. Set during the turbulent 1960s and early 1970s, the book chronicles Rodriguez's days as a gang member in an East Los Angeles barrio. By the time he was sixteen, he had abused heroin and other hard drugs, was shot at by his own gang, and suffered mental and physical abuse at the hands of a corrupt police force. As a teenager, he also served time, on several different occasions, in the Los Angeles County Jail.

Rodríguez's life turned around when he discovered writing. Working first as a journalist, then exploring poetry, he published his first book of verse, *Poems Across the Pavement* (1989), to critical acclaim. *The Concrete River,* released in 1991, won the PEN Oakland/Josephine Miles Award for Poetry and established Rodríguez as a powerful new Latino voice eager to challenge the status quo. His memoir solidified this reputation and thrust him into the foreground of political and social activism.

This conversation took place on February 3, 2000, in Boone, North Carolina. In the interview, Rodríguez

SUGGESTED READING

Poems Across the Pavement
(Chicago: Tía Chucha Press, 1989)

The Concrete River
(Willimantic, Conn.: Curbstone Press, 1991)

Always Running: La Vida Loca, Gang Days in L.A.
(New York: Simon and Schuster, 1993)

América Is Her Name
(Willimantic, Conn.: Curbstone Press, 1996)

Trochemoche: Poems
(Willimantic, Conn.: Curbstone Press, 1998)

It Doesn't Have to Be This Way: A Barrio Story
(San Francisco: Children's Book Press, 1999)

Hearts and Hands: Creating Community in Violent Times
(New York: Seven Stories Press, 2001)

The Republic of East L.A.: Stories
(New York: Harper Collins, Rayo, 2002)

discusses his interaction with prisoners and his thoughts on the American penal system, which he argues must be transformed completely. He also comments at length on his art and addresses a number of other pressing issues facing our country today, especially the injustices suffered by many Latinos and other marginalized groups. He concludes the interview by discussing the ten weeks he spent in North Carolina as a writer in residence.

⌄ *You keep referring to poetry as "soul talk." Can you elaborate?*

It has to do with people not being able to reveal themselves, for a lot of reasons. If it's because people expect others to have a certain face, a professional stance, propriety, whatever—people just aren't being honest. They're relating, but you can't get a deep, emotional connection. Most language that you get from ads, TV, and newspapers takes out that part of it, that honest, open connection. Ads play with it, but they exploit it by trying to sell you something. Newspapers are completely void of it. Adults, teachers, and professionals won't even talk about it. You can't trust most politicians and spin doctors. You have teachers in front of the classroom, but very few of them feel they can relate from a deep and honest place. They won't tell you that they've had a bad day. Kids would appreciate that, but the class goes on as usual.

So where is the place that people really soul-talk? It doesn't have to be great language. It just has to be real, honest, where you're opening up. Maybe around friends. Maybe among family. My thing is that we need to have a public discourse where that's its function. Poetry is really the best place for that. Not that novels or essays can't do it, but that's really what poetry is. It's condensed language. It's musical, it's rhythmical. It has an emotional edge and emotional power underneath the words and the lines. That's where it can happen. Some contemporary poetry is slipping from that. But I still think that poetry has that quality of telling the truth, no matter what. We have to have a very conscious, aware space in our culture where people can be totally open and honest. It doesn't have to be a chat on the Internet, where people don't even know who it is they're talking with.

⌄ *How did your own soul talk evolve? Were there certain poets, certain inspirations?*

Obviously, every writer is influenced by other writers. Pablo Neruda is my favorite poet. I discovered him later, when I was already in my twenties. And García Lorca.

But I'm not just turning to these poets because they're Spanish-language poets. I think I've missed that Spanish-language literary tradition. I find them emotionally moving, more so than some of the English-language poets. You can't beat Neruda for imagery, and there's emotional power under it. I read a lot of poets. I read a lot of Native American writers—Joy Harjo, Sherman Alexie. I like Charles Bukowski. He's influenced me a lot. He could be a little more poetic at times, but he was a no-bullshit kind of guy—hard-nosed, this is my kind of life, I drink, I suffer. We don't have enough of that. The Italian American writer John Fante also influenced me a lot. He's not that well known, but he has a cult following. Fante wrote a number of novels and screenplays about L.A., where he moved during the Depression. He was a white guy who was also emotionally open. In his book *Ask the Dust,* the protagonist is a very lonely, hungry, starving writer who falls in love with a Mexican girl. She rejects him. Some of my friends say, "How can you like this kind of writer? He's racist; he hates Mexicans." But when the woman rejects him, he's honest. I didn't see him as racist. I saw him as a white man who is rejected. He fights back. He's poor, he's hungry. Some people turn to racist ideas when they're desperate. This is the kind of writing I like. I'm also influenced by Jewish writers, especially writers from the 1930s. Like Mike Gold. I started eating that up. The immigrant writers coming out of Chicago and Dos Passos and Theodore Dreiser. As I mention in *Always Running,* there were also many African American influences. African Americans, Native Americans, Italian Americans, Jewish writers— all were influential. They could grab your heart and still keep poetic, literary distance. And there's still humor.

⌄ *How do you feel, then, about labeling writers? Is being called a Latino poet or a Chicano poet something that you accept or reject?*

If it's done in context, I don't mind. Obviously, I'm a writer. Some can see an American writer, especially if you broaden what America means. I don't see America as just the United States. You could say all kinds of different things about me. I wouldn't have any problem if someone tried to label me a "native" writer, too, but nobody ever says that about Chicano writers. I feel connected to that as well. I'm also an urban writer. But I think it depends on the context. When people use the term *Chicano writing,* they mean a certain kind of writing. Sometimes it can be good, sometimes bad. Sometimes people say I'm an English-speaking poet in the United

States. And it's true: I'm an English-speaking poet in the United States. I could be Robert Bly, for that matter. It's a complicated issue, but I think it's important to address it, not deny it.

> ∨ **Always Running** *is a vivid account of your gang days in East Los Angeles. Would you comment a little on how you used writing to work your way out of the barrio, which you describe in your book?*

I had just gotten out of jail. I had been shot at by my own homeboys. I was getting very frustrated. I was still doing heroin. I had no idea how addicted I was. There was a law in L.A. at the time where the police could get you for marks. You had to shoot up in all kinds of body parts because the police could stop you and check your veins, and if you had marks, they could put you in the county jail. We had to find ingenious ways to shoot it, to try not to get collapsed veins, which is something you couldn't help because the more you use it, the more your body suffers. But I didn't pay attention to that part of it. I wasn't going to stop. My attitude was, if someone overdosed on drugs, those were more drugs for me. "That's some good stuff there, man. Let me get it." We didn't care. So killing myself was not going to stop me from using drugs.

But I also had these friends—teachers and mentors—who were saying, "Here's your opportunity to leave this kind of life; the judge gave you a break; you're out of jail. You've been shot at by your own homeboys, so you don't owe them anything." Which I took badly because I didn't want to leave the neighborhood, but it made sense. And these friends said they would help me get off drugs. So they took me for two months to a San Pedro housing project, kept me away from everything, and rehabilitated me. They fed me well. They gave me a lot of books to read, too. Revolutionary books by Che [Guevara], Franz Fanon, George Jackson, Karl Marx. They were trying to intellectualize me. The one thing that people weren't giving gangs was intellectual activity and stimulation. And I think that's important. They convinced me that I needed to stay away from drugs, not just because it was the moral thing to do, but because drugs were spiritually and culturally destroying our people. That was powerful.

> ∨ *So you were hearing this from Chicano friends?*

Yeah, actually they were mixed up. All of them revolutionaries. An African American guy, an older guy, had been mentoring me for years. They were talking to me, trying to help me, trying to work with people in the community, to broaden their political and social awareness.

> ∨ Is this when you started finding books like **Manchild in the Promised Land** and others that you mention in your memoir?

Actually, those I discovered earlier. I went to those on my own. I found them on the library shelves. That literature was popular in the 1960s. Malcolm X's *Autobiography,* Piri Thomas's *Down These Mean Streets,* Julius Lester, Eldridge Cleaver. They were talking about oppression—where it comes from, how to educate yourself about these problems. This was important for a kid like me. I had never been given that kind of knowledge before. It was the kind of thing I needed at the time. It wasn't institutionalized. My mentors were also trying to get me to work. It kept me away from crime.

When I got out of jail, I had to learn how to work, to keep a job—in factories, construction, steel mills. I learned a lot of skills. All this was keeping me off drugs. If I'd gone back to the neighborhood for one day, I would have started back on heroin. It was that easy. Staying away from the environment was extremely important for keeping me clean. Unfortunately, the working-class people I was hanging with drank like crazy. So I went from one addiction to another. I had met a beautiful girl in East L.A. When she was eighteen and I was twenty, we got married. She gave birth to two of my kids. I had a family, I had work, and my life was starting to turn around, and it was good. But I still drank too much. There was too much hassle between my wife and me. Three years later we broke up. It was painful because I thought that she was part of my salvation. It was destructive. You idealize these things when you try to get out of something. And I almost killed her. I wrote about that in my poem "Always Running." I was waiting in front of the house with a shotgun. I was waiting to blow her away. Fortunately, she didn't show up.

> ∨ The poems about love and the pain associated with it are some of your most powerful poems.

The rage is there. You have to learn how to deal with it. But what I realized was eating at me, and I'd been realizing it for seven years working in industry, was that I wanted to be an artist. I'd had a taste of it, and I knew that if I didn't go that way, I would end up like my father, who was completely out of it. Ten years before he died, he went crazy. His dreams had been crushed. He was a broken, diminished man. I couldn't end up like that. That was one of my decisions that I made on my own. I upset a lot of people, though. I got fired from a chemical refinery, so that was my way to never go back. I had been making five hundred dollars a week—seven hundred dollars with overtime—and I wanted to trade it all in to write. So I started writing for a newspaper, which paid me only one hundred dollars a week.

ⱽ *You wrote community columns in a local paper?*

It was a bilingual newspaper that was passed out freely in the community. They had columns. And then they also had articles on the community, in East L.A., right in the barrio. Every once in a while they would send me out to do stories. I was also a photographer. Once I had a boxing column, which was cool because at one time I was an amateur boxer. I also covered scandals, disasters, and fluff stories. What happened is, things started to escalate. I knew I wanted to be a writer, but just because I wanted to write didn't mean that I knew what I was doing. I went to East L.A. College at night. I took creative writing, journalism, and poetry classes. I got into a summer program for minority journalists. I was one of the few people they ever let in without a degree. I was very persistent. I sent them all my articles, and they let me in. That was great. It was in Berkeley. I interviewed people. I photographed people. I had about five or six stories a week. I graduated and got my certificate. I was valedictorian of the class.

Then I got into my first daily newspaper job in San Bernardino. I covered crime. It was a crazy three years because the city had the second-highest murder rate per capita in the country—and mostly in the Mexican and black community. Then they had all these disasters—the worst car crash in years, the worst fires where five hundred homes were destroyed, earthquakes. It was great training for journalism. It was even better training than the neighborhood. I saw more dead bodies than I ever cared to see.

ⱽ *This was in the early 1980s?*

Yeah, and then I started working with literary material. I started participating with a group called the Writers' Association, in East L.A. We started organizing readings, started doing a magazine, of which I was an editor. We started doing workshops in barrios and prisons, which really was a good way to get back to the past. I started doing workshops in the old barrio itself. By 1985, I had moved to Chicago, where I worked as an editor, writer, and photographer.

⌄ *You moved to Chicago for a specific job, then?*

Yes, someone told me to come over. I was leaving someone I call my third wife. We weren't married, but we were that close. I was still drinking a lot. I quit the newspaper, which was a bad thing because they blacklisted me in L.A. I couldn't get a job in daily newspapers anymore. So I moved to Chicago. A couple of years after I got there, I became involved in poetry slams. By 1989, I had published my first book of poetry. I did it myself. I'd worked as a typesetter and knew how to work with books. That was also how I started Tía Chucha Press. I'd been very active in the poetry scene, so I set this up as a company to publish poets from that scene.

⌄ *Can you talk about Youth Struggling for Survival? It has received a lot of publicity over the years.*

Well, we started out in Chicago with two hundred people. That was the founding group. I knew that I couldn't work with two hundred kids—we didn't have enough adults—but it was good that there were so many people into the organization. I would say that on the average we have about thirty kids and ten adults. Right now, at the moment, we probably have about fifteen kids, and the "kids" range from ages eleven to twenty-four. There are about eight adults. But we've been around since 1994.

⌄ *What is the basic concept of Youth?*

The basic concept is for adults and young people to work together for the benefit of youth. I saw that the community was very severed. I saw that the rise in gangs was reflected by that community's fracturing. Economic life wasn't prospering. Parents and families were severed. Schools and other adults were not working together. There was too much police presence, too much abandonment. So Youth tried to rethread some of those threads of the community. I had to do it by example. I couldn't just talk about how to work with youth. We had to do it. We deal with the holistic development of youth, so we usually have one adult to three kids. Again, it's been hard because youth come and go. The youth who really hang with us and stick it out are the ones who have really benefited. We ask adults to stay with it, but it's really hard work. There's no money in it. It's all volunteer. Most of the adults have stayed for the duration, though.

> ˅ *Like Big Brother?*

No, that's a good way to start, but it's deeper than that. The attitude isn't just "I'm an older person, I'll take you to the mountains." I'm talking about adults who can guide, support, who can interact with youth, mirror them. We were trying to develop the kids' leadership skills, their artistic skills, and to get them culturally trained and knowledgeable about their own roots and traditions. Sometimes a kid is involved in rituals in the community or goes to events, like demonstrations against the growing prison rate. We want to get the kids involved in the political, economic, and social life of the community. We have both gang and nongang kids. We wanted to mix it all up. So it's that holistic approach. They need to be engaged emotionally, psychologically, culturally, intellectually, and spiritually. All of those needs must get met.

> ˅ *The name Youth Struggling for Survival suggests "at-risk kids."*
> *Your own children have been part of the organization, haven't they?*

Yes. My oldest son and my daughter were founding members. My other two sons are doing much better than their brother did, but I thought it would be better for my younger sons to meet some of these kids and other adults so that maybe they could find mentors other than their dad. I think that's an important part of it. I think kids should be able to turn to other people in the community.

> ˅ *Do you have other branches of Youth Struggling for Survival?*

Right now we have four chapters, three in the city and one in a suburb of Chicago that has the fastest-growing gang population in the country. Mostly Mexican kids. Very heavy-duty gang situations. The group might spread beyond that, but that's all we have now.

> ˅ *In **Always Running**, you describe your own struggle to survive.*
> *You talk a lot about law enforcement and brutality. With the recent*

investigations of the Los Angeles Police Department [LAPD], which have
resulted in federal lawsuits, indictments of police officers, and the dis-
trict attorney's office reviewing more than three thousand cases, do
you feel that your plea for justice is finally being heard?

This is probably the biggest thing they've done to try to change the abuse I describe in *Always Running*. The same thing's going on in New York with the Diallo case. But one thing you should know: the corruption I talked about in my book was not just the LAPD. The L.A. Sheriff's Department was probably more corrupt. Those are the ones I was targeting in my book. They're related, but they're not the same thing. A lot of the trouble I had was with the Sheriff's Department because we were part of the county. Half of East L.A. and Watts—a lot of these areas—were county territory; we were part of the L.A. area but not part of L.A. city. The sheriffs also run the county jail.

I don't think cops should abuse or kill people. That should be adamantly opposed. But at the same time, I wonder about a society that allows human beings to be in a situation where their humanity has to be on the line. What I'm interested in is what we are doing as a culture. A lot of people think that the more cops we have, the safer we'll be. They're buying into a lie.

I had this retreat once where gang members were mixed with other men from the community. The gang kids were very articulate. They scared some of these white, middle-class guys who showed up. This one kid was describing the death of his friend, and this white guy was getting very frustrated. Finally, he gets up and says, "Well, I didn't shoot that guy. I didn't do it!" I pointed out that this guy's friend was killed by the cops, that somewhere he had participated in the consensus that says in a community, gated or otherwise, one can live a fairly decent life as long as someone can keep down these blacks, browns, poor whites, or whoever else they happen to be. And that someone is the cops, and most people have accepted that. What we've done is given cops a license, in our name, to kill. When you change the skin color of the cop—a brown on brown, for example—the dynamic is often intensified.

> v *But isn't it ludicrous to send four white cops into a neighborhood,*
> *such as the Diallo situation in New York?*

Of course it's ludicrous, but sometimes you have black cops going into a neighbor-hood, and they're just as brutal. The dynamic hasn't changed. Basically you still have an elite power structure. What they, white cops, demand is that black and brown cops prove themselves. They have to prove that they are not like the gang people, that these gang folks are the "ugly" blacks and browns who are giving the "best" of the blacks and browns a bad name. You know, a lot of those cops being indicted now in L.A. are Chicano cops. They've been brutalizing people for years. My experiences were with white cops. I don't defend black and brown cops' bru-talizing either. We should have a diverse police force, sure, but what remains is that there's a dynamic that they're falling into and that we support. And that's hurting kids. That's what I'd like to have us look at. Personally, I feel we need to change the whole concept of the police system. The death penalty should be completely stopped. Everything should be reexamined. That's part of my mission.

⌄ *The racism that you're talking about became a major issue in the
O. J. Simpson trial, didn't it?*

Police in big cities dealing with a lot of people don't care about doing that exhaus-tive work resolving crimes. There are good detectives that come in, sure. But they're not that exhaustive because their basic conception is that if we have a murder, we'll get the nearest possible suspect. Most of these victims can't defend themselves, unlike O.J., who had lots of money. They [the police] just want a conviction rate. So in the barrios or in the communities that are very poor, if somebody's mur-dered, who's the next closest possible suspect? If you get that guy, whether he did it or not doesn't matter. If you can get an indictment, the guy's gone.

⌄ *The Hurricane Carter story.*

Exactly. This is why in Illinois, half of the twenty-four people on death row were released, when DNA and other factors helped prove they were innocent. And now the governor, who is a Republican, had to put a moratorium on the death penalty. An amazing thing. As much as he might want the death penalty, because he's said he's for it, he knows that the system is killing innocent people.

Why was O.J. found innocent? The reason why is that the police, who have got-ten away with this flimsy police work for decades, could not get away with it with

O.J. It was flimsy police work that destroyed that case. O.J. is presumed innocent according to the law. You have to prove someone killed, and if you don't have all the proof put together, you cannot convict the guy—even if you believe he did it. That's the way it works. That case proved that. In the Jon Benet Ramsey case, the police can't figure out who killed the girl. The errors that the police committed in that case are making it so that they may never find the killer. The police pretend they do a good job finding the evidence. If you don't have any money and power, then you get convicted. It doesn't matter. When you have these high-level crimes, the police aren't doing a very good job. I'm not putting them all down. There are some pretty good detectives out there. Forensics is outstanding. But there are also brutal police officers as well. They hurt people; they've done it for years; they've killed people and never thought twice about it. And now it's just starting to come out. The O.J. case is just the tip of the iceberg.

 ⌄ *This is what you talk about in your poem "The News You Don't Get*
    at Home," isn't it? This sense of naïveté that permeates our society?

Naïveté, yeah. And when I was talking to a group of teachers recently at your university, I started talking about the lies that this country is based on. That's not to say that I don't love the people and the country. This is home, and it's all I know, but you have to look at both the good and the bad. You can't have only an idealized history, a distorted one, where it's all Anglo-American, the powerful, and the rich. You're lying to the kids. You grow up in your home, and you tell your kids, "Don't lie." But the books we have them read are based on lies. If Native American, African, Mexican, Cuban, and Puerto Rican are peripheral, then it's a big lie. Even Anglo-American history as it's portrayed is a lie. It's all idealized. How do we get closer to the truth of our time? The truths of our experiences? This is the soul talk I was talking about earlier.

 ⌄ *You conduct writing workshops all over the country, in many different*
    settings. Much of your time is spent working with prisoners. Can you
    talk about some of the things you do with these men and women?

Poetry workshops in prisons have been going on for awhile now. I know a number of people who've been doing them for decades, and I've been doing them since the 1980s. There's something rich about that experience. You notice the transformative, transcendent power of words. Most of the prisons I go to don't have too many outlets or literary programs going on. But when you have a writing workshop, it really inspires these men and women. And beautiful things come out of there. Just like if you give an easel to some of these prisoners, some of them come out fantastic artists. They've got the time, but also I think these people are tapped into their creativity, and they're not willing to fall into a void.

> *v How do you motivate prisoners to believe in their art when many*
> *of them know that they're not going to get out?*

As I mentioned, tap into the creativity. They're limited and constrained by society, but there's a part of them that is abundant, inexhaustible. This helps them become fuller human beings. And I've met these guys who have done forty, fifty years, and they're the best people you ever want to hang with. They're also some of the most creative people you'll meet, too.

> *v So nihilism doesn't set in?*

It could—if you don't give them an outlet, if you punish them so badly that it becomes totally inhuman, where life is meaningless. Then they will see it that way. But I think that these workshops do some pretty good things. A lot of these prisoners help other prisoners. Ultimately, prisons and crime are mixed together with politics, poverty, racism. That's why prisons are worse than anyone can imagine. People say, "Well, you commit a crime, you should go to jail." But if it's mixed in with politics and sociology and economics, well, it's just not that simple.

> *v Recently the Republican governor in New Mexico came out in favor*
> *of legalizing certain drugs. Are things changing?*

Eighty percent of all federal prisoners are in for drug-related crimes. Men and women are getting these terrible prison sentences nowadays for selling drugs. Something has to change. Drug abuse is manipulated and created by major industries, with the support of the government. The fact that it's in communities means that, somehow, somebody powerful allowed it to happen. The other side of the argument is that when you're on drugs, hard drugs, basically you need help; you need treatment. If you're terribly addicted to drugs, you can't even help most of your actions. A lot of people who are making money off of drugs, except for the big-time dealers, are merely trying to survive. A lot of these ghetto or barrio drug dealers aren't making lots of money. Obviously, they're better off than some others—maybe they have a four-wheel drive, but that doesn't mean they're living in a mansion. Some of them are barely able to pay rent. They have families. Some of the people in those communities can't make money any other way. Some of them don't want to sell drugs, but they have to because there is no other opportunity in their communities. People have to see some of this drug dealing as rational behavior.

Still we have all this talk about fighting drugs. It's just creating another industry—cops, helicopters, more guns. That won't sweep away the drug problem because this policing does not reflect what is really happening. It doesn't reflect the history, the economy. So I say prison is the worst way to deal with it. What addicted people need, first, is treatment, then economic opportunity. It's that simple.

˅ Do you still see heroin as a major problem in the cities?

Yes, it's still a problem. The biggest AIDS rise among Latinos and blacks is because of heroin. There are people trying to do the needle exchange, but they're under attack. When I was twenty, the issue was hepatitis. There were always risks when you were shooting up. With AIDS, it's gotten worse. In East L.A., you have three, four, five generations of heroin addicts. It used to be that the drugs mostly made it into East L.A., Spanish Harlem, Black Harlem. Get it to the blacks and browns, and don't think twice about it. Now that it's affected other sectors of society, it's a big problem, but they're still not dealing with it the right way. They're still trying to put offenders away. You have middle-class kids of all colors who got involved with drugs, and now they're doing twenty, twenty-five, thirty years. It's insane.

˅ Do you ever fear that people might call you too idealistic?

Some people do call me idealistic. The reason my arguments can't wait, though, is that I'm speaking from some hard, brutal experience. I have proved, however, that under certain circumstances, that with certain ways of relating to people, things change. All these things I've mentioned are already being put into place. It's not that idealistic anymore. We have to interact and interconnect. As some wise person once said, in the essentials we can have unity, in the nonessentials liberty. I want the same beautiful, just, creative, liberating world that everyone else wants. Some people say it can't happen. Some people say it can. Part of my goal is to write, to speak, to teach, to help make it happen. It's about moving our imaginations, our ideas, toward action that truly reflects our best ideas. We have to move our dreams to reality.

> ⌄ *If possible, I'd like to finish with your comments on the North Carolina residency. How has it been so far?*

The residency has been a tremendous experience. I've talked to a cross section of the state's population while also enjoying its varied terrain: from mountains to farmlands to industry to oceans. I've spoken at public schools, universities, churches, prisons, juvenile facilities, ESL [English as a Second Language] classes, conferences, community centers, drug treatment centers, hospitals, the Cherokee Reservation, and once at a bedsheet-manufacturing plant. They speak in English, in Spanish, and even in some eastern European or Southeast Asian tongues. All races, all cultures— which says a lot about how rich and diverse this state is. This should be valued and not just for literature, but also in politics, the economy, and the culture. I've not had a bad experience with any audience. As it is, I don't believe there's such a thing as a bad audience, although some can be quite challenging, as it should be.

> ⌄ *Are there any specific highlights you can point to during your travels?*

There are so many, but I recall fondly when several elementary school children in the Hickory area presented me with handmade books of art and writing that they'd created based on my children's book, *América Is Her Name*. I almost fell into tears. Also, the prison visits where I talked with some of the prisoners about their creativity and poetry were rewarding. There were some great talks in churches, great openings of dialogue and issues that I will remember for a long time. The workshops with teachers I had as well as the university readings—they were all memorable. But mostly it was the little things, like a young girl, about twelve, who read her poetry at a workshop I did for mostly adults. She also presented me with a poem on pink paper, covered in plastic, and then tied with a ribbon. So much care. Again, I think about this, and I begin to feel sorrow because it's hard to have so much poetry, so much ache of creativity, and still know we don't yet have a fully embracing society that will make a real and lasting place for this.

> ⌄ Have you had many opportunities to communicate with the Latino
> population in North Carolina?

Yes, especially with the community organizations trying to meet the needs of this rapidly growing population. I spoke at ESL classes and after Spanish-language services in churches that allowed me to converse with many people. I also did writing workshops with Spanish-speaking children, mothers, and migrant workers. We've had some intense talks. There are some real concerns here—from how to handle the few people wanting them to disappear to crime, but also issues of balancing their values and traditions with the fast-paced, more materially driven culture that seems to permeate this country. Many felt that they had to come here; they didn't have a choice because of the economic or political realities of their home countries. Some harbor feelings of returning, although I believe most will stay. They also know they need to know English and become properly integrated into the political and social life of North Carolina. The thing is, they don't need to lose their original languages, their essential values, or their cultural roots to do this. Things will change naturally for them, as well as for the rest of the state, because of their presence. Most of this, by the way, will be for the good. But Latinos need to learn how to adequately balance the many challenges confronting them, although I know it's a hard thing to do. Unfortunately, they are being given mostly either-or choices, and I believe this ultimately hurts any new people coming to this country. Different countries, social classes, races, and concerns exist among Latinos. There's a lot to unite us, but there's also a lot to recognize and celebrate as differences, nuances, accents, and histories. It's important for people to appreciate what countries they come from and, in places like Mexico, what state or region. They are all quite interesting.

> ⌄ The schedule for the residency has been demanding. One wonders
> where all of your energy comes from.

While I will have spent ten weeks total in North Carolina, there was a two-week break in the middle where I returned to Chicago, to my family and to the work I left behind. I also have brought my laptop to help me continue my writing, includ-

ing a journal of my residency, and many books and magazines. I don't need much
to relax except quiet, water, good fruit, and a good book. For someone who has lived
a pretty unhealthy and addictive life for so long, it feels good now to take care of
myself and enjoy the small and wholesome pleasures that the world has to offer. I
also take walks and, if I can, exercise. Although some days were more hectic than
others, people were most gracious to allow me my space to relax the best way I
could. I know many writers who would never do what I do. They won't speak as
often or to as broad a group of people. But I thrive on it. I love talking to and relating with all kinds of people. So while all of this is work and does require a lot of
attention and energy, I also get much enjoyment from doing it.

Benjamin Alire Sáenz

*B*enjamin Alire Sáenz was born in Picacho, New Mexico, in 1952. After working as a priest for four years in the American Southwest, Texas, and Louisiana, he studied literature at the University of Iowa, then Stanford, where he won a Wallace Stegner Fellowship in poetry. He currently teaches in the bilingual creative writing program at the University of Texas, El Paso.

This interview took place at Appalachian State University, in Boone, North Carolina, April 20, 2001, after Sáenz's reading. Sáenz talks about his training as a priest and how theology inspires his writing. Disillusioned with Christianity in this country, he argues that Americans "don't want to think about suffering at all." They "want that empty Cross, where Jesus somehow is up in heaven, and there's nothing but this corpseless Cross. No suffering, just resurrection." He discusses this "suffering" as well as his artistic craft, the literature of other prominent Latino writers, and the influence of the desert on his writing.

SUGGESTED READING

Calendar of Dust
(Seattle: Broken Moon Press, 1991)

Flowers for the Broken
(Seattle: Broken Moon Press, 1992)

Carry Me Like Water
(New York: Hyperion, 1995)

Dark and Perfect Angels
(El Paso: Cinco Puntos Press, 1995)

The House of Forgetting
(New York: Harper Collins, 1997)

*A Gift from Papá Diego/
Un regalo de Papá Diego*
(El Paso: Cinco Puntos Press, 1998)

*Grandma Fina and Her
Wonderful Umbrellas/
La Abuelita Fina y sus
sombrillas maravillosas*
(El Paso: Cinco Puntos Press, 1999)

Elegies in Blue
(El Paso: Cinco Puntos Press, 2002)

> ⌄ *You left the priesthood in 1984. The next decade you published a*
> *remarkable amount of writing: a collection of short stories, two novels,*
> *two children's books, and two collections of poetry. Had this literary*
> *voice been pent up, waiting to explode?*

I would say that you have to find different forums, at different times in your life, to say the things you need to say. When I was a priest, I had a particular kind of forum; when I left the priesthood, I had no forum at all. I needed to find a forum. I had always wanted to be a writer. I guess I had always been a writer in the sense that I was always writing down my thoughts. It was easy for me to articulate myself and express what I needed to say in the written form, and so after I left the priesthood, writing took on a new urgency—the need to be in dialogue and to articulate the things that you see, the things that you feel, the things that you're interpreting in the society and world around you. I was always a very political person, but, for someone like me, I didn't see any sense in being a politician. It made perfect sense to bring all of my views together in my writing, so I would say that I was really ready to write. I was also old enough and mature enough to have had experience in life and to have something to say.

> ⌄ *You say that you've "always been a writer." When did you first start*
> *writing? How far back do you go?*

I'm working on an essay on writing, as we speak. I think that what happens is we don't think of ourselves as writers because we are not publishing. But I have a long résumé as a writer. I'd written a master's thesis; I'd written papers in graduate school, in undergraduate school, in high school. I was always writing, and in my day we were expected to write a lot. And so I had experience in expressing myself in writing and was quite successful at it. But, in that way, I don't think that most people consider themselves writers. I think, though, that if people have a lot of experience in writing things down, expressing themselves on the page, then in some very real ways they're writers. They just don't consider that as their vocation.

> ⌄ *Did you publish your poetry first?*

Yes, I did. My first book was a book of poems.

v *How do you determine when your writing fits a particular mode? Do*
you work on one book, publish it, let it rest, then go on to another
genre?

It varies. I don't think I have a plan. I think that I have an idea for something, and if I have an idea about a woman who gets kidnapped and her captor erases her identity, it doesn't sound like a poem to me. That's a novel. So I start off with an idea, and the genre becomes very apparent. I don't sit down to write a poem. I sit down with an idea and say, "I want to write about this." And usually, immediately, it comes to me that this should be a poem or this should be a novel or this should be a short story or this should be an essay. It's just obvious to me.

v *When do you know that you have a collection of poetry? In the new*
book of poems you're working on at the moment—the one you were
discussing [at the reading] last night—a thematic thread connects
many of the poems. The whole idea of visiting the graves, for example.
The collections that came out in 1991 and 1995 also express that theme.

I very much write *books* of poems. In the new book you mentioned, one section is called "Elegies in Blue." A good many of the poems are elegies—about visiting graves, about exploring one's past, about being an archaeologist, about having a dialogue with history. But all of my poems, books of poems, are dialogues with history. It's just that they take on different forms. My first book moves from the cycles of death and life; we move from death and exile to a kind of resurrection, and it's in three sections. There's a movement in the poems, and I very much wrote a *book* of poems, which I called *Calendar of Dust*. At the time, I was thinking of a book; I threw out poems that I had written that didn't fit in. It's the novelist in me that works on a book of poems. The second book moves, too; it's seasonal. It moves from winter to spring, and again it's the same movement as the first book in that sense. They're very different books, but the movement is the same. It moves from exploring death and renewal. And so my books are very cyclical.

This new book is very different because it doesn't move cyclically. The first two sections are not cyclical. They're thematic. The first part is entitled "Learning to Do Philosophy," the second "Now No One Knows Why You Fought." The third one is entitled "Elegies in Blue." While the third part is a section of elegies, you could also say that the first two sections are elegiac in nature. In the second section, there are lots of "poems of address" to people, to important people whom I consider influential in my life: James Baldwin, Denise Levertov, César Chávez. I write poems of address to them and also to my wife, so some of them are a little bit personal in nature, and, broadly speaking, they're addressing people who were either writers or people who were bringing about social change. I'm addressing poems to them. The first section of the book is about how you learn to think, how you learn to be political in the world. One of the poems is entitled "The Boy Learns to Ask Important Questions." Another poem is entitled "The Boy Learns about Names," which is about discovering all of those issues in American history, such as the House Committee on Un-American Activities and the names on the Vietnam Wall and all of these histories that you discover outside of the classroom. In the classroom, they don't teach you American history. So, really, "Learning to Do Philosophy" is a section that's about learning to be political. When you are learning to be political, it's always elegiac because you're learning that our legacy is one of killing, one of death, one of dying—a legacy of erasure.

The second section addresses people who have sought to address these issues in one way or another. My wife is a social activist, a judicial activist. Denise Levertov was a poet, a political activist. César Chávez, of course, was trying to bring about social change for farmworkers in America. James Baldwin was one of the most astute political writers this country has ever known and a writer I greatly admire for the fact that he could speak about his rage in such articulate and meaningful ways. And then someone like the poet Saul Fishman, who changed his name to Edwin Rolfe. He fought in the Abraham Lincoln Brigades. So I address these people, and the section title "Now No One Knows Why You Fought" is from a line in the César Chávez poem. It refers to the fact that we remember these people as historical figures, and, as such, we show them the shallowest form of praise, the shallowest form of political erasure because we revert to heroic individualism instead of to the communal changes these individuals sought to bring about. No one indeed knows why they fought; no one gives a damn about the farmworker, but they love César Chávez, which I find not only ironic but repulsive. You admire César Chávez *because* of why he fought, not as just another hero. We reduce him to a sports figure in that kind of politics, if that's what you want to call "a politics." And I'm very much against that. The next section is about burial places. I suppose, in some ways, I politicize elegies. Yet, interestingly enough, I think of this book of poems as my most lyrical book of poems. Certainly I consider it my best book of poems.

> ∨ You mentioned that all of your writing is fixed in a historical
> moment. In **Calendar of Dust**, all but one of the poems is prefaced
> with a setting in time and place. In your next book of poetry, you
> don't include these prefaces. Is there a reason for this?

Well, yes, there is. What really ties the first book together is not just the movement that I was talking about earlier—the cyclical movement, moving from exile to resurrection—but that I was also playing with the idea of history, of journal keeping, of calendar. All of those kinds of things that can be either public history or private history, so that each poem becomes a way of placing a date on it and making it smaller, but also making it larger at the same time. I was trying to be intimate, where I didn't privilege the poems in terms of "Oh, this was a public event and therefore more important than this private, more personal event, which is also historical." It's our understanding of the event that is always fluid—that these things happened. And in some ways, my first book was very much a kind of rewriting of history in poetic form.

> ∨ And of narrative form, too?

Yes, I would say a lot of the poems in my first book are narrative poems. In my second book, I had one long poem that was certainly narrative. Actually there are many narrative poems in my second book as well. There are very few, if any, in this new book of poems.

> ∨ The second book includes a great deal of dialogue between
> characters.

Well, yes. I always use dialogue in my work. Certainly. I use several voices in that book.

> ∨ I'm thinking specifically of "El Paso County Jail," "I Wouldn't Even
> Bleed," "Meditations."

I like using dialogue in poems. Again, it's the novelist in me, the short-story writer in me. I believe you can use dialogue to great effect in poetry, at least when it's appropriate. But it's not something that I'm necessarily thinking of when I write a poem. I often use quotes in a poem as opposed to dialogue. In my first book of poems, I have a poem called "Exile," which is mostly all dialogue, about a man and a woman speaking to each other. So there are times when you think that that is exactly the right strategy to use, but it actually doesn't arise that often.

> ⌄ *When you say that it's "the short-story writer in me" or the novelist speaking, do you see yourself as one or the other? Do you feel yourself as a poet first or as a novelist first, or do they overlap so much that you can't really distinguish between the two?*

Well, put it this way, I consider myself a writer. A writer. I don't think that it's more important for me to be a poet or that it's more important to be a novelist. It's just important to me to be a writer, and so I consider myself a writer who kind of weaves in and out of genres.

> ⌄ *You quit the priesthood when you were thirty. Did you feel stifled and thus unable to become the writer that you wanted to be?*

I think that's part of the reason, but I don't think that's everything. I just needed to live my life in a different way. That included writing, but it also included a lot of other things. I just needed to drop out, and I did. It was really important for me to express myself in other ways that the priesthood did not allow. The priesthood isn't just a stifling thing; it frees you to do lots of other things. It's just that I didn't quite fit in that mode. It wasn't the way I was meant to live my life. I knew it, and I had to do something about that.

> ⌄ *Despite this change in professions, there's still an obvious spiritual side to much of your writing. Biblical references, for example, especially the Gospel according to John. Are you conscious of these references when you write? Or, as time passes, do you leave them behind?*

No, I don't think you leave things behind. I think things change. It's like language. Do you leave English behind? No, your English changes, but you don't leave it behind. I was trained in Western philosophy and theology. I know Scripture. I use it. I always will. My references to Catholic culture are very important because I come from a Mexican American culture where those kinds of reference points are very important to understanding the culture. I'll never leave Catholicism behind because I have no need to leave it behind. It's just a part of the way I think, the way I feel. It's part of the imagery that I use. I use a lot of Catholic imagery, but I use a lot of desert imagery as well because I'm from the desert. I'll never leave any of those things behind. Rather, I'll expand on them.

I think it's fair to say that calling me a Catholic thinker doesn't insult me. I think there are some people who wouldn't particularly care for that. That's a label that they might want to run from. I'm certainly not a dogmatic Catholic. I never have been. I'm unorthodox in many ways. I'm unorthodox about a lot of things. But I don't run from the label, any more than a Jewish writer would run away from that label. If someone said, "I'm a Jewish thinker," no one would say anything about that. I think we still have a lot of issues with Catholicism in this country. I think that writing—for lots of writers, not just for me—is a salvific kind of thing. Salvific as in theology and Catholicism. I don't use it specifically that way, but to say that writing saves me is also a religious thing. That's religious terminology—like when one says "art saves lives." That is not humanistic; that's very theological thinking, actually. And I do think art saves lives. It saves some people's lives, at least. I think we can overstate that, but I think it saves some people's lives. I think it saves artists' lives, if no one else's. I don't know if it saves the rich people who purchase art, but I think that in many ways writing has saved my life. So I consider it a holy thing. That's religious; that's the way I think. And I think other writers think that. I think many writers think that way, and other writers say the same thing in nonreligious terms because they haven't grown up in religious environments. But I have, and I accept that. I embrace that.

> ⌄ *Despite this religious background that you bring to your writing,*
> *you also write about a heartless God, a God who allows someone to*
> *kill another human being. In "Meditation Winter," one of your speakers*
> *says that God "is a set of jaws that bites down on your heart."*

I think that one always struggles with life, and whether you do it in a religious context or not, you want to look for harmony, and you can look for that kind of harmony in a religious context, whether it be through Catholicism, Judaism, Buddhism, or Islam. And it's never easy; in fact, one of the things that draws me to Judaism and Catholicism is that the struggle itself is really important. The mystics all have their dark night of the soul, and you need to have that. Otherwise, it's shallow: sweet, nonsensical, Hallmark Christianity. I have no use for that, absolutely no use for it. "Jesus loves me this I know, 'cause the Bible tells me so"—I think those people should get a life. It's very difficult to come to terms with ugliness in the world. And when you do it through a religious lens, there are many difficulties and incongruities. Faith doesn't make your life easier; it makes it harder, in fact.

The whole paradox of the Cross is that people die. The crucifixion is real. What I sometimes resent about North American Christianity and even North American Catholicism is that people think that somehow the whole notion of death is blood-less. When people go from the United States to Mexico and they see all these bloody saints, they think, "How garish!" Well, my response is, "What the fuck do you think?" I wrote a poem that says, "In Mexico, where any saint worth praying to is adorned with blood as well as gold." I really mean that. I take that blood seriously. What do people think? They don't want to think about suffering at all. They just want that empty Cross, where Jesus somehow is up in heaven, and there's nothing but this corpseless Cross. No suffering, just resurrection. Not in my world. Not in anybody's world I know. People die. It's a hard world, and that has to become a part of the way you think about the world.

As I said, in living you have a lot of what the mystics call the "dark night of the soul." There are moments when this notion of resurrection does not exist because this is the stage of death and darkness. I think many writers write about all of those moments. But the darkness has to be real darkness in order for anything that we want to call regeneration—whether you want to call it resurrection or not, any kind of renewal—to happen. There's got to be a winter, and winter is very real.

⌄ Is that why you chose the title **Dark and Perfect Angels**?

It's alluding to that; it's alluding to lots of things. Also to dark people, Mexicans. Angels are always presented as these white figures, but in my world they are very earthy and a lot browner. A lot darker.

⌄ Speaking of titles, why the title **Calendar of Dust**?

Because a calendar is made of days, but it is also made of the earth and of the earth passing, and dust represents that. Not only the storms and the desert, but it kind of connotes dirt, earth, dust, death—a passing of days. There's the Ash Wednesday expression, "Remember, man, that you are dust, and to dust you shall return." People don't say that anymore. Not the church. They have other expressions, now. But when I was growing up, that's what the priest said. Now they say, "Repent and believe in the good news," or they say other things, but when I was growing up, it was "Remember, man." It was real sexist, it didn't say "Remember, woman," but "Remember, man, that you are dust, and to dust you shall return." And I don't think that the return to dust is such a bad thing—I don't find that depressing. It's good to go back and become part of the earth from whence you came.

> ⌄ *Much of your poetry explores the past along the border. The picture is generally grim and bordering on hopeless. Is this your role as a poet or at least your role in a book such as **Calendar of Dust**? To expose the historical mistakes, to capture the darker side of life on both sides of the border?*

Well, maybe it's the darker side, but my writing could be a lot darker, frankly.

> ⌄ *Some of the historical pieces, though, set in the nineteenth century?*

Well, I just think at a certain point you have to tell the truth. You can't erase all that poverty. You can't erase all that oppression. You can't erase all that racism. You observe it, and you write about it. I don't think that's necessarily hopeless; I just think that you certainly can't create change if you don't even see the problem. On an institutional basis, Christianity has never been very successful at solving these problems that plague us. Christians are very good at pointing out individual faults. Protestantism, Catholicism, and Judaism, for that matter, can be quite successful at accusing the self of faults and sins and shortcomings. Western religions—and perhaps Eastern religions, too, I suspect—are very bad at dealing with things like institutional racism. Do you think, for all its great claims, that the United States is a Christian country? We have to address issues like slavery, which we've never really come to terms with in our country. You would think that somehow Christianity would create that dialogue.

I don't think that Eastern religions, though, have helped in a country like China either, quite frankly. We often romanticize Eastern religions because we are not connected to those regions' histories. But in fact, historically speaking, China has oppressed her own people terribly, and Japan, too. Apparently, no religion has been able to deal with these institutional issues of inequality. I don't quite know why, but I do know that one of the great things about the prophets was that they said, "We have a problem here; we have a serious problem, and we gotta address it." And people did not like the prophets. Prophets were not popular in the Old Testament. They were not loved because they were accusing the people. You know, a prophet went up to David and asked, "What do you think of a man who owns all these sheep, and this other man has only one sheep, and the owner of the number of sheep takes that one sheep as well?" And David said, "Bring me that man that I might punish him," and the prophet said, "*You are that man.*" His remark didn't make him all that popular with David at that moment.

> ⌄ In one of your poems, a character says that **tomorrow** is a word the "gringo made for us," that "tomorrow is a word for the poor."

Tomorrow is a word for the poor. We don't deal well with poverty in this country, period. We just don't. We don't like to acknowledge it; it's difficult for us to address that issue. I resent the fact that the racist notions of Mexicans and Mexico was mañana, the land of mañana. Mexico, the land of mañana. But it's the powerful who are always telling people to wait. We tell poor people to wait; we tell anybody who's not rich and wealthy that they can wait. Wait in line. Wait. Wait. Wait. We are always telling people mañana.

I'm a real critic of the country I live in, but that doesn't mean that I don't love this country. I'm a utopian thinker. We need to address these issues of democracy seriously. I take democracy very seriously. Democracy is important, and anything that opens up a space for democracy and that lives up to this whole notion that all people are created equal—I take that very seriously. And I'm very critical of institutions that don't take that seriously, and I think a lot of people in power don't take democracy seriously. Democracy is messy. And I think a lot of politicians don't want to solve the problems. We don't want to make it possible for Ben Sáenz to be president because the system right now makes it a lot easier for someone like George W. Bush to be president. And that's not about merit. We don't know that he's smarter than I am. We don't know that he is more qualified than I am. But he's poised to be president. Because the society I live in has put him in a particular position, he is closer to that goal. And it is easier for him to achieve precisely because he has money. Poor men and women are never going to be president. They're not. Ever. Unless they completely sell out, and then we don't want them. We want real democracy. And so, I think, when I deal in my work with moments like this, I think that I'm being very political; I'm making a comment on the world I live in. And I do believe that a real democracy is possible. I just don't think that we are willing to work for it.

> ∨ *Last night you mentioned that you teach a course in El Paso on*
> *autobiography. You've led an interesting life. Have you ever thought*
> *about writing your own memoir?*

You know, I really think that I write what I need to write. I don't need to focus in on my own life to say the things I need to say. There are really important issues that are confronting this country and our communities, my Mexican American community, my community in El Paso and Juárez. We're poor. We have issues I need to explore, that I need to write about. They're really urgent. I don't consider getting my story out very important. But we do live in a culture that teaches us to focus on the individual. The problem with writing a narrative about oneself is that we all become heroes in our own narratives. I don't think that I live a very heroic life. I live a very ordinary life. I think that I meet people who do, though. I think that I meet people who struggle a great deal more than I've struggled. I see things that capture my imagination, and I need to write about that. I don't want to focus in on my own individual talent or writing, though. I want to focus on the communal. I want to focus in on other things that are much more important than my own life story. My own life story is supremely important to *me,* in my life, because it is *my* life, and I love being alive. I do. I love my life. I quit smoking because I don't want to die. Obviously, living my life is very important to me, but I don't think that other people need to be subjected to reading it. We are saturated with narratives of self-aggrandizement. When we write about the self, we are privileging the self. It just can't be helped. And even though I read autobiography and teach it to students—and some of these stories are very good—I can't imagine anything more boring than for me to sit and write my life story.

ᵛ *But the autobiography or memoir must speak to a larger issue if you
teach an entire class on it.*

I can use autobiography in the classroom, but these writers have already written
something that addresses issues of identity in the United States. If I want to write
a book about identity, I can write it, but it doesn't have to be my autobiography. I
can say, "Look, these are the issues," and I can frame the issues in different ways
without using me.

ᵛ *Have you ever considered writing a collection of essays?*

Yes, and in fact I am working on a collection of essays at present. And I'm certainly
in those pieces, as I am in everything I write. I don't try to absent myself from my
work. In fact, they're all about my passions. But that's enough for me. Right now, I
have enough material to write about until I'm an old man. I want to write more
novels, more stories, more poems. I want to write more essays. And there's plenty
of Benjamin Alire Sáenz in all of those books for people to get their fill.

Virgil Suárez

$\mathcal{A}$n only child, Virgil Suárez was born in Havana, Cuba, in 1962. In 1970, he moved with his mother and father to Madrid, Spain, where they lived for four years. The family finally settled in Los Angeles, California, where Suárez grew up and attended public school. He eventually received a B.A. from California State University at Long Beach and an M.F.A. from Louisiana State University.

A former student of Edward Abbey and Vance Bourjaily, Suárez is the author of four novels, a collection of short stories, and five volumes of poetry. He also has edited several groundbreaking anthologies on Latino writers, among them *Paper Dance: 55 Latino Poets,* with Victor Hernández Cruz and Leroy Quintana. Suárez teaches creative writing and Latino literature at Florida State University.

This conversation took place by e-mail September 1, 2000. In the interview, Suárez talks about his transition from fiction to poetry, his memoir *Spared Angola,* Cuba as subject matter, and his role as a publisher of other Latino writers.

SUGGESTED READING

Latin Jazz
(New York: William Morrow, Simon and Schuster, 1990)

The Cutter
(Houston: Arte Público Press, 1991)

Welcome to the Oasis and Other Stories
(Houston: Arte Público Press, 1992)

Iguana Dreams: New Latino Fiction
coedited with Delia Poey (New York: Harper Perennial, 1992)

Havana Thursdays
(Houston: Arte Público Press, 1995)

Paper Dance: 55 Latino Poets,
coedited with Victor Hernández Cruz and Leroy Quintana (New York: Persea, 1995)

Little Havana Blue: A Cuban-American Literature Anthology
coedited with Delia Poey
(Houston: Arte Público Press, 1996)

Going Under
(Houston: Arte Público Press, 1996)

ᵥ *You started out writing fiction, then switched to poetry. Can you talk a little about the transition and how, at least in your last four books, poetry is a more appropriate form for your writing?*

I had always been writing poetry. As a matter of fact, I wrote poetry first. Very bad love poetry. I have a few journals filled with poems I had written to my first girl-friend, who'd been emotionally draining and exhausting for me. When I started in my senior year in high school, I showed a few poems around to some of my teachers, one Spanish teacher in particular, who then introduced me to Neruda, Nervo, Paz, Borges, Min-stral—a whole new world of poets. When I read those poets for the first time, I knew two things: one, that I was writing very bad poetry, and two, that I wanted to continue writing poetry. During my first four years as a student at California State University, Long Beach, I took mostly poetry workshops. Elliot Fried was my mentor there. I also fell in with an interesting crowd of students and teachers. We read our work out loud all over Los Angeles, including some really tough places where the audience could have cared less about poetry. Biker bars. Punk bars. Singles' bars. We read from skid row to the Laguna Beach Public Library. We exposed our work to different audiences. All along, we lived and breathed and wrote poetry. I have been writing poetry since 1978 or so. I had always done it.

Of course, then I started writing fiction, too, because I took a fiction workshop and immediately started writing *The Cutter,* my first novel. My first learning novel. I worked on it for one whole year, then put it away, and kept coming back to it until I published it about ten years after I had finished the first draft.

I write poetry every day. I revise poetry every day. Some poems take forever to make right; some never make it. I love the energy of poems, the fact that you have to say what you mean in a shorter space. I've been writing more poetry these days because it suits my lifestyle perfectly. I have a family now. I have responsibilities that call me away from my desk. Every day, though, I get up at the crack of dawn and work on my poems. If I have time in the afternoon, I come back to them and revise. I'm always revising. It's a lot more fun and rewarding to revise than it is to write a first draft of a poem—though that's exciting, too, because I seldom know what a poem will be about. Ishmael Reed described it best when he said "Writin' is fightin'." I love that. It's my motto. I see myself writing to fight back time, awareness of mortality, bad things happening to good people everywhere. Writing keeps me going.

v ***Spared Angola**, your memoir, is a unique blend of poetry, narrative, and nonfiction. Can you discuss how poetry works in this book?*

It wasn't until I worked on *Spared Angola* that I thought of using poems as an appropriate link in my work. In this book, I wanted to give the reader nice little rest places between the longer essays and stories. It just happened, too, that a lot of my memories about childhood took the form of poems. I was really happy with the way those poems took shape because many deal with these brief moments in my life I felt I couldn't devote a whole essay to. It worked out just fine in poems like "Cuca," "Uncle Isidoro," "The Dirt Eaters," "Lolo," and many others. It also provided me with a way to bring in an assortment of memories that wouldn't have been written about and exposed otherwise. *Spared Angola* gave me the confidence that my poetry mattered; people reacted to it very strongly, and I liked that. When I read those poems from that book to audiences everywhere, I could tell I was making contact. I found out, too, that my poems could be funny, that they could make people laugh, and this was a releasing experience for me. For years, I tried too hard to make my poems sound formal, and it wouldn't work. That's not my true voice. I like poems that make me think but then also chuckle along the way. I like comic-serious stuff. That's why I always gravitate toward the work of people like Alurista, Gustavo Pérez Firmat, Judith Ortiz Cofer, Alberto Ríos—poets who are not afraid to let a little humor into their lines. I sit down every time to write the kind of poem that will please me first as an audience member. So many poets out there, many considered great poets, are so precious with their own work that they kill it when they read in public. They lull you to sleep. Their stuff falls flat at their feet because they are thinking "this is lasting poetry, this is poetry with a capital P, this is too much for anyone to understand." Pure rationalization on their part. Poetry lives in two worlds—that of the spoken, oral, and that of the page, that vast white space we invite folks to come swimming in.

> ⌄ *You quote Reinaldo Arenas at the beginning of your collection*
> **In the Republic of Longing**: *"We have no homeland, so we have to invent it over and over again." Is this what you're doing in the four books of poetry you've published over the last three years—inventing the Cuba of your past "over and over again"?*

Very much so, though I know that many of the things I write about, in particular my childhood, are true. I mean, what I remember people saying might be completely different than what they might have actually said, but it is part of what I imagine. In this way, it is absolutely a construct. Call it pure imagination. I had to free myself from thinking that no one would believe this stuff or that it wasn't valid to write about the things I tend to write about. In this way, Reinaldo Arena's memoir *Before Night Falls* is one of the most brilliant books I've read in a long time. He holds nothing back. Raw honesty in his voice. This is where the book draws its power. Knowing that he is dying, he keeps nothing from the paper and by extension from us. It's a beautiful book. Sad and raw and wonderful. It is one of my favorite books. It's funny for me because I normally don't read or enjoy the kind of baroque fiction that Arenas wrote, but I love his memoir because it is direct in what it wants to say. No beating around the bush. It's what I always try to do in my own work. I sit down and think, "Today I'm going to write that poem about the bullfrogs that terrorized me in my childhood at my aunt's house," and I can do it because I no longer think, "Well, this is not going to appeal to anyone," because I've learned to make it appeal. Craft isn't everything, but on a dark, stormy night it's like bright headlights. It guides you where you need to go.

> ⌄ *James Baldwin once said that "you can never leave home," that "you always carry home with you." Is this why you have this nostalgic yearning for a Cuba you left some twenty-five years ago?*

I met Mr. Baldwin once in New Orleans at Vance Bourjaily's house during a party. He was a warm, sweet human being. It was a small party, so we got a chance to chat a bit. He said to me that he had always turned down invitations to go to Cuba, and I found this to be endearing because someone like Baldwin would definitely know what was going on there—what is still going on there—in particular with the treatment of homosexuals and of blacks, too. He was one of these folks you like right away. When the party was over and he left, he reached out and kissed me. The only man who's ever kissed me on the lips, you know, and what was I to say to James Baldwin?

To get back to your question, I wouldn't call it "nostalgia." I think of it more in terms of what I want to turn to record—what I want to keep, or sometimes purely what I want to bring out of myself to look at. I would agree you never do leave. I keep coming back, and every once in a while I think, fear rather, that I'm going to run dry on material. I've lived a good life, but I want to keep living. Those eight years I spent in Cuba are a great resource for me. The four years I spent in Spain, too. I have lived more than three-quarters of my life outside of my native country. I live in the United States. I am a citizen. I consider myself a contributing member of this country's society. I pay my taxes. I work. I love no other country as much as I love Cuba and the United States. I have learned, as Gustavo Pérez Firmat would put it, to live "on the hyphen." I nourish myself there.

> v *Several of your most powerful poems are about your father. Did his*
> *death trigger a longing for your childhood?*

My father's passing (and normally I say "dying," but "passing" has stronger connotations) did make me focus much more on my own life and by extension on my own life through his eyes, perhaps. Or on our life of exile through his eyes, ideas, and words. My father had always been a source of inspiration for me. I have a great deal of respect for the man, which keeps getting stronger because I can't imagine having to uproot my life, my girls' life, and flee to another country. This takes all the guts in the world. My father was a man of high principles. He liked his world clean, honest, devoid of ugliness and pain. What I learned best from my father is that you act; you don't sit around thinking about things. If a man keeps his mind busy, then he's got no time to be depressed. Another direct influence on me. I have become three times as prolific because if I don't write every day, I'm at the risk of falling prey to these dark, bitter thoughts. Call it existential angst. Sure. Writing keeps me focused. Writing poetry is a religion.

My father died of a massive coronary thrombosis, and we never really got a chance to talk about anything spiritual, like whether he believed in a god or whatnot. He went to church with my mother, but my father never really got on my case about beliefs. I respected that about him, too. Not once did he say I was doing the wrong thing because I never set foot in a church. My father, like a lot of men I know, myself included, was skeptical, but, you know, we are not going to take any chances. As I said, poetry is my religion, as corny as that may sound, and going back to my childhood is like entering a temple. I know this is where the memory spirit lingers. I have to coax it to dance with me. I have to get its attention to take me to moments I might have forgotten or moments I'm repressing for some reason. My father's death also had an impact on me because of all the ways I've seen people die, his was the best. Quick. Really quick. I can't imagine my dying any other way. I want to go from this world to the next in lightning speed. In this way, I think the act of writing (and certainly writing poetry) serves as a bridge, something that helps visualize how the mind moves without needing the body. I think imagination is what makes us travel from this life to . . . well, whatever we call the afterworld. I always like to think that my grandmother, who gave my father his name and mine, was thinking of Dante's Virgil—I'm sure she was because she was a schoolteacher and a lover of the classics—when she named us. I see myself in that next world as an usher. I want to accompany folks to where they yearn to go and then be able to tell their stories. Something like that. Hell wouldn't be all that bad if I knew I had friends waiting for me. Then we could play cards, shoot the breeze, eat, and have a heck of a laugh.

⌄ *You celebrate the father in the Cuban section and the mother in the American section of* **In the Republic of Longing**. *Why is this? Was your father more adamant and anti-Castro? Was your mother better able to adapt or assimilate?*

The struggle over Cuban politics between my father and mother influenced me throughout my teenage years. My father, who had left little family in Cuba (a sister and her three children), didn't ever want to return. He was pro-embargo. He wanted Castro out at whatever cost. My mother, on the other hand, had all her family in Cuba, six brothers and sisters, her mother, who up until 1994 was still alive, and her father, who is ninety years old and very sick. She has returned several times. My mother has always put family over politics. Her courage has always amazed me because she followed my father here to the United States. Early on, my father knew he wanted to get out of Cuba, maybe as early as 1957 or so. He smelled something about the revolution, he always liked to say. My father always loved the United States, though he knew that life was very hard here. My mother, I hope, will one day return to live in Cuba with the rest of her family. I am an only son, and sometimes I wonder what keeps her here. Me and two granddaughters. Are we enough? My mother turned sixty recently. She could easily, I hope, live to be ninety. She comes from a genetically strong family. People in her family tend to live well into their nineties; some of her great aunts and uncles lived to be older than one hundred. My mother has a fighting spirit. My father did, too. My politics, though, are in-between. I will not return to Cuba while Cuba is not free, a democratic country, but by the same token I believe in helping the Cuban people somehow. My mother does it by sending medicine. Care packages. A little money. I tend to focus on the human drama, of course, which at times includes the political.

The Cuban Revolution was needed, but all power corrupts absolutely, right? A new revolution is needed. It's needed all over the world. The working class, it seems, will never make gains without revolt. Capitalism is squeezing the life out of the world. Is there a better way? I'm pessimistic. I think we've tried it all, and the form of government we share in the United States is about as good as it gets. Unfortunately, in order for the few to live well, the many (the poor) need to be exploited. I like the way Kurt Vonnegut puts it, which has to do with overpopulation. We are certainly putting too much stress on the earth, on ourselves—something has to give.

v *There seems to be a political shift in your poetry that one doesn't find in your fiction. The poetry is more politically direct, more confrontational, more willing to take chances. And more anti-Castro. Are the Castro poems you include in "Destierro" the result of your thinking about your father and what he never got to see again, dying as he did in a foreign land?*

Yes, there is more of a political awareness in my poetry because I feel freer to say what I want. Fiction restricts you because you are creating characters who might not think the way you do. With my poetry, there are no masks, no pretenses. I call it as I see it, so to speak. Castro has had a devastating influence on everyone, every place, everything. There are more Cubans living in exile or who have been killed because of the revolution than are actually living currently on the island. I wrote a poem titled "Diaspora," which I dedicated to Nancy Morejon because we once met in a conference in San Antonio, and we argued about the word *diaspora* as concerns Cubans and Cuban Americans. Of course, we didn't agree because she stuck to the strictest connotation and meaning of the word, which pertains to African diaspora, not Cuban. I find that arguing with people over politics is a big waste of time. I would much rather let my work do the talking. I never once heard my father say that he wanted to return to Cuba to die there. My father was very proud of being an American citizen. He loved this country more than many people I know who were born here.

> ˅ **You Come Singing** is a memory—of Cuba, of Spain, of Los Angeles,
> of dying loved ones, of traveling across America to a home unknown.
> Like **Spared Angola**, is this book a conscious tribute to the past?

All of my poetry seems to be rooted in the same material, I think, because I think it is given the same voice. I tend to go in circles in terms of those themes I keep coming to. It's allowed me to look at experiences again and again, sometimes (I hope) from different angles, different stages of my life. I think my poetry has allowed me tremendous growth as a human being, more understanding—certainly more so than the fiction. As I said earlier, I come to it with an open heart, no masks, no pretenses, no baggage. It allows me glimpses of old selves—I am astonished about my own innocence. The fact is that most of the writing I do keeps me out of depression, out of trouble.

> ˅ In a poem titled "Luis Navarro Rubio Comes Singing," you mention
> "this bi-cultural / bilingual ambiguity and nightmare." Do you still
> see your own immigration experience this way? In your opinion, is
> this a common experience for Latin American immigrants? Does it
> always linger?

It lingers because I want it to linger. Remember, this is where my material comes from. In this poem you mention, I was making reference to someone I knew and loved. Luis Navarro Rubio was my best friend's grandfather in Los Angeles, the man who served as the real-life model for Esteban Carranza in *Latin Jazz,* one of my novels. He felt the break between his life in the old country and his life in the United States. He felt it everyday, and so he talked about it all the time. His life in Cuba was something that kept him going. Those memories. The people he knew. The places.

We are all bicultural, I think, at least in that we grow older each day, and we have to live thinking about the person we were yesterday and the person we will become tomorrow. America is a land of gypsies. If we could place a little monitor inside everybody, then have a satellite take pictures of where we go, we'd see these comings and goings, much like ants. You have to get used to movement because movement means you are still alive. Movement means possibility, change, chance—you are going somewhere. Immigrants get used to this moving around. They come to the United States from all over the world, and they have to go where the jobs are, where they can find kindred spirits, family, love—all those human basics. Then again, that is true of the young people who are born here and leave for college, run away, find their own way into the country. That's why I love cities like Miami, Los Angeles, New York, Chicago. Everyone finally arrives there, looking for something or someone. The arrival is always breathtaking and exciting. Of course, it's also very sad because more often than not, things do not go right. People lose their way. The American Dream isn't guaranteed to everyone. You have to fight for it, and even then it doesn't mean you'll achieve it. But it means living in a country where at least you get to gamble for it. You can make it, maybe. We all can, somehow.

> *Slaughtering animals is a vivid motif in many of your poems.*
> *Can you discuss this recurring image?*

I grew up helping my parents slaughter all kinds of animals. We had to do it in order to survive, to feed ourselves. It's all over my work because at no other moment in life are you more connected to the animal world, to your own world, as when you have to kill something in order to eat and survive. It is pure, raw experience. Our children grow up disconnected from that knowledge since we buy everything already killed and prepackaged at the market. I was fortunate enough to have witnessed it all, including the roundup the Cuban government conducted one day in 1969 because they said there was a German virus in swine. The army came through the neighborhood and picked up all the animals people kept in their backyards (in our case it meant the chickens, rabbits, and a pig) and burned them all at a corner pit. Amazing. To this day I still think about it, and I myself don't believe it. Killing animals to survive also meant that the family would get together to eat, so whenever we killed chickens, goats, or pigs, it was also a good family occasion—people getting together, talking about their lives. I was in the middle of a very busy life in Cuba. Crowded in by people. What better environment for a single child with an overactive imagination? I thrived on it then, and I still do. I still think about cousins I haven't seen in thirty years. It's a gift time and living conditions bestowed upon the writer.

> v *Occasionally you write the "odd" poem—"Auto Erotica," "JFK for a Day: The Tour," "Monks of Mood." Any response?*

These "odd" poems—I like the word and it fits just right—are ongoing series I have on subjects that I find in the papers or that I hear about on the radio, TV, practically anything that grabs my imagination. I often feel like they are a different kind of work than I usually do, but I love to write such poems in part because I always find something interesting and worthwhile in scope. I like the energy I often tap into in these kinds of loose subjects. "JFK" was like that for me. I read a human interest story in the paper, and, bingo, I had to write something about it. Another poem called "The Valet's Lament" I wrote upon hearing that Richard M. Nixon's personal valet was Cuban, and so I thought, "What would it feel like to tell about the president's last few days in office from Manolo's point of view?" I would call these flights of fancy, really, because I seldom write about these kinds of things, but I like to do it to stay warmed up.

> v *And the poem that focuses on the smallest moments, such as "Trace" and "Song in Praise of the Colada"?*

These, too, I write because I sometimes sit down to write the shortest poem I possibly can. I sit down with a goal, telling myself that I need to write about something minuscule. A big influence with a lot of my song poems, of course, comes from Lorca and Neruda, but the Chinese poets, too, Tu Fu and Li Po. I love to be precise, to measure the words carefully. What's that carpenter's logic: measure twice, cut once?

> *ᵥ Very few of your poems seem to focus on nature. Instead, they are intimate portraits of your family and friends, of a boy growing up without brothers and sisters. You seem more concerned with human relations. Is this an accurate assessment of your poetry?*

Sure, I'm concerned with the human, but no, I write about nature, too. Humans in nature. Living in Tallahassee in the woods has helped me become more aware of the natural world. The cicadas, the walking sticks, the thousands of frogs, turtles, egrets, cranes, geese—the list goes on. I've been writing nature poetry since I lived in Miami in the mid-1980s—particularly in Coral Gables, where I came across so many strange and tropical fauna and flora: iguanas, geckos, tropical fruit like mamey and guanabana. Mind blowing, and so a lot of it has been filtering into my work. I love it. Most of the time, though, I am aware of my own presence in nature, and so I like to write about nature, but from a human's point of view, in part because as a reader of nature poetry I like the relationship. I like the references. Without them, well, then it would be too detached, too distant from that point of convergence I'm interested in.

> *ᵥ Is it fair to say that your poetry is one long autobiographical poem?*

This is a brilliant question. I love it. You're the first person to think about it. I have been thinking about my own output for a few years now, and part of me believes that I am working on a single volume that, if you were to drop the titles, would tell the story of my life. That would please me tremendously if readers would see it like that. Certainly if I ever get around to doing my collected poems, it's the design I have in mind. I have three more books of poetry lined up, and then I plan to put together a selected volume. I might try it then. Maybe simply number the poems. Of course, many of these other types of poems would drop completely. That's all right. If I can do a book of poems with the kind of narrative drive I often put into my fiction, I would be very pleased.

> ⌄ *Part of the benefit of the immigrant and exile experience is that you*
> *present a varied landscape. We get glimpses of Cuba, of Spain, of the*
> *United States. Is this a welcome irony or something you would trade*
> *for a different past?*

No, I would not trade my past for anything. It's enriched my life considerably and my imagination, too. I love to travel and see different things, and I have been blessed with being born on an island. The craving for water is strong, though I enjoy the freshwater of rivers and springs. I like the ocean, too. Each of these countries I lived in made a mark on my psyche, on my being. I love them for what I saw in them. I continue to travel, and my writing facilitates such travel. I like to travel in the company of friends and family, though. I don't tend to be as adventurous when I'm alone. When I'm alone, I find myself mostly writing—so many hours writing. But who's keeping track when you're having so much fun?

> ⌄ *You are also an editor and publisher of Latino poets. I'm thinking*
> *specifically of **Paper Dance: 55 Latino Poets**, which you coedited*
> *with Victor Hernández Cruz and Leroy Quintana. Is there a conscious*
> *"networking" of these poets? That is, do you feel these poets and others*
> *are aware of Latino poets as an ethnic force or voice? As a distinct*
> *entity? Or are these fifty-five separate poets speaking their own*
> *personal brand or style of poetry?*

Editing keeps me in touch with everyone I know in the field. Also it keeps me in tune with the new voices. Besides, I love to read and share other folks' work. Yes, I think there is a strong literary tradition in Latinos and Latinas to keep reading each other's work. The problem is still finding the right outlets, publishers, distributors. Most people like to buy their books at the major chains or at the great independents like Books & Books in Coral Gables (where I do all my book shopping) or on-line. If they can't find the books there, then they might pick them up at a reading. Many ethnic writers have learned to travel with their own books, promote their own collections. Car Trunk Poets, as I like to call them. They buy a few hundred of their books, then hit the road. That's the way I've been doing it for a long time. Just now the bookstores are getting my books. Then again, I've been lucky to have the publishers who've worked with me. In particular, Arte Público Press and

Tía Chucha—they've taken good care of my work, promoted it, gotten it into the hands of the readers. I like the diversity one sees in poetry. It's always been more democratic. Fiction, novels in particular, tends to be more of a market commodity. You know, what's hip sells and then influences more hip. Poets are navigating alone for the most part. Sure, we influence one another, but the work doesn't carry the burden of commercial expectations. In poetry, everyone knows that if you sell five hundred copies, you are doing well. I like that. I like the small community feel of it. Everyone knows each other. Everyone reads everyone else.

Source Acknowledgments

INTERVIEWS PREVIOUSLY PUBLISHED:

"Interview with Judith Ortiz Cofer." *Cold Mountain Review* (fall 2000): 58–75.

"Conversation with Gustavo Pérez Firmat." *Michigan Quarterly Review* (fall 2001): 682–92.

"Conversation with Aleida Rodríguez." *Cold Mountain Review* (fall 2001): 32–47.

"Conversation with Luis Rodríguez." *North Carolina Humanities Council* (winter 2002): 32–49.

PHOTOGRAPH CREDITS:

Martín Espada photograph by Paul Shoul

Sandra María Esteves photograph, © 2002 Sandra María Esteves

Victor Hernández Cruz photograph by Néstor Barreto

Demetria Martínez photograph, © Douglas Kent Hall

Pat Mora photograph, © Cynthia Farah

Ricardo Pau-Llosa photograph by Lew Wilson

Gustavo Pérez Firmat photograph by Mary Anne Pérez Firmat

Leroy Quintana photograph by Gabriella Motta-Passajou

Benjamin Alire Sáenz photograph, © Cynthia Farah

About the Interviewer

$\mathcal{B}$ruce Allen Dick is an associate professor of English at Appalachian State University in Boone, North Carolina. He teaches African American studies, Latino literature, American literature, and film. He has coedited books on Ishmael Reed and Rudolfo Anaya and recently published *The Critical Response to Ishmael Reed*. He lives with his wife and two children outside of Boone.